Russia's Muslim
Frontiers

Indiana Series in Arab and Islamic Studies
Salih J. Altoma, Iliya Harik, and Mark Tessler, general editors

RUSSIA'S MUSLIM FRONTIERS

New Directions in Cross-Cultural Analysis

EDITED BY

DALE F. EICKELMAN

INDIANA UNIVERSITY PRESS

Bloomington and Indianapolis

The paper used in this publication meets the minimum requirements of American
National Standard for Information Sciences—Permanence of Paper for Printed
Library Materials, ANSI Z39.48-1984.

Manufactured in the United States of America

Library of Congress Cataloging-in-Publication Data
Russia's Muslim frontiers : new directions in cross-cultural analysis /
edited by Dale F. Eickelman.
p. cm. — (Indiana series in Arab and Islamic studies)
"Originated in workshops held in Moscow and Leningrad in August 1990
and in a conference held in Hanover, N.H. and Washington, D.C.
in April 1991"—Pref.
Includes bibliographical references and index.
ISBN 0-253-31939-0 (cloth : alk. paper). — ISBN 0-253-20823-8
(pbk. : alk. paper)
1. Soviet Central Asia—Politics and government—Congresses. 2. Middle
East—Politics and government—1979– —Congresses. 3. Islam and politics—Soviet
Central Asia—Congresses. 4.Islam and politics—Middle East—Congresses. 5. United
States—Foreign relations—Middle East—Congresses. 6. Middle East—Foreign
relations—United States—Congresses. 7. Soviet Union—Foreign relations—Middle
East—Congresses. 8. Middle East—Foreign relations—Soviet Union—Congresses. I.
Eickelman, Dale F., date. II. Series.
DK859.R87   1993
958—dc20   92-43844
1 2 3 4 5 97 96 95 94 93

CONTENTS

Part IV: Pakistan

PREFACE

This book originated in workshops held in Moscow and Leningrad in August 1990 and in a conference held in Hanover, New Hampshire, and Washington, D.C., in April 1991. Soviet and U.S. scholars who study the Muslim societies of the Middle East, South Asia, and Central Asia met to share the results of their research, to assess the strengths of their respective approaches to understanding political and religious developments in the Muslim world, and to develop future collaborative projects. The project brought together scholars from anthropology, political science, history, and religion, with U.S. and Soviet—as they were then called—scholars paired by topical and regional interests (see Eickelman and Pasha 1991).

The project was an early beneficiary of the changes *glasnost* brought to the working conditions of Soviet academics. In 1990, for the first time, Soviet scholars were granted greater control over the dissemination of their scholarship, which allowed for open, uncensored exchanges with foreign scholars. Soviet and U.S. scholars had an opportunity and an incentive to work together to evaluate their respective approaches to understanding Muslim and Middle Eastern societies. One observer at the conference noted: "Many parts of the Islamic world, especially the Middle East, have been of enormous strategic importance to both the Soviet Union and the United States in the twentieth century. But until recently, Soviet and American scholars of Islam have had virtually no contact and opportunity to benefit from one another's understanding of Islamic religion and politics" (Coughlin 1991).

The lack of prior contact provided a major initial impetus for the project. The Russian literary critic Mikhail Bakhtin (1990: 22–27) writes of the "excess of seeing," by which he means that another can see things behind our backs that we cannot see and vice versa. If we share our perspectives, we can overcome the limitations created by being situated in a particular place and context. The multiple perspectives represented in this book—Muslim, Middle Eastern, Russian, Central Asian, and U.S.—are not mutually exclusive. The focus on the Muslim majority regions of Central Asia and the adjoining areas—especially Afghanistan, Pakistan, and Iran—evolved as the project developed. The regions were especially interesting to our Soviet colleagues, but the focus also serves as a reminder of the ties that bind scholarship to policy concerns in both Soviet and U.S. academic traditions.

In 1990, several of our colleagues in Moscow pointedly began to use the term "Russian" to characterize their scholarship instead of "Soviet," and I defer to that usage here. Russian scholars offer their Western counterparts a distinguished tradition in the study of Muslim societies. Even when focused on policy issues, most of our Russian counterparts received early training in a strong tradition of analysis of classical Muslim texts and a commitment to the mastery of "Eastern" languages, which is often superior to that offered in Western training. Soviet studies of Muslim societies have not been compartmentalized as "area" studies, as has U.S. scholarship. Soviets have viewed the "foreign Muslim East" as a whole and not as a collection of regional subspecialties, although they have been hampered by the ideological necessity of distinguishing between the "progressive" Muslim populations of the Soviet Union and those of the "foreign Muslim East," where ideological obstacles were more readily ignored. U.S. scholarly efforts to think of the Muslim world in its entirety, as Muslims do, are becoming more common (for example, Hodgson 1974; Eickelman and Piscatori 1990; Canfield 1991), but these approaches are still rare.

The workshops in Moscow and Leningrad, held August 21–31, 1990, were funded by the Soviet Academy of Sciences, the Rockefeller Center for the Social Sciences at Dartmouth College, and the International Research and Exchange Board (IREX). A conference entitled "Other Orients: Soviet and American Perspectives on Muslim and Middle Eastern Societies and Politics" was held in Hanover, New Hampshire, April 4–8, 1991, and in Washington, D.C., April 10–11, 1991. It was sponsored by Dartmouth College and supported by grants from the National Endowment for the Humanities (Grant RX-21281–89), the John Sloan Dickey Endowment for International Understanding and the Howland H. Sargeant Fund at Dartmouth College, the Smithsonian Institution, the Soviet Academy of Sciences, and the Soros-Foundation, Moscow. The views expressed in this book, however, are those of the authors alone.

In addition to the contributors to this volume, I wish to thank Jon W. Anderson, Shaul Bakhash, James A. Bill, Karen I. Blu, Robert L. Canfield, Norman Cigar, Jill Crystal, John Esposito, Cornell H. Fleischer, Clifford Geertz, Yvonne Y. Haddad, Sergei Kan, Alexandr K. Lukoianov, Ian S. Lustick, Dimitri V. Makarov, Mikhail B. Piotrovsky, A. Kevin Reinhart, and Irina Zviagelskaia for advice and support which contributed materially to the realization of this volume. I owe special thanks to Vitaly V. Naumkin, Deputy Director of the Institute of Oriental Studies of what is now the Russian Academy of Sciences in Moscow. Political vicissitudes notwithstanding—our last meeting in Moscow took place weeks after the attempted coup d'état of August 1991—our Russian and Central Asian colleagues offered, and delivered, essential support at every stage of the project, when less committed scholars would have had every justification to neglect the ordinary rhythms of academic work. Throughout the editorial process, Vyacheslav Belokrenitsky, one of this volume's contributors, assured coordinated editorial work at the Moscow end, no easy task in the absence of reliable postal communications.

Leonard Rieser and George Demko of Dartmouth College facilitated the project at crucial points, as did Robert McCormack Adams, Secretary of the Smithsonian Institution, and James O. Freedman, President of Dartmouth

College. Anthony Olcott translated the chapters by Victor Korgun and Alexei Malashenko. Alla Kan and Barry Scherr provided translation assistance throughout the conference, and Kamran Pasha served as conference rapporteur. Preparations for the U.S. end of this project, involving two cities, were especially complex. Karen Kiesel at IREX-Princeton and Elizabeth McKeon at IREX-Moscow provided communications facilities which facilitated this volume's timely appearance. Thanks at Dartmouth are due to Margot de l'Etoile, David Lindgren, Maureen Lobacz, Linda Hathorn, and Cynthia Michalowski. Special acknowledgement is due Deborah Hodges, who provided vital administrative support, in addition to her ordinary responsibilities, and served as the editorial consultant throughout. Nancy M. Fenton prepared the map.

At the Smithsonian in Washington, Francine Berkowitz, Mary Combs, Eulette George, and Cheryl LaBarge, together with Andrea Harris, made the event run smoothly. Ambassador Christopher Van Hollen of the Middle East Institute and Nancy B. Dishaw of the Middle East Studies Association also provided facilities and advice, as did Christine Kalke, Program Officer at the National Endowment for the Humanities. The editor was in Rabat, Morocco, during the final stages of the editorial process and is grateful to Dr. Evelyn A. Early and Nadia Ettibari of the United States Information Service and Edward H. Thomas of the Moroccan-American Commission for Educational and Cultural Exchange for facilitating communications. Janet Rabinowitch, Senior Sponsoring Editor at Indiana University Press, not only provided advice throughout the project but twice met with contributors in Moscow.

References

Several passages of the preface and introduction have appeared in earlier form in Eickelman and Pasha (1991) and are incorporated into the present text with the permission of the Middle East Institute.

Bakhtin, Mikhail Mikhailovich (1990). *Art and Answerability: Early Philosophical Essays by M. M. Bakhtin*, ed. Michael Holquist and Vadim Liapunov, trans. Vadim Liapunov. Austin: University of Texas Press.

Canfield, Robert L., ed. (1991). *Turco-Persia in Historical Perspective*. New York: Cambridge University Press.

Coughlin, Ellen K. (1991). "In Landmark Effort: Soviet and American Scholars Share Fruits of Research on Muslim Countries," *Chronicle of Higher Education*, April 17, pp. A5, 13.

Eickelman, Dale F., and James Piscatori, eds. (1990). *Muslim Travellers: Pilgrimage, Migration, and the Religious Imagination*. London: Routledge; Berkeley and Los Angeles: University of California Press.

———, and Kamran Pasha (1991). "Muslim Societies and Politics: Soviet and U.S. Approaches—A Conference Report." *The Middle East Journal* 45, no. 4 (Autumn): 630–47.

Hodgson, Marshall G. S. (1974). *The Venture of Islam: Conscience and History in a World Civilization*. Chicago and London: University of Chicago Press.

NOTE ON TRANSLITERATION

Any book that draws upon materials in Arabic, Persian, Urdu, Pashtu, Dari, and Turkic languages, as well as Russian, poses considerable problems of transliteration, especially as many contributors stress colloquial rather than literary usages. The system employed here, with as much consistency as possible, is that adopted by the *International Journal of Middle East Studies*, except that diacritics have been omitted. As suggested by Judith Butcher's *Copy-Editing: The Cambridge Handbook*, the plural of words has been formed by the addition of an "s" to the singular, except in such cases as *'ulama'* (Muslim religious scholars), in which the transliterated plural form has become standard.

Russia's Muslim
Frontiers

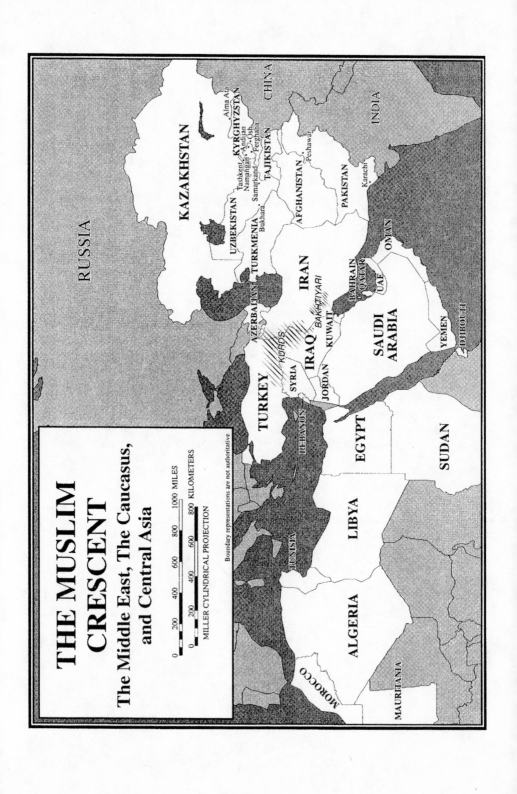

THE MUSLIM
CRESCENT

The Middle East, The Caucasus,
and Central Asia

0   200   400   600   800   1000 MILES

0   200   400   600   800 KILOMETERS

MILLER CYLINDRICAL PROJECTION

Boundary representations are not authoritative

RUSSIA

KAZAKHSTAN

KYRGHYZSTAN

Alma Ata

Tashkent   Andijan

UZBEKISTAN   Namangan   Osh

Samarkand   Ferghana

TAJIKISTAN

Bukhara

TURKMENIA

CHINA

Peshawar

AFGHANISTAN

PAKISTAN

Karachi

INDIA

AZERBAIJAN

IRAN

BAKHTIYARI

KURDS

OMAN

BAHRAIN

QATAR

UAE

TURKEY

SYRIA

IRAQ

KUWAIT

JORDAN

SAUDI
ARABIA

YEMEN

DJIBOUTI

LEBANON

EGYPT

SUDAN

LIBYA

TUNISIA

ALGERIA

MOROCCO

MAURITANIA

Introduction

THE OTHER "ORIENTALIST" CRISIS

Dale F. Eickelman

For Western scholars and their public, studies such as Edward Said's *Orientalism* (1978) heightened awareness of the subtle links between the dominant organizing frameworks of scholarly perceptions of Middle Eastern and Muslim societies and the social and political contexts in which they are produced. The collapse of state authority in Lebanon and the Iranian Revolution brought home to Western policymakers and the general public the weaknesses of conventional organizational frameworks for understanding the Middle East and Muslim societies.

These frameworks had been based on "modernization" theories of the 1950s and 1960s, which assumed that religious belief and practice would become privatized and recede from public political life (Binder 1986). In the memorable, if misleading, phrase of a leading protagonist of modernization theory, Middle Eastern societies faced a stark choice: "Mecca or mechanization" (Lerner 1964: 405). Other modernization theorists saw the Muslim world as facing an unpalatable choice: either a "neo-Islamic totalitarianism" intent on "resurrecting the past" or a "reformist Islam" that would open "the sluice gates and [be] swamped by the deluge" (Halpern 1963: 129). This intensely negative view of the possibilities for "evolution" in Muslim societies betrayed an inherent preference for such militantly secularizing reformers as Turkey's Mustafa Kemal Atatürk (1881–1938) and the Pahlavi Shahs of Iran, Reza Shah (1878–1944) and his son, Mohammed Reza Shah (1919–80). In the 1970s, assumptions about Islam's role in the development process continued to be similarly stark: "In an industrializing nation, the gap between political and religious authority . . . becomes progressively greater. . . . Islamic influence and control are strongest when maintaining the status quo in a backward community" (Bill and Leiden 1979: 69).

I wish to thank Vyacheslav Ya. Belokrenitsky, Deborah Hodges, Theodore Levin, and James Piscatori for comments on an earlier version of this introduction.

The Iranian revolution pointed up an urgent need to find more satisfactory ways of understanding Muslim social and political movements and how they redefine boundaries of sect, language, ethnicity, and nation. In the rush to understand the political implications of the Muslim-majority republics of Central Asia and the Caucasus, however, now that they are recognized as independent states, echoes of the old framework of modernization are resurfacing in policy circles. Turkey, for example, has reassuringly emerged as a secularized, democratic Muslim state in which religious sentiment and practice pervade public life but do not eclipse it. Despite Iran's brilliant diplomacy during the 1990–91 Gulf War, which apparently convinced both the U.S.-led coalition forces and Iraq of its neutrality, Tehran is again seen primarily as a revolutionary state dominated by traditional clerics. Presumably, it is prepared to spread fundamentalist unrest throughout the region. If destabilization occurs, it can conveniently be imputed to Iran and not to the internal political processes of the new republics.

The residual framework of modernization theory facilitates the adaptation of established conventional wisdom to the poorly known regional politics of Central Asia and the Caucasus. The contributions of Richard W. Cottam and Georgy M. Korniyenko in this volume demonstrate how the conventional wisdom from the early years of the Cold War established stereotypes so powerful that evidence of contrary behavior was misinterpreted or ignored; there is now a risk in Moscow and Washington of seeing Islam—or at least an ill-defined Islamism or Islamic "fundamentalism"—as a monolithic destabilizing force.[1] Desperately seeking economic aid, the leaders of several Central Asian republics—for the most part old-regime survivors who have good reason to be wary of mass political movements and democratization—have appealed for assistance, often successfully, from Saudi Arabia and the Gulf states to counter Iranian-inspired revolutionary themes (Tyler 1991). Thus an intra-Islamic "great game" has begun in the region, and one of the sides has wary U.S. encouragement.

The Soviet "Orientalist crisis" occurred in relative isolation from Western scholarly debate. Conventional Soviet frameworks for analyzing political, social, and economic processes were as inadequate as their Western counterparts in explaining the Islamic revolution in Iran and the rise of Islamic political activism and other religious movements as forces in world politics. Yevgeny Primakov, formerly director of Moscow's Institute of Oriental Studies (IVAN)—and since December 1991 head of the Russian Intelligence Bureau, the so-called new KGB—sought to reconcile Soviet social science theory with the new Muslim politics of the 1980s in the Middle East by reconceptualizing the social

---

1. One op-ed writer has gone so far as to depict the "vast arc of Moslem-controlled territory" from the Straits of Gibraltar "across the Balkans and right into Central Asia" as a "belt of tension" in which "fundamentalist theocracy is taking over" (Johnson 1991). Fuller (1991, 1992a) provides a view free of the conventional clichés on Islamic "unrest."

and political aspects of religion within the framework of Marxist-Leninist theories of development. However, the analyses of IVAN scholars eventually persuaded Primakov that the Soviet view of the inevitability of "progressive" Marxist revolutions in the "foreign Muslim East" was wrong. Primakov, in turn, played a role in persuading Soviet President Mikhail Gorbachev to abandon Moscow's strategy of aiding "revolutionary" regimes in the Middle East.[2] Primakov left IVAN in late 1986 to become head of the Institute of World Economic and International Relations (IMEMO). In the late 1980s, he was also elected as an alternate (not full) member of the Politburo and for a period served as speaker of the All-Union Supreme Soviet. Thus he left others in IVAN to fill the conceptual void that Gorbachev's "new thinking" had produced.

In 1988, the study of Islam within the boundaries of the Soviet Union was added to IVAN's responsibilities and removed from state organizations concerned primarily with antireligious propaganda. Alexei V. Malashenko (this volume), whose prior work was principally concerned with North Africa, became head of IVAN's Department of Religious Studies, a unit which had previously been concerned with antireligious propaganda within the USSR. Under his direction, the unit focused on understanding religious and political developments in the Muslim regions of the former Soviet Union.

Russian scholars recognized the crippling constraints of official ideologies on understanding religious trends within the former USSR. At the 1990 Moscow workshop, Mikhail Piotrovsky commented: "Twenty years ago we considered religious beliefs to be dying. Now we are reaping the harvest of this neglect" (Eickelman and Pasha 1991: 632). The former Soviet Union had the fifth largest Muslim population of any country in the world—over 55 million—500,000 in Moscow alone (Anderson and Silver 1990: 164). The concerns of the Muslim populations of Russia and the former Soviet republics in Central Asia and the Caucasus in many ways parallel those of Muslims elsewhere, making Islamic nationalism a potentially powerful post-Communist force (Malashenko 1992).

Recent political developments within the Commonwealth of Independent States, including explicitly acknowledged linkages between Islam and national consciousness in Azerbaijan and the Central Asian republics, provide added urgency to the Russian need to understand Muslim politics. The Soviet "Orientalist crisis" was made visible to Soviet policymakers and the public by what they saw as "external" developments in Iran and Afghanistan. These events were subsequently recognized as posing an "internal" challenge, inexplicable by conventional Soviet analysis, because the relative isolation of Soviet scholars had hindered their efforts to identify and apply non-Marxist social theories

---

2. Olcott (1989) describes this conceptual transition and provides an account of IVAN's organizational structure and its implications of producing scholarship according to a hierarchically directed "plan."

and conceptual frameworks. Now that the Muslim-majority republics of Central Asia and the Caucasus are strengthening their ties with the Middle East, the sense of frontier in the region, formerly thought to be relatively impermeable between the Soviet and non-Soviet zones, has rapidly dissolved, and linkages of trade, regional rivalries, ethnicity, language, and religion are rapidly being reconfigured, as are scholarly—and policy—understandings of these processes.

John Comaroff (1991: 673) notes that the Soviet system, like colonial orders elsewhere, engaged in a sustained effort to siphon value from periphery to center, creating an economic system workable—at least in principle—only through reference to the center. The Soviet system also created elaborate notions of nation and ethnicity (Bromley and Kozlov 1989; Shanin 1989), together with a politicized ethnographic bureaucracy to study these entities, which often served to keep the peoples of the periphery (as seen from Moscow) distinct and divided, so that reliance on Moscow would be seen as part of a "modernizing" process. Russian studies of Muslim societies in the "foreign Muslim East" were not compartmentalized by geographic regions and ethnic groups, as has often been the case in the West, but no such advantage accrued to studies of the "peoples" and "nations" within the former Soviet Union. Only now is this scholarly legacy gradually being overcome.

In this volume, Cottam and Korniyenko trace the remarkable parallels in U.S. and Soviet assessments of each other's intentions and the extent to which developments in the Middle East were overshadowed by superpower rivalry. Cottam argues that U.S. policymakers developed stereotypes concerning Soviet intentions and conduct early in the Cold War and that these stereotypical assumptions, especially concerning Soviet expansionist intentions, were sustained in subsequent decades, despite mounting evidence to the contrary.

U.S. objectives for the Middle East crystallized into three goals: contain the Soviet Union, secure an uninterrupted flow of oil to the West, and guarantee the security of Israel. In the early years of the Cold War, the United States supported secular and populist nationalists, such as Iran's Musaddiq and Egypt's Nasser. Such leaders could be counted on to oppose Soviet imperialism, but their support for nationalization of resources, their emnity toward Israel, and their anti-imperialist attitudes were seen as a threat to Western interests.

To the surprise of the United States, the Soviet Union, which shared a 1,200-mile border with Iran, took no action after Musaddiq's fall. Cottam writes: "One need only reflect on the probable American response to a parallel situation in Mexico to recognize the startling nature of such a picture." Subsequent events, such as the Soviet refusal to supply Iraqi President Saddam Hussein with ammunition to suppress the 1974 Kurdish rebellion at a time when he was considered to be a Soviet client, also failed to alter U.S. perceptions of Soviet intentions. The overthrow of Musaddiq and interventions elsewhere, however, shattered the image of the United States as a supporter of democracy and national self-determination.

Cottam argues that the 1953 U.S. Central Intelligence Agency-supported coup in Iran was one of many interventions in the affairs of the region—including the failed CIA coup against Syria in August 1957 and the landing of U.S. troops in Lebanon in July 1958—to secure Western interests or to neutralize the Soviets' effect through proxies.

Korniyenko agrees with Cottam that Soviet and U.S. conduct in the Middle East fits the spiral conflict model, where each party perceives the "defensive responses of the other as *offensive*," so that conflict spirals to "ever more lethal levels." Thus U.S. policymakers saw the Soviet invasion of Afghanistan as the opening wedge and reacted accordingly. He acknowledges that Soviet policy, like that of the United States, was often blinded by ideological constructs. Cottam, the government official turned political scientist, writes elegantly of an enduring political "formula" emerging from "a long and often fiercely competitive policy process in the early years of the Cold War." Korniyenko, a consummate senior diplomat, expresses surprise that outsiders would see the "isolated, poorly coordinated, and sometimes contradictory" Soviet actions in the Middle East, for which he provides examples, as coherent and consistent.

Korniyenko believes that the greatest threat to coherent Soviet policy was the ideological factor. The most spectacular failure of Soviet policy, he argues, was the ill-fated decision to send troops to Afghanistan in December 1979. It was based on the conviction of Communist Party ideologues that Afghanistan was ready to become a full-fledged socialist state. The near-unanimous objections of Soviet diplomatic and military professionals were overridden. In Korniyenko's view, ideological distortions also clouded Soviet economic and political objectives in the Middle East. As a senior member of Morocco's Communist Party confirms (interview, Casablanca, April 17, 1992), Soviet intervention in Afghanistan played a major role in discrediting Soviet influence throughout the Islamic Middle East.

If, as Cottam and Korniyenko argue, much Soviet-U.S. conduct in the Middle East was based on sustained reciprocal misperceptions, parallel misperceptions appear to color events in Central Asia. Turkish and Iranian initiatives are already being interpreted in language suggesting a late twentieth-century "great game" much like Russian and British economic, political, and military rivalries in Central Asia and the northern Indian subcontinent in the late nineteenth century. In the new, intra-Islamic great game, at least as perceived by the West, Turkish initiatives are seen as stabilizing, secular, modern, and Western (Keatley 1991), while those of Iran, notwithstanding Iran's sensible mediation in the Nagorno-Karabakh dispute between Armenia and Azerbaijan in early 1992, are perceived as destabilizing, religious, traditional, and anti-Western (Faroughy 1992; Seib 1992).

The equally strong "interests" of Pakistan and India—not to mention China—have yet to be integrated into the dominant imagery of a competition spearheaded by Turkey and Iran. This imagery also neglects Pakistan's encouragement of religious fundamentalism in Afghanistan and Central Asia prior to

1991 (*The Economist*, February 22, 1992) or U.S. and Saudi support for fundamentalist movements in Afghanistan, relics of the recently extinct "great game" of the Cold War. Specialist reporting on the region (for example, Robbins 1991a, 1991b) stresses that Turkey's goals are to make itself a commercial entrepôt, not only for Central Asia and the Caucasus and Central Asia, but also for Iran. Although rumors of Iranian political activity in Central Asia proliferate, benign interpretations are possible for the trade, communications, and educational agreements announced so far, as the Central Asian republics seek to extend trade beyond the Commonwealth of Independent States.

Martha Brill Olcott's essay provides a guided tour of the region's republics, a sketch of their recent political history, and the responses of regional leaders to the collapse of central authority (see also Fierman 1991). The emerging picture is a complex one. One conventional image is that Central Asian peoples were in what Olcott calls the earliest stages of "consolidation" when the Russian Empire collapsed in 1917, with only the elite participating in nationalist, pan-Turkic, and pan-Islamic movements. Yet other accounts of regional history, including Allworth (1990) on Uzbekistan and Gross (1991) on Central Asia suggest that these "early stages" were not very different from those found elsewhere in the Muslim world at the same time—for example, North Africa under colonial rule. As Abduvakhitov (this volume) and others note (for example, Allworth 1990: 174–76), the study of nationalist movements was suppressed or distorted under Communist rule. Inevitably, as after the independence of North Africa, one of the first fruits of independence in Central Asia will no doubt be a rewriting and reinterpretation of the events of this century.

Olcott portrays the vicissitudes of the existing elite of Central Asia and the southern Caucasus, most of them members of families who have been in power since the purges of the late 1930s. As she makes abundantly clear, the leadership remains the same, although in most instances it bases its right to rule on different ideologies. The Moroccan historian Abdallah Laroui (1977: 348) wrote that his country's independent government was not a "resumption of the precolonial past" but a continuation of the colonial regime, with much the same beneficiaries. At the other end of the Muslim Middle East, in Pakistan, a leading nationalist editor remarked that the immediate effect of independence was to elevate the indigenous elite "from the position of intermediate and indirect domination to that of primary and direct domination." The Pakistani elite also soon "discovered that their survival depended on the perpetuation" of the institution of British rule (Gauhar 1979: 266).

Such comparisons may not be exact, but Olcott cautions that the elite secular visions of nationalism, fueled in part by the exemplar of Turkey, may not be shared by all parties in each of the new republics. Will continued economic control of the economy by "powerful, family-based patronage networks," called the "party mafia" by two contributors, remain unchallenged if a transition to mass participation in politics take place in the new republics?

In some instances, as Abduvakhitov avers, religious networks offer a framework for effective opposition to the old order, as they have elsewhere in the Middle East (Rouadjia 1990). The old order may strike back at this threat to its domination by labelling Islamist opposition as "fundamentalist" or, worse still, supported by "foreign" (Iranian) elements. In the short term, the United States, Russia, and conservative Middle Eastern regimes may be tempted to support the old regime in the name of "stability" and the protection of Western "interests," postponing the inevitable dislocations which mass political participation—democracy?—is likely to bring.

Malashenko's essay offers a fascinating contrast to Olcott's conjectures and a somewhat conventional view of Islamic politics from Moscow, the former seat of All-Union rule. He asks whether Islam in the Soviet Union became a "Soviet" Islam or whether it remained "traditionally" Islamic. Many might contest his thesis that "Islam was able to preserve its influence at all levels of society" while the Russian Orthodox church was not. Yet the reasons he gives for the evident strength of "an Islamic form of life" warrant careful scrutiny. Malashenko argues that Islam and Communism bear many resemblances, a common assumption since at least the 1970s among officially recognized Muslim clerics in Central Asia (Theodore Levin, personal communication, March 5, 1992). Malashenko writes that the "egalitarian" concepts of Islam favor collective values over individual ones, and in both systems "power is personified by a strong political figure who is an ideological or spiritual leader."

The tenacious resistance offered by Islamic leaders and their followers in Afghanistan, Iran, Algeria, and elsewhere to land redistribution schemes (see Korgun, this volume), among other "egalitarian" measures, suggests that we should be wary of deducing political comportment from asserted doctrinal tenets or imputing a single, uncontested doctrinal tenet to a world religious tradition. Malashenko, Abduvakhitov, and Olcott forcefully concur that Communist political comportment cannot be deduced from doctrinal tenets, which were in any case undergoing constant revision. How much more difficult, then, to try the same exercise for Islam, which lacks a formal clergy and a hierarchy authorized to interpret doctrine.

Malashenko provides a useful summary of official Soviet policies toward Islam, which ranged from the elimination of religious leaders and suppression of religious practice to efforts to coopt them. He argues that until the last decade of Soviet rule, "Islam and the official political structures were so tightly interwoven that there was no possibility of opposition" to "formal," or state-recognized, religious structures. With *perestroika*, however, "Muslim educators" emerged—comparatively young, often secularly educated—who worked for the government during the day and pursued their "Islamic work" at night. Malashenko traces the growing schism among these "educators," the rising nationalist movement, and the "official" Muslim clergy, who continued to speak against religious politics.

He recognizes that the term "fundamentalist" is "somewhat artificial" because there are many different Islamic movements, but his claim that some of these movements called themselves "Wahhabis" after the founder of the eighteenth-century movement for the revival of Islam that originated in the Arabian peninsula, is contested by Abduvakhitov, who suggests that this label was first used by Russian scholars who were asked to report to Moscow on the growing strength of political Islam in the 1980s.[3] As in the semantic choice of whether to call religious militants "strugglers for the faith" (*mujahidin*) or "bandits" (*basmachi*), religious labels count, and that of "Wahhabi" carries the connotation of intransigent fanatic and, in the former Soviet Union, foreign-sponsored and foreign-directed.

The problems of describing the tenets of the new Islamic movements notwithstanding, Malashenko acknowledges their growing strength and the efforts of secular authorities to coopt them or hold them in check. His account, based primarily on a careful reading of press accounts and the literature of these groups, is incomplete, but no doubt accurately reflects what is known in Moscow, where Malashenko regularly offers newspaper analyses of Islamic trends within the new Commonwealth (for example, Malashenko 1992).

Abdujabar Abduvakhitov's account of Islamic revivalism in Uzbekistan offers an interesting counterpart to the papers by Malashenko and Olcott. Like Malashenko, Abduvakhitov was commissioned to study the growing Islamic movement, although his sponsors were Uzbek, not Russian or All-Union. Although his paper does not present an account of Islamic movements from the "inside," it goes farther in identifying the organization and sources of strength of Islamic activist movements. Abduvakhitov sees the origins of present-day Islamic activism in the reformist movements of Central Asian intellectuals in the late nineteenth and early twentieth centuries and in the organizational frameworks offered by Islamic brotherhoods, which were intertwined with the fortunes of the leading families.

The portrait he offers of these movements bears an uncanny resemblance to the fate of maraboutic (*sufi*) orders in Algeria. Long thought to have been discredited because of collaboration with French colonial officials, by the late 1960s, the leaders of key maraboutic families in Algeria emerged as strong Islamic activist leaders (Rouadjia 1990). Abdüvakhitov offers a similar image of a framework of religious leadership that was never quite extinguished during the years of Soviet rule. Of course, this image may be the product of an understandable historical revisionism, but as such, it offers a harbinger of histories now in the making.

---

3. Contradictions abound in the claim that this term is self-descriptive. Members of the "Wahhabi" movement elsewhere in the Muslim world refer to themselves as "unitarians" (Arabic, *al-muwahhidun*) to avoid elevating their founder, Ibn ʿAbd al-Wahhab (1703/4–1792), to the status of cult leader. It is worth noting that the "peculiar synthesis of folk and doctrinal Islam" which Malashenko imputes to the movement runs counter to "Wahhabi" doctrines, a central tenet of which is a purification of Islamic beliefs and practices from what they consider to be unsanctioned accretions.

Who are the Islamists in Uzbekistan? By the late 1970s, the policies of the Communist Party, Abduvakhitov explains, brought about growing economic and social inequalities, so that even some party cadres had become demoralized. Young urban people in the middle- and lower-income groups "felt that the situation was especially disastrous," and the policy of monocrop cotton production in the countryside also caused hardships. For some, an appeal to Islam was an appeal to self-determination, although the state-recognized religious leaders had little to do with this "parallel" Islam.

In the late 1970s, Islamists stressed religious education to the exclusion of politics. The leaders who emerged were young and had no formal religious training, making them, in many respects, like the Islamic leaders who have emerged in the Middle East, Southeast Asia, and elsewhere. They opened "clandestine" schools (although it appears that the authorities turned a blind eye to most of them) and used state presses to print their literature, binding religious tracts in covers with titles such as *Materials of the XXVth Congress of the CPSU*. Although state authorities imprisoned some leaders of the "parallel" Islamic movement and harassed others, the movement continued to grow, although, according to Abduvakhitov, it received no external support.

As in Malashenko's account, there is an indirect accolade to the skills of the state-recognized religious hierarchy, some of whom appear to be making their peace with the "parallel" activists in an effort to retain their status. Ironically, it is these "official" leaders, not the "parallel" activists, who are seeking external support from donors as diverse as Libya, Saudi Arabia, and Pakistan. Far from being advocates of terror, the militants of regions such as Uzbekistan's Ferghana Valley appear to be keen on sustaining public order as state authority crumbles or where the holders of state authority are responsible for instigating disorder. Although his narrative of recent disturbances is not firsthand, Abduvakhitov contextualizes the elements needed to understand these events.

Finally, his comments on the prospects for nonindigenous inhabitants of Central Asia, although not overly optimistic, suggest that an appropriate comparison could be made with French settlers and technicians in Tunisia and Morocco after independence—rough but basically peaceful transitions—as opposed to the more pessimistic analogy with Algeria. The strength of Abduvakhitov's account is a narrative of how Islamic activists are achieving their political objectives, not just reliance upon ill-considered doctrinal pronouncements. His suggestion that the activists are already enmeshed in political negotiations, even as the scales are weighted against them, offers more hope for future political stability than reliance on doctrinal pronouncements or deductions from supposed "religious characteristics."

As with the essays on Cold War superpower misperceptions and political developments in Central Asia, Victor Korgun and David Edwards offer significantly different perspectives on the efforts to introduce secular socialist rule in Afghanistan. Korgun acknowledges the failure of Soviet policies in Afghanistan, but his analysis suggests the perdurance of older frameworks. The corruption of successive Afghan governments, the refusal of private investors to put capital into industry, and efforts to "democratize" public life were all "stillborn," with the parliament continuing to be dominated by "feudal landlords."

In April 1978, a coup d'état brought a revolutionary council to power, which advocated such measures as land reform, the "liquidation" of feudal relations, the eradication of illiteracy, and the "democratization" of public life. By June 1978, 11 million peasants were "freed from debts to moneylenders and land-owners." These basic reforms, writes Korgun, were "doomed to fail, primarily because the country was unprepared for the revolution and its radical trans-formations," which occurred without popular support. The revolutionary elite relied upon its reading of popular sentiment and not upon mass participation to achieve its goals. Basing his argument on an implicit schema for political evolution (which is not without its echoes in Western modernization theories), Korgun believes that the "level of productive forces" and "the political capa-bilities of the [Afghan] party leaders" were not yet ready to create "a society free of exploitation of man by man." The Soviet model was introduced without regard for the "national specificity" of Afghanistan, and subsequent events showed the Soviet model to be "bankrupt."

Government leaders, Korgun continues, committed a "social and psycholog-ical error in overestimating the significance of social contradictions." Peasants, formally freed from moneylenders and landowners, were forced to turn to them again because the government organized no alternative. Moreover, the peasants were reluctant to renege upon their debts because doing so violated Islamic law and threatened the complex ties of tribe, clan, and family, in which villagers and land-owners were equally enmeshed. Peasants and land-owners were not antagonistic classes. Peasant dissatisfaction was paralleled by splits within the military and the ruling regime. As reforms accelerated, dissatisfaction grew, and party leaders became increasingly isolated. Even Soviet military interven-tion could not save the "revolution from above" and, indeed, "had a destabi-lizing influence on the political processes of the country."

Korgun's view of the failed "revolution" of 1978, skillfully interpolating the view of the masses, contrasts with Edwards's perspective, which is firmly situated in the periphery of the "masses." His concern is less with formal ideology than with popular perceptions of government acts and intentions, yet he also assesses the shortcomings of Korgun's analysis. One of the elements in this critique is Korgun's "tendency to view people as passive and ultimately reactionary rather than active and assertive." Peasants, because of "their limited stage of social advancement, . . . could not possibly assess the benefits of a socialist revolution on their own."

The alternative which Edwards suggests is to view the Afghan conflict "as an unfolding set of actions and responses, at any stage of which alternative actions would have led to different outcomes." In most Western accounts of the Afghan revolution, as in Korgun's analysis, direct testimony of Afghan views is absent. Edwards seeks to provide this through intensive analysis of

Afghan popular poetry from the early years of the Afghan revolt onward. In Afghanistan, as elsewhere in the Middle East, poetry is "one of the traditional channels for the articulation of political beliefs."

Edwards's analysis of this poetry suggests that a main theme in the early years of the revolution was the deviation of the Marxist regime from the notion of political "hierarchy as an extension of tribal structure," in which rule is an entitlement of birth. Usurpation of "just" rule is seen as analogous to "the murder of the Prophet Muhammad's grandchildren by Yazid on the plains of Karbala."

Nur Muhammad Taraki, described by official party biographers as "the kind of man with whom millions of poor Afghans could identify" because of his humble origins and by Korgun as "a typical Eastern ruler of the patriarchal type," is a target of popular outrage in the poems. Government propaganda was seen as an effort to arrogate importance to Taraki and the "new order" of the revolution as an inversion of the "moral understandings" on which Afghans had, until then, "based their acceptance of government rule." Local officials were seen as petty tyrants, "seduced by the trappings of power and prestige."

Yet, as Edwards argues, there was nothing inevitable about resistance to Marxist rule, for there was widespread discontent with President Daud at the time of the Marxist revolution. It was not Taraki's subscription to Marxist ideas that fueled popular resistance to the Marxist ruling clique, but the "conscious and avoidable decision to *portray* themselves as Marxists," including a boastfulness about Taraki's humble origins, and to identify with their Soviet sponsors.

Gene R. Garthwaite's paper offers an historical perspective on the development of "tribe" and national identities. The chapters on Central Asia and Afghanistan all presume the persistence of tribe and clan loyalties, and Garthwaite offers an account of what such political loyalties imply in two contrasting settings. Unlike the Kurds, Iran's Bakhtiyari are seldom categorized by Middle Easterners and outsiders as "national minorities," although both groups have significant internal divisions of religion, language, and ties with neighboring ethnic groups.

In the case of the Bakhtiyari, imperial Qajar rule enhanced the role of paramount tribal rulers in exchange for subordination to royal authority, legitimated through a cooptation of religious authority. These ties were further strengthened by intermarriage. Under Pahlavi rule, Bakhtiyari leadership was eliminated, although "some of the Bakhtiyari elite survived as part of the Pahlavi national elite," continuing their "traditional patronage roles" on a lesser scale. Since 1979, Iran's religious leaders, like their Pahlavi predecessors, have required an "unchallenged loyalty alongside an Iranian loyalty." Nonetheless, Garthwaite argues that the "self-image and representation" of tribespeople remains unchanged at "levels" of social organization lower than that of the former tribal political confederation.

Among the Kurds, the role of various *sufi* leaders, together with discriminatory state policies, provided the impetus for a political organization that united rural and urban Kurds, shopkeepers, and other urban residents with tribal leaders. Garthwaite argues that the higher level of urbanization has contributed significantly to a rejection of "traditional" leaders in favor of those who claim a national identity and the access that the Kurdish elite has had to education since the time of Ottoman rule. The sustained repression of Kurdish nationalist aspirations has itself provided an impetus toward nationalism.

As other papers in this volume—notably those of Malashenko, Abduvakhitov, Korgun, and Edwards—remind us of the perdurance of supposedly suppressed or obliterated religious and national identities, Garthwaite's analysis suggests the strength of subnational identities and allegiances and the conditions in which they might reemerge as politically significant. The collapse of Marxist rule in Kabul and its replacement by an Islamic government raises the question of whether more than a decade of fighting a common foe has forged dominant new, transregional, transethnic identities in Afghanistan. Many of Afghanistan's ethnic identities—Pathan and Tajik, for example—cross international frontiers into Pakistan and the neighboring Central Asian republics (Fuller 1992b; Philip 1992). Garthwaite's analysis pertains to Iran alone, but an analysis of the situation there provides insight for understanding the current situation in Afghanistan and Central Asia, as well as a fresh look at Iran's own complex of ethnic, linguistic, and religious affinities (see also Banuazizi and Weiner 1986).

In dealing with Islamization in Pakistan, Vyacheslav Belokrenitsky and Dimitri Novossyolov emphasize what might be called a "top-down" Islamization, while Richard Kurin places more emphasis on the implicit dialogue between the state center, which promulgates Islamization decrees and attempts to implement them, and the local, highly contextualized understandings that can redirect or give new meanings to state initiatives or provide "unauthorized" initiatives independent of state authority.

Belokrenitsky skillfully provides an historical overview, suggesting how British colonial rule ironically provided form and impetus to Islamic revival, then deals with the way that Islamization—not a crucial issue immediately after the creation of Pakistan—became increasingly important with the advent of military rule in the 1970s. In part, as Masud notes (Eickelman and Pasha 1991: 643), Islamization in Pakistan can be seen as the government's assertion of control over political and economic structures, with virtually no effect on the nature of the political-military elite. As John Esposito (Eickelman and Pasha 1991: 643) comments, the irony of Islamization in Pakistan and elsewhere is that its first effects are repressive—taxes and punishment. One consequence of Islamization, with its implications for reinforcing government control, is to reduce the potential for the emergence of ethnic nationalisms, a possibility which could be devastating for the survival of Pakistan as a state.

The papers by Novossyolov and Kurin are almost mirror images in approach. Novossyolov, in large part because of restrictions placed on his movements in

Pakistan by both Soviet and Pakistani authorities, assesses the consequences of Islamization through an analysis of the working of the *zakat* [alms] tax after the government made it mandatory. He traces how the *zakat* committees (over 36,000 of them in 1988, with 250,000 persons participating in administration of the tax) became increasingly an instrument of patronage and political mobilization. He also notes the links between regulations and the implications of bureaucratic structures.

Kurin, in contrast, carefully traces the implications of Islamization on individual lives, stressing what Muslims do rather than deducing conduct from doctrinal tenets. He chooses two figures—a *sayyid*, or descendant of the Prophet, who was also a landowner and a village religious leader, and a woman dancer from Karachi—and documents how their lives and careers were affected by Islamization. He invokes traditional Pakistani notions of person and self to explain the codes of morality and conduct through which his subjects interpreted what "being Islamic" meant and how they explained their personal choices, "empowering" some and making others increasingly difficult.

In the concluding paper, Masud, a scholar in Islamic law, draws on the literature of political science, urging scholars to go beyond the "impressionistic and general" in analyzing Islamic politics. In presuming that the proper domain of political science is the nation-state, for example, scholars assign a fundamental significance to control over a delimited territory, although language, ethnicity, and culture rarely coincide with territorial boundaries. In some parts of the world, moreover, the state is merely one political actor among many, and not necessarily the strongest.

Masud also notes that most contemporary Muslim states originated, not from the breakup of medieval Muslim empires—the Ottoman Empire excepted—but from states carved out of "colonial non-Muslim empires." Nonetheless, many analyses of Muslim politics have employed "deterministic" frameworks, asserting a diminished role for religion in contemporary political life, while arguing that the political conduct of Muslims can be deduced from religious doctrines. Because Muslims themselves sometimes assert that all Muslim conduct derives from authoritatively interpreted Islamic principles, analysts take them at their word, although few scholars would assign an equivalent role to other world religious traditions. The political principles of the Muslim world are highly varied—there are vigorous debates over just which principles are "Islamic"—and not all advocates of Islamic conduct place equal stress on political participation. It is not just pragmatism that creates "diversity" in the Muslim political process, but a degree of doctrinal and organizational diversity which Muslims themselves are often reluctant to recognize.

Masud calls special attention to the limitations of studies of Muslim politics that are "studies of scholars by scholars for scholars"—an elitist view which allows some to deduce, for example, that if a medieval Muslim jurist is favorably interpreted by a contemporary Muslim activist in one context, then the literal words of the medieval jurist are similarly binding on contemporary

Muslim activists. An understanding of Muslim politics involves more than focus on "literary, official, and elite sources." One thinks, for example, of the contrasting perspectives on the Palestine Liberation Organization provided by leaders of the movement's component organizations and that provided by Arabic-speaking Jean Genet (1986), who lived for an extended period in a camp with young *mujahids*. Similarly, the views of the leadership of the Muslim Brotherhood or other activist organizations do not necessarily represent those of their followers.

Masud notes the contrasts provided in this volume between scholars basing their work on official records and those using unofficial or indirect sources, including, in the case of Edwards, cassette poetry. He notes too the importance of language and labels, where one government's bandits are the people's "freedom fighters" or vice versa. The language used to describe Islamic movements is beginning to change, as ideas of "acceptable" representations of other people's politics also change. The same is true for regions of Muslim domination, where Masud notes the limitations inherent in a view that non-Muslims have no role to play in the analysis of Muslim issues.

One final note on the content and approaches of the contributors to this volume. A major difference between the U.S. and Soviet participants lies in the theoretical assumptions and organizational frameworks used for interpreting political and religious movements. U.S. participants generally note the theoretical assumptions implicit in their analyses of topics as diverse as foreign policy and ethnic, national, and religious identities; Soviet contributors do not. As became clear in the conference that preceded this volume, Soviet scholars tend to view "theory" with skepticism, partly because of the term's misuse in Marxist doctrine. One participant commented that Soviet problems were too "real" to be concerned with "theory" and "speculation." Others felt that learning Western concepts and techniques for analyzing ethnic, national, and religious identities offered a sounder base for approaching these issues than existing Soviet ones. As Masud indicates, a sensitivity to language, concepts, and perspectives enriches not only the understanding of concrete situations but also offers the possibility for better political understanding—and awareness of the limits of scholarly knowledge—for the future.

References

Anderson, Barbara A., and Brian D. Silver (1990). "Growth and Diversity of the Population of the Soviet Union." *Annals of the American Academy of Political Social Sciences*, no. 510 (July): 155–77.
Banuazizi, Ali, and Myron Weiner, eds. (1986). *The State, Religion, and Ethnic Politics: Afghanistan, Iran, and Pakistan*. Syracuse: Syracuse University Press.
Bill, James A., and Carl Leiden (1979). *Politics in the Middle East*. Boston: Little, Brown.
Binder, Leonard (1986). "The Natural History of Development Theory." *Comparative Studies in Society and History*. 28, no. 1 (January): 3–33.

Bromley, Julian, and Viktor Kozlov (1989). "The Theory of Ethnos and Ethnic Processes in Soviet Social Sciences." *Comparative Studies in Society and History*, 31, no. 3 (July): 425–38.

Canfield, Robert L., ed. (1991). *Turco-Persia in Historical Perspective*. New York: Cambridge University Press.

Comaroff, John (1991). "Humanity, Ethnicity, Nationality: Conceptual and Comparative Perspectives on the U.S.S.R." *Theory and Society* 20, no. 5 (October): 661–87.

Faroughy, Ahmad (1992). "L'Iran à la recherche d'une politique régionale." *Le Monde Diplomatique*, May, p. 7.

Fierman, William, ed. (1991). *Soviet Central Asia: The Failed Transformation*. Boulder: Westview Press.

Fuller, Graham E. (1991). *Islamic Fundamentalism in the Northern Tier Countries: An Integrative View*. Santa Monica: RAND (R-3966-USDP).

——— (1992a). "Our Fear of Islamic Politics Is Exaggerated." *Washington·Post*, January 16.

——— (1992b). "Afghanistan's Jagged Mosaic." *The New York Times*, March 23.

Gauhar, Altaf (1979). "Mawlana Abul Aᶜla Mawdudi—A Personal Account." In *Islamic Perspectives: Studies in Honour of Sayyid Abul A'la Mawdudi*, ed. Kurshid Ahmad and Zafar Ishaq Ansari, pp. 265–88. Leicester: The Islamic Foundation.

Genet, Jean (1986). *Un captif amoreux*. Paris: Gallimard.

Gross, Jo-Ann, ed. (1991). *Muslims in Central Asia: Expressions of Identity and Change*. Durham, N.C.: Duke University Press.

Halpern, Manfred (1963). *The Politics of Social Change in the Middle East and North Africa*. Princeton: Princeton University Press.

Johnson, Paul (1991). "Another Moslem Invasion of Europe." *The Los Angeles Times*, December 20.

Keatley, Robert (1991). "Turkey's New Image Is Suddenly Making It a Mideast Role Model." *The Wall Street Journal*, December 31, pp. A1, 4.

Laroui, Abdallah (1977). *The History of the Maghrib: An Interpretive Essay*, trans. Ralph Mannheim. Princeton: Princeton University Press.

Lerner, Daniel (1964). *The Passing of Traditional Society: Modernizing the Middle East*. New York: The Free Press.

"Looking North" (1992). *The Economist*, February 22, p. 29.

Malashenko, Alexei (1992). "L'Islam comme ferment des nationalismes en Russie." *Le Monde Diplomatique*, May, p. 4.

Olcott, Martha Brill (1989). "Islam and Ideology: IVAN's Political Agenda." Report to the National Council on Soviet and Eastern European Research, revised, May.

Philip, Bruno (1992). "Afghans d'abord." *Le Monde*, April 22, p. 3.

Robbins, Gerald (1991a). "Turkish City Pursues Rebirth as Trade Center." *The Journal of Commerce* (Washington), September 6.

——— (1991b). "Turkey Seeks Role as Trade Conduit to Soviet Union." *The Journal of Commerce* (Washington), November 20.

Rouadjia, Ahmed (1990). *Les frères et la mosquée: Enquête sur le mouvement islamiste en Algérie*. Paris: Karthala.

Said, Edward F. (1978). *Orientalism*. New York: Random House.

Seib, Gerald F. (1992). "Iran Is Re-Emerging as a Mideast Power as Iraqi Threat Fades." *The Wall Street Journal*, March 18, pp. A1, 10.

Shanin, Theodor (1989). "Ethnicity in the Soviet Union: Analytical Perceptions and Political Strategies." *Comparative Studies in Society and History* 31, no. 3 (July): 409–24.

Tyler, Patrick E. (1991). "Saudi Arabia Pledges $1 Billion to Soviet Union." *The New York Times*, October 9, p. A9.

Part I

International and Regional Perspectives

I

UNITED STATES MIDDLE EAST POLICY IN THE COLD WAR ERA

Richard W. Cottam

The forty-year Soviet-American conflict, which we came to call the Cold War, is over. It was a conflict unique in the world's history. One of the dimensions most responsible for this unique quality was nuclear weaponry. This was the first intense conflict between powers equipped with weapons capable of administering damage at a level so terrible that neither side could justify a decision to initiate the use of such weapons. Yet the conflict was at a level of intensity which in the past would have led to all-out warfare. Unwilling to pay the price of unleashing a nuclear holocaust or risking escalation to the nuclear level, yet determined to deny the enemy expanded world influence, both countries engaged in conflict at low violence or subviolence levels. The internal politics of third powers became central arenas of conflict. Regions such as the Middle East, which were judged strategically critical, became, in effect, primary battlegrounds between the warring powers (Cottam 1967; Treverton 1987).

With the passing of this great conflict, the time is propitious for making a preliminary assessment of how the conflict was expressed in the Middle East. This chapter identifies the strategic thrust of United States policy in the Middle East in the Cold War era and the impact of this strategy on Middle East politics, economics, and society. Finally, it asks what, if anything, has been learned from this history by those making contemporary policy in the region.

Evolution of a Policy

The prominent role of the United States in the Middle East was accepted with some reluctance in the early years of the Cold War and only after the British had concluded they could no longer play such a role. There were major interests at stake, and the involvement of the United States became intense and persisting. Despite the lack of American experience in the area, a formula for

dealing with the Middle East region emerged within a few years. That formula
endured in its general form throughout the Cold War era. Successive administrations found that the formula served critical American interests in the region
reasonably well.

There were three primary interests in the area which no American administration could ignore. The first and most compelling interest emanated from a
perceived threat by the American public from the Soviet Union and international Communism. By the early 1950s, the perception was widespread that
the Soviet Union would seek to gain dominance of the Middle East and would
do so largely through political subversion. All the administrations of the Cold
War era therefore gave top priority to containing and deterring this perceived
Soviet expansionism. The second interest, closely related to the first, was to
maintain the free flow of Middle East oil to Western industry. This was essential
for maintaining the Western industrial base. But there was also an interest in
defending the large financial investments of American oil companies in the
area. The third interest developed from the concern of a major public-interest
group in the United States with the security of the newly formed state of Israel.

The discovery of a policy formula which could serve all three interests did
not come easily. Indeed, the formula emerged from a long and often fiercely
competitive policy process and not from the planning tables of a few strategists.
The task was seriously complicated by the fact that the Middle East was an
area undergoing change at an accelerating rate. Throughout the area, traditional leaders were being challenged and internal stability threatened. The
challenge came primarily from two emerging and competing forces, each of
which sought immediate change in somewhat different directions. These were
(1) secular nationalist movements among the various peoples of the Middle
East and (2) Islamic movements. The major thrust of United States policy,
concerned as it was with the internal politics of Middle Eastern states, was
inevitably shaped by decisions on how it should deal with this leadership
struggle.

Both secular nationalism and political Islam had the potential to become
major vehicles of political populism, but in the early days of the Cold War, the
secular nationalists were the most important focus of populist appeal in most
regional states. The question of how to relate to regional nationalist leaders
had to be faced by American decision-makers, but it was viewed within different
local contexts, and no one familiar with the policy process should have expected
the emergence of a clearly explicated formula. Rather, a range of differing
patterns should have been expected and in fact did appear.

There was little difficulty in developing a policy toward Turkey. The modernization process was more advanced there than among Arabs and Iranians.
By the beginning of the Cold War, the traditional-modern struggle had been
won by the modernists. Secular nationalism was well ensconced in the Turkish
political system, and its leaders were natural allies of the United States. They
were reacting, much as the Americans were, to a perceived threat from the

Soviet Union and viewed the emergence of strong anti-Soviet sentiments in the United States with satisfaction.

The situation in Iran and the Arab world was more complicated. To be sure, major nationalist figures had emerged among both peoples. Muhammad Musaddiq in Iran and Gamal Abdul Nasser in Egypt and the Arab world were seen by members of the American decision-making community as counterparts of their Turkish allies. Musaddiq was a charismatic spokesman for Iranian secular nationalism and Nasser the accepted leader of Arab nationalism in wide sections of the Arab world. The case for supporting Musaddiq and Nasser related most clearly to the American goal of containing perceived Soviet expansionism. As Mustapha Kemal Atatürk had been in Turkey, Musaddiq and Nasser were determined to defend the independence of their peoples from any challenger, including the Soviet Union. The case for supporting them was particularly strong in terms of the form of expansionism the Soviets were expected to follow—for example, political subversion. The popularity of nationalist leaders, in contrast to the limited appeal of traditional political leaders, could be expected to reduce significantly the potential for political subversion (for an explication of this rationale, see Copeland 1969).

The attraction of supporting Iranian and Arab nationalist leaders was less apparent with regard to Western oil investments. Musaddiq was recognized as the leading proponent for nationalizing the Anglo-Iranian Oil Company. Egypt was not a significant source of oil, but Nasser's allies in the oil-producing areas of the Arab world favored nationalizing oil production. Thus, whereas the nationalists could be expected to resist any Soviet challenge, they also demanded the elimination of all foreign control of their oil.

The policy of support for Iranian and Arab leaders had no attraction with regard to the third United States objective, that of defending the security of Israel. Both Musaddiq and Nasser viewed Israel, as did their supporters, as a manifestation of Western imperialism. For Musaddiq and the Iranians, opposition to Israel was not likely to go beyond hostile rhetoric. For Nasser and his Arab followers, however, Israel was a focus of the struggle against imperialism. Self-determination for Palestinians had become an article of faith for Arab nationalism generally. Inevitably Nasser, the leader of Arab nationalism, came to be viewed in Israel as their most dangerous regional opponent. Americans who feared for Israel's security shared this view (Finer 1984).

Two major decisions by American policymakers set the stage for a strategic formula for dealing with the Middle East. The first was made by the newly inaugurated Eisenhower administration in 1953, shortly after the death of Joseph Stalin. That decision was to execute a coup d'état in cooperation with the British and Iranian opponents of Musaddiq (Gasiorowski 1987). The decision was audacious in the extreme. Musaddiq had established his credentials as an incorruptible and uncompromising foe of imperialism. His appeal to progressive nationalists in Iran was charismatic. But Iran was undergoing rapid change, and probably no more than 10 percent of its population could be considered politically participant. The majority of Iranians entertained little thought of challenging the traditional elite structure. Thus, even though Musaddiq was overwhelmingly popular with those who were politically participant, he was vulnerable to a challenge from an established elite which was supported financially, logistically, and politically by the United States and Great Britain.

Like Iranian nationalists generally, Musaddiq viewed the United States as the one Western polity that was true to its ideological commitment to national self-determination. Indeed, pro-Soviet Tudeh Party newspapers described Musaddiq and his national movement as agents of American policy. The Truman administration had viewed Musaddiq as a difficult individual but concluded that good relations with his populist movement served the American anti-Soviet purpose (see British Foreign Office [1952] for one such appraisal). But Eisenhower's Secretary of State, John Foster Dulles, had different ideas. Musaddiq had associated his regime with Third World leaders such as Nehru of India, who felt that a policy of nonalignment best served the interests of people just emerging from prolonged imperial domination. Dulles had no sympathy with such a policy. He saw Musaddiq, as he saw others in the nonaligned camp, as too weak and too naive to provide a defense against a ruthless Soviet subversive campaign. Musaddiq's tolerance of a vigorous Marxist press and the pro-Soviet Tudeh Party demonstrations served to confirm the Dulles view that Musaddiq's behavior was indistinguishable from that of Soviet satellites. In addition, America's closest ally, Great Britain, was determined to reverse the nationalization of vital oil interests, and Dulles was sympathetic. The decision was made shortly after Eisenhower's inauguration to join Great Britain in overturning Musaddiq. The Eisenhower administration thus broke completely with Truman's view that an association with Iranian nationalist leaders served American security and economic interests (Cottam 1988: 103).

The most extraordinary aspect of this decision lies in what it revealed about official American perceptions of the Soviet Union. A major operation, one which could never escape the attention of the KGB, was being launched to replace a popular, pro-American but nonaligned Iranian prime minister with a regime fully dependent on American support for its survival, and the coup was to occur in a state which shared a 1,200-mile land border with the Soviet Union. Yet there was no expectation that the Soviet Union would respond violently to the imposition of what could reasonably be seen as an American satellite regime on its most vulnerable border. Nor was there an expectation that the Soviet Union would take advantage of the American action to establish close relations with ousted Iranian national-movement leaders. One need only reflect on the probable American response to a parallel situation in Mexico to recognize the startling nature of such a picture.

Why should an American leadership which viewed the Soviet Union as ineluctably expansionist maintain such expectations? One possible explanation lies in the view of the Soviet Union held by Dulles, a view that approximates the "diabolical enemy" stereotype identified in perception theory (Holsti 1967). In this view, the ineluctably aggressive enemy is also highly rational and, if con-fronted with will, determination, and strength by its intended victims, would adopt a nonthreatening posture. It would then wait patiently for a new set of leaders to conclude they had nothing to fear and lower their guard. This so-called paper tiger picture is an integral part of the diabolical enemy image (White 1966). In point of fact, these American expectations were realized. Far from responding in a threatening way, as one not holding such a stereotypical view might have expected, the Soviet leaders established relations with the new regime, which soon became closer to the Soviet Union than the obstreperously nationalistic Musaddiq had been. The Soviet leadership turned a deaf ear to the pleadings of the pro-Soviet Tudeh Party of Iran to endorse a popular front with the Musaddiqists, and from this point on, the United States showed little hesitation in engaging in major anti-Soviet activities on the Soviet-Middle East border.

The American decision regarding Musaddiq and Iranian nationalism did not forecast a parallel decision with respect to Nasser of Egypt and Arab nation-alism. Indeed, Kermit Roosevelt, the self-proclaimed executor of the coup against Musaddiq (Roosevelt 1979),[1] was a major supporter of the policy of good relations with the Egyptian dictator. Ironically, the authoritarianism of Nasser may have added to his appeal. Whereas the liberal Musaddiq refused to go far in suppressing Iranian Communists and was allied with Islamic political activists, Nasser dealt harshly with both Communists and religiopoliti-cal activists. The break with Nasser would occur, but not until two years later and as a consequence of an Israeli raid into the Egyptian-occupied Gaza Strip, which dealt Nasser's forces a humiliating defeat. Nasser's response to this debacle was to request that the United States sell him more effective military equipment. The request posed a serious dilemma for the American government. How could it be supportive of Israel and Israeli security concerns while pro-viding a friendly and useful Nasser with military equipment which might well be used against Israel? For several months the administration procrastinated, and finally an exasperated Nasser turned to the Soviet Union with a request for arms sales. The Soviets agreed to the sale of Czech arms to Nasser. Following that transaction, continued close relations with Nasser were impossible for the United States (Love 1969).

The final policy shift away from Nasser came after the Suez Canal crisis (October 1956) in the form of the Eisenhower Doctrine, which offered support to any Middle East state requesting aid to oppose a threat from the Soviet Union, acting directly or through the agency of a regional surrogate. Specific policy applications made clear the administration's assumption that Nasser's Egypt was the primary regional Soviet surrogate. The support given King Hussein's royal coup of April 1957, the failed CIA coup against Syria in August

---

1. Roosevelt (1979) is an excellent source for viewing extreme stereotypical thinking regarding the Soviet Union and its supposed satellites.

1957, and the landing of troops in Lebanon in July 1958 were the most visible manifestations of this policy.[2] Its purpose was to isolate and, if possible, overturn Nasser, now the symbolic leader of Arab nationalism.

The United States policy formula had thus crystallized. A functioning alliance system emerged but, because of internal contradictions, could not be formalized. However, its structure remained relatively constant. The allies were Great Britain, Israel, Turkey, the Shah's Iran, and those Arab regimes which felt threatened by the forces of Arab nationalism. The membership of this last group shifted in response to internal developments. The most shocking developments came in 1958, when a coup d'état in Iraq, until then the mainstay of the conservative Arab bloc, moved that state out of the alliance, and in 1978, when Anwar Sadat, Nasser's successor, moved Egypt into the American alliance (Quandt 1986).

This alliance system reflected an implicit operating assumption that the political environment of the Middle East was favorable for achieving the objectives of containing the Soviet Union, insuring the free flow of oil to Western industry, and providing for the security of Israel. The forces of change, represented initially by Iranian and Arab nationalism, were treated as endangering those objectives. American involvement in the internal politics of states in the area therefore took the form of reinforcing a favorable status quo. Change was acceptable, but change at a controlled and managed pace. A combination of technocratic management and planning and entrepreneurial freedom resulted sometimes in impressive economic growth. But the nationalistic legitimacy of Iran and friendly Arab countries was always in question.

After 1958, instances of gross American interference in the internal affairs of regional states declined rapidly. There was only one major clandestine effort to overturn a regime that opposed the alliance. That was the attempt in 1974, in alliance with Iran and Israel, to trigger a Kurdish rebellion to destabilize the Iraqi regime in which Saddam Hussein was the dominant figure.[3] Generally the focus was on isolating and containing such regimes, which were viewed as satellites of the Soviet Union.

Disintegration of the Policy Formula

The Camp David Agreement of 1978 between Egypt and Israel marked the high point of this policy formula. The list of Soviet clients had been reduced

---

2. These episodes have yet to be described well in the literature. For one good account, see Seale (1965). George and Smoke (1974) includes a case study of the Lebanon episode.

3. This case has yet to be analyzed adequately. The Pike Committee of the House of Representatives, commissioned with the task of investigating clandestine diplomacy, summarized the documentation on the Kurdish case. Sections of that documentation were leaked to a Manhattan weekly, *Village Voice*, where they appeared on February 16, 1976, in a 24-page supplement.

to three Arab regimes—Syria, Iraq, and the Peoples Democratic Republic of Yemen—plus Afghanistan. There was some uncertainty about Iraq's placement on that list, given the lack of support it had received from the Soviet Union in the 1974 Kurdish uprising and Saddam Hussein's stubborn independence. The pro-American camp, buoyed by Egypt's critical presence, was the more impressive regional bloc.

How can this asymmetry in favor of the United States be explained? The Soviet Union, still perceived by Americans as expansionist, was a superpower whose boundaries extended geographically into the Middle East, whereas the United States was several thousand miles away. In a geopolitical sense, the Middle East could be described as part of a natural Soviet sphere of influence. From the perspective of political realism, particularly as expounded by Hans Morgenthau (1967), the United States could be described as having committed the crime of overextension and ignoring the legitimate power interests of the Soviet Union. But the Soviet Union seems not to have been seriously concerned by American intrusion in the Middle East, even, as we have seen, when American influence was felt on the Soviet border.

In verbal terms, American officials continued to describe the Soviet Union as a diabolical enemy, but American policy tended more and more to deal with the Soviet Union as if it were following an essentially status quo policy. This conclusion became particularly obvious as one of the most important developments of the Cold War era began to take shape: the Iranian revolution. September 1978, the month of the Camp David conference, marked the climactic point of American influence in the Middle East, but it was also the month when it became apparent that a new regime was about to appear in Iran, one of the most vital United States allies in the region. The tendency throughout the Cold War era was for Americans to see any development detrimental to American strength in the area as Soviet-orchestrated. This was indeed the view of National Security Advisor Zbigniew Brzezinski, and President Carter accepted Brzezinski's thinking regarding Iran (Sick 1985). But the prevailing view in the State Department was that the revolution was a product of indigenous forces. Following the revolution, the behavior of the Iranian regime convinced even Brzezinski that the new Islamic government was bitterly anti-Communist. Indeed, prior to Iran's taking American diplomats hostage, Brzezinski saw the Khomeini regime as a potential ally in serving the anti-Soviet purpose.

The Soviet occupation of Afghanistan in December 1979 came as a shock to the Carter administration. That this should have been so is instructive. The Soviet Union, perceived as an ineluctably aggressive superpower, had a friendly socialist regime on its southern border, but that friendly regime was perceived by the Soviets as politically vulnerable and in danger of being replaced by an unfriendly regime, possibly one under American influence. Given such a picture, why should anyone have been surprised when the Soviet Union intervened in Afghanistan? The answer seems to be that Soviet passivity and acquiescence in the face of similar challenges had come to be the expected pattern. That acquiescence was seen as a natural response to an American resolve which the Soviets could not deny. In other words, the Soviet Union was viewed as successfully contained even in an area (such as southern Central Asia) where the Soviet geopolitical advantage would seem to be greatest. But the occupation of Afghanistan restored an image of a Soviet Union both aggressive and uncontained (Brzezinski 1983; Carter 1982).

Fears that the Soviet move into Afghanistan would be followed by moves into more strategically important areas to the south were expressed in the next few months. The focus of greatest concern was briefly on the Persian Gulf area, but when no serious movement occurred in that direction, American policy responses began to return to preoccupation patterns. The American response now came to focus on the Afghan theater of operations, and the Soviet occupation forces became the primary target. It took the form of support to Afghan resistance groups, usually in cooperation with the Pakistani government. Recipients of this support included a number of *mujahidin* groups which represented diverse elements within a political Islamic context. Assistance seems to have been distributed largely on the basis of military effectiveness. Within months of the Soviet occupation of Afghanistan, the United States, in cooperation with Pakistan, was giving support to elements representing an Islamic political resurgence. It was doing so on a Soviet border halfway around the world from the United States. Such a policy once again reflected an assumption of a Soviet Union which understood it was contained and acquiesced in an obtrusive American presence deep within its geopolitical space.

The major anomaly that appeared in this relationship was the United States' apparent willingness to deal with a dynamic and radical Islamic political assertiveness. The case is made above that the policy formula that had crystallized in the late 1950s was based on an assumption that the existing political environment was favorable and that the status quo should be maintained. The target of that period had been populism, in the form of secular nationalism, in Iran and the Arab world. Now, a generation later, populism, in the form of religious nationalism in Afghanistan and possibly in Iran, was being treated as a natural ally. Did this portend a fundamental shift in strategy and an acceptance of a new policy formula where the agents of change would be supported rather than suppressed or isolated?

United States policy toward the Iran-Iraq War suggests that the answer to that question must be no. When that war ended in a cease-fire in 1988, the United States' tilt toward Iraq had become a virtual alliance. Furthermore, Reagan administration statements regarding the United States' role reflected a determination to contain the forces of revolutionary Islam, which threatened to undermine the stability of the area. Yet that same administration was strengthening its ties, through Pakistan, with Afghan leaders such as Gulbuddin Hikmatiyar, whose political philosophy differed little from Khomeini's. There had been no crystallization of a new policy formula but, rather, a disintegration of the old formula and the adoption of compartmentalized formulas for dealing with different crisis situations in the region.

Policy toward the Gulf Crisis

Iraq invaded Iran on September 22, 1980, only days after the Carter administration had received a highly credible signal that the Iranian regime was prepared to negotiate the release of the American hostages. The administration judged correctly that the invasion would complicate, if not destroy, the basis for negotiations. Since Carter's reelection prospects would be enhanced by a quick resolution of the hostage crisis, the invasion could not have been less propitious.

It should also be kept in mind that the regime in which Saddam Hussein played the dominant role had been regarded by American officials as a primary instrument of Soviet policy through the mid-1970s. Triggering the Kurdish rebellion in Iraq in 1974 was part of an effort to destabilize the Hussein regime. So were the close collaborations with the Shah of Iran and the government of Israel. The Soviet Union's failure to give Iraq arms and diplomatic support was in accord with expectations.

When Iraq invaded Iran, however, the American response was surprising. The Soviet occupation of Afghanistan had taken place in December 1979 and had been greeted as a reaffirmation of Soviet aggressive intent. Then, nine months later, a regime which had been regarded as a regional instrument of Soviet policy invaded Iran, a state widely regarded as the strategic prize of the region. The invasion should have been seen, one would think, as a continuation of Soviet expansionism in a more subtle form. The damage done to the American effort to extricate itself from the hostage crisis could easily have been described as serving the expansionist Soviet purpose as well. Yet the United States' response did not fit these patterns (Cottam 1988: 237–40).

In contrast to the later reaction against "aggression" when Iraq moved into Kuwait, there were no serious protests regarding Iraqi aggression in the eastern Gulf area. Nor was there any effort to depict the invasion as tied to Soviet expansionism in south Asia. American attention focused primarily on the hostage crisis and its implications for the 1980 election. In the nine months since the Soviet move into Afghanistan, American fears apparently had faded. Iraq had condemned the Soviet move into Afghanistan, and that, plus the Soviet Union's failure to give assistance to Iraq in 1974, may have led to a view that Iraq was an independent actor. In any event, when Ronald Reagan was inaugurated, he did not depict Iraq's aggression against Iran as an indirect move by the Soviet Union acting through a regional surrogate. But neither was there a clearly expressed preference for Iraq over Iran.

When the fortunes of war shifted in the Gulf arena, so did the American attitude. In 1982, after the failure of Iraq's offensive in southwest Iran, Iranian

forces began to move into Iraq. The American press began to paint scenarios
of a victorious Iran turning south into the Arabian Peninsula after it disposed
of the Iraqi regime. Reagan administration spokesmen quickly made clear their
determination that Iran would not be allowed to destabilize the Gulf region
(Murphy 1984). Although officially denied, the administration's tilt toward
Iraq was accepted as an established fact. Diplomatic relations with Iraq were
restored, and it was removed from the list of states giving support to terrorism.
In the meantime, the Soviet Union had resumed arms shipments to Iraq and
continued to treat the regime as a friend and ally.

Within the Reagan administration there was considerable unease regarding
this alliance. As would become clear in 1986, William Casey, Director of
Central Intelligence, and Robert McFarlane, National Security Advisor, were
among the officials who favored an altered relationship with Iran. The logic
of their position, given the acceptance of a Cold War world view within the
administration, was compelling. Iran's oil wealth and geopolitical position gave
that state strategic importance. To be sure, the regime had been guilty of
unforgivable behavior in the hostage situation, but it was stable, and its attitude
toward the Soviet Union and Communism left little to be desired. Its policy
toward Afghanistan coincided with that of the United States, in terms of giving
support to the *mujahidin* forces, and it had taken the lead in mobilizing
opposition in the Islamic world to the Soviet occupation.

Iraq, as they saw it, remained a close friend of the Soviet Union and was
doing the Soviet cause a service by attempting to weaken Iran. Colonel Oliver
North's statement to Iranian leaders that the American administration understood that Saddam Hussein must be eliminated (Tower Commission Report
1987: III, 18), though probably unauthorized, suggests that the tilt toward Iraq
would have been abandoned with alacrity had those involved in "Irangate"
succeeded in changing United States policy. Then–Vice President George Bush
(1986) advised the Arab Gulf states of the advantages for them in a shift of
American policy toward Iran. The rationale, of course, was that Iran could
play a major role in keeping the Soviet Union contained, which would make
it unable to extend into the oil-producing areas of the Arabian Peninsula.

The oil-producing Arab Gulf regimes found this an unconvincing argument.
As their spokesmen made clear, there was little fear of a Soviet move into the
Gulf. There were, in contrast, real fears regarding the strength of political Islam
within the Arab world. Iran's success on the battlefield could encourage local
leaders of resurgent Islam and might lead to the demise of the conservative
Arab friends of the United States. These regimes understood equally well the
risks of cooperating with Iraq. Saddam Hussein saw them as weak dependencies
of American policy. They had no place in his plan to unite and lead a much
expanded Arab nation. But the threat from a politically resurgent Islam was
more imminent. The Gulf regimes reached deeply into their financial reserves
to support Iraq in the war.

Those Reagan administration officials willing to move toward Iran saw their hopes destroyed by the untimely revelation of their willingness to trade arms for hostages and to use the money received from Iran to finance the Nicaraguan contras. This left the policy field open to those who advocated a continuation of the tilt toward Iraq. In fairly short order, that policy evolved into a de facto alliance with Iraq.

The official American rationale for this policy was never that of defeating a challenge from politically assertive Islam. At an Arab meeting in November 1987 in Amman, the decision was made that Iran, rather than Israel, now constituted the primary threat to the Arabs (Foreign Broadcast Information Service 1987). There is little to indicate that the Reagan administration understood that the Arab presidents and kings were really saying that the primary threat was from Islam. The stated rationale for United States policy was twofold: first, to prevent the Soviet Union's getting a foothold in the region, which would allow them to interdict or control oil supplies, and second, to maintain free navigation of the Gulf. Why an alliance with Iraq, which had a friendship agreement with the Soviet Union and against anti-Communist Iran, would serve the first purpose was not explained. Nor was any serious note taken of the fact that Iran was willing to agree to a cease-fire in the Gulf waters (which would be to its advantage) and that Iraq saw attacks on shipping headed for Iran as an essential part of its battle plan.

I am not arguing that the Reagan administration attempted to conceal its true purpose in the Gulf by a logically untenable rationale. Rather, the proposition is that the policy and its rationale were reflections of the disintegration of the world view on which the Cold War was based. The policy formula that had evolved to deal with a perceived Soviet threat had as a critical element a close working relationship with a group of conservative Arab regimes, most of them oil-producers. This policy led to the appearance of a web of interests—economic, military-strategic, and bureaucratic—tying the United States to these regimes. A threat to their stability thus was a threat to these interests. The suggestion that United States interests, especially in containing the Soviet Union, would be better served by allying with Iran, which opposed any external inroads in the area, was without appeal to those tied to these interests. A shift toward Iran could only have occurred if the perceived threat from the Soviet Union remained at a first degree of intensity. The real author of the policy was the rapid decline in the intensity of that perception of threat from the no-longer diabolical enemy.

Impact of the Cold War on the Middle East

The Cold War occurred at a time in Middle East history when the forces of revolutionary change were gaining major momentum. For purposes of this analysis, the aspects of change that were most critical were, first, the shift in political identity from parochial foci, such as the extended family and clan, to large, politically relevant communities which could serve as a basis for large, modern nation-states. Among these large identity communities in the late 1940s and early 1950s were ethnic groups, religious sects, and the wider Islamic community. Leaders of ethnic communities and religious activists sought to replace traditional leaders who struggled to preserve the old structures. Second, there was a growing predisposition within publics to participate actively in the political life of their communities. The right of traditional leaders such as landowners or tribal leaders to make decisions for them was being challenged. These two trends suggested that an era characterized by mass politics was not far distant.

Much of the impetus for change of this dimension and speed came as a result of the interaction with Europe. But the European powers, having played a catalytic role in producing change, became increasingly uneasy with the impact of change on the region and their position in it. The instability associated with rapid change was damaging to their economic interests and to their relations with each other. In the post–World War I period, the French and British acted to slow the tempo of change. They did so directly, through the mandate system, and indirectly, working through traditional and conservative elites. The Cold War era saw a persistence of this pattern. United States policy, in particular, took the form of strengthening regimes that followed slow and controlled change strategies. Arab and Iranian leaders who attempted to move their peoples more quickly were opposed or overturned (as with Musaddiq) but more frequently isolated and weakened (as with Nasser).

The trends of identity change and a predisposition to participate actively in the political process were much too strong to be halted or reversed by external intervention, however. At most, they could be deflected and their tempo slowed. This did in fact occur. The most significant impact was on the fortunes of secular nationalism in Iran and the Arab world. At the beginning of the period, secular nationalist leaders were the primary focus of populist appeal. They were also the primary targets of American interventionist policies. By the end of the era, they had been discredited and were no longer viewed as capable of leading their peoples. The focus of populist appeal then fell on leaders speaking for religious rather than ethnic communities. The most important were those who advocated a political resurgence of Islam. But minority religious communities, such as the Maronite, the Druze, and the Shiʿi communities of Lebanon, with their own populist leaders, began behaving as mininations. This enhanced the danger of intercommunal conflict, sometimes at the genocidal level, among these assertive communities. In addition, there was a growth in the attraction of leaders in small and often artificially created Arab states, reflecting the development in the Arab world of state nationalism. In Egypt the appeal of an Arab identity, so strong in the Nasser period, declined sharply for Egyptian secularists. But the attraction of identifying primarily as Muslims grew.

The predisposition to participate in politics continued to develop. The Iranian revolution was a manifestation of populism at an unparalleled level. Iran, since the revolution, has witnessed countless mass demonstrations, and even though the regime has lost much of its popular support base, there is no question that Iran has entered the era of mass politics. Mass participation in the political life of most Arab states was constricted by authoritarian leadership, but liberalization in the late 1980s in Jordan, Tunisia, and Algeria produced a level of mass participation that suggested the days of constricted political participation were nearing an end in the Arab world generally. The elections that occurred in the above three states provided evidence for the contention that the newly participant mass would look primarily to Islamic political resurgence for its leaders, at least in the immediate future.

The case cannot be made with any certainty that, without American intervention in the Cold War era, there would have been a unification of much of the Arab world, but the belief that this is so is widely held by progressive Arabs throughout that world, and that belief is marked by deep public anger and hostility. The view that the United States, working with Israel, seeks to maintain its control over the resources and territory of the Arab and Muslim world for the foreseeable future is pervasive in the region. Those Arab leaders who solicit American support—particularly the leaders of the oil-producing states in the Arabian Peninsula—are viewed as agents of American-Zionist-Atlantic imperialism.[4] Without question, emerging populist leaders in the Middle East will ground their appeal in this worldview. Any assessment of the impact of the Soviet-American Cold War on the region must include this attitudinal consequence.

Regional Power Alterations

The appearance of a militarily overwhelming, essentially American force in the Arabian Peninsula in response to the Iraqi invasion of Kuwait on August 2, 1990, and the attack on Iraq on January 16, 1991, underlined the power advantage of the United States. Were capability assessments based solely on military power, the United States was in a class by itself and had the option to impose its will on the settlement of any dispute. However, capability assessments must be based on an analysis of all, not just military, aspects of power. In the early Cold War years, for example, the United States had the power to involve itself in the internal affairs of target states and to effect desired outcomes. Clandestine political power instruments granted a capability to overturn some regimes and to strengthen others. By the end of the Cold War, such power instruments had lost their effectiveness. Confronted with the Iranian Revolution

---

4. This is the litany of the anti-American bloc. The imagery was well developed in Saddam Hussein's speech to the nation, in which he announced his withdrawal from Kuwait (Foreign Broadcast Information Service, February 21, 1991: 21–24).

and the threat to the Shah's regime, which had played a critical surrogate role for the United States, the United States government was unable to sustain its influence in the country. In Lebanon, following Israel's invasion of 1982, the United States government sought to gain control of internal political develop-ments to construct a favorable political milieu. But it was soon apparent that achieving this goal required the massive application of military power and a semipermanent occupation of the country. The Reagan administration under-stood that it could not mobilize the necessary public support for so costly an enterprise, and this ability must be a central aspect of any capability assessment. That American citizens were virtually excluded from two great Middle Eastern cities, Beirut and Tehran, by 1985 was symbolic of a declining American ability to project its influence in the Middle East.

The coincidence of the disintegration and the termination of the Cold War with the appearance of an assertive public in the Middle East had combined to alter the political balance of power in the region. Presumably, had the threat of a possible Soviet takeover of the region maintained its early high intensity, the American public might have been willing to accept a long-term military presence in the area, but once the interest in containing perceived Soviet expansionism faded, there was no foreign-policy interest sufficient to sustain such a presence.

As regional leaders—in particular Saddam Hussein—took note of this change in power relationships, they perceived policy options that previously had been denied them. As was the case in Eastern Europe, the passing of the Cold War in the Middle East meant that a political status quo which had appeared for over a generation to be frozen now could be seen as malleable. Saddam Hussein, earlier than most, had understood that the Soviet-American Cold War was losing its determining force in world politics. Yet he made the astonishing mistake of mounting a challenge that induced the United States to use its military power, the one area in which American capabilities were still expand-ing. Other Middle Eastern leaders interested in reducing the American role in the region are unlikely to repeat that error.

Conclusions

The era of the Cold War coincided with an era of exceptionally rapid sociopolitical change in the Middle East. In the first decade after World War II, much of the Middle East, especially the Iranian and Arab sections, was just beginning to emerge from a traditional system. Popular leaders had begun to appear, but typically they could count on full support only from a small percentage of the population. The currents of change were strong, however, and the Iranian and Arab worlds were about to follow patterns already seen in Turkey.

This was also the decade in which United States policy was most obtrusive.

Involvement in the domestic affairs of regional states reached the level of overturning regimes only occasionally, but it was sufficiently significant to be described as "political engineering." By the end of the decade, a clear pattern in regime preference had emerged. Most favored were regimes willing to accept political change at a slow and controlled pace and willing to grant a fair amount of entrepreneurial freedom. Most opposed were regimes which moved quickly to replace the traditional order and were willing to experiment with political freedom. Not coincidentally, regimes that were opposed tended to be regarded by their politically active publics as having nationalistic legitimacy. As a consequence, United States policy came to be viewed by many Iranians and Arabs as indistinguishable from the policies of the European imperial powers in previous decades. Favored regimes were seen, at best, as American dependencies; at worst, as lackeys of Western imperialism.

In an effort to counter American policy, regimes that felt threatened solicited support from the Soviet Union. The hope was obviously to balance the threat from one superpower with the support of the other. The Soviet response to these solicitations was often favorable and typically took the form of a willingness to sell arms on favorable credit terms and to give limited diplomatic support. However, there remained an asymmetry in the degree of support given by the two superpowers: the United States was far and away the more reliable ally. Still, the support given by the Soviet Union provided regimes such as that of Hafez al-Asad in Syria with the leverage to stand up against the alliance associated with the United States.

The final decade of the Cold War, as it related to the Middle East, was marked by two developments that forecast basic change in the post–Cold War period. First, the clusterings of regional states around the competing superpowers, which had been fairly stable throughout the 1970s, began to unravel. The primary associates of the Soviet Union, Iraq and Syria, were bitterly opposed, and the latter maintained a friendly alliance with Iran throughout the Iran-Iraq War. Iraq was now closely associated with Arabian Peninsula states which it had earlier described as "American lackeys." Even more telling, Saddam Hussein had become a de facto ally of the United States while maintaining a friendship agreement with the Soviet Union. Second, both superpowers suffered political defeats in the region which suggested their declining ability to influence the course of events. The United States was unable to keep the Shah of Iran in power in the face of an almost bloodless revolution and failed in its effort to play a stabilizing role in Lebanon. The Soviet military was unable to establish firm control of Afghanistan in the face of popular resistance.

In late 1989, the region began to understand that the Cold War was over, but very different expectations were expressed regarding the new era. Hafez al-Asad, for example, viewed the event primarily in terms of the collapse of the Soviet Union as a significant world power. He believed that this would deny the Arabs their only external base of support and hence sharply reduce their bargaining strength. The primary consequence would be the weakening of Arabs in their struggle with an aggressive Israel, which was likely to receive undiminished support from the remaining superpower. Saddam Hussein, in contrast, saw the end of the Cold War in terms of the end of the era of superpower domination in the region. In his view, the post–Cold War era would be one in which Iraq's options were greatly enlarged. He could now think in terms of unifying major sections of the Arab world and ultimately mounting a military challenge to Israel. The policy line he later followed suggests that he saw an Arabian Peninsula no longer protected by the United States, whose major interest in the area—the containment of the Soviet Union—was no longer relevant.

In the long term, Hussein's deductions may prove more correct than those of his Syrian rival, but he underestimated the United States' commitment to its Arabian Peninsula Arab friends. Unlike that of the Soviet Union, American military power remained unimpaired. Saddam Hussein's miscalculation and the extraordinary response it produced almost certainly prolonged, possibly for years, the period of a major United States presence in the region. With regard to the long term, however, a very different conclusion can be considered. The United States, now that the perceived threat from the Soviet Union had evaporated, no longer had interests serious enough to sustain a major and costly presence in the region.

Of course, the free flow of Middle Eastern oil to American industry remained a critical interest. One need only recall the world crisis that accompanied the rise in oil prices and the selective application of an Arab oil boycott in 1973 and 1974 to appreciate that importance. For a few months that oil consumer-producer conflict seemed likely to replace the Cold War itself as the preeminent world crisis. However, as that response suggests, the oil interest in the post–Cold War era is best viewed in terms of the global economic system. The economies of major oil producers and consumers alike are intricately interwoven in that system. Furthermore, the economic development programs of the oil producers, which are essential for their political stability, require a sustained and predictable oil production level. The threat to cut oil production for political purposes, therefore, is losing credibility. The fear that an aggressive superpower would interdict the flow of Gulf oil, a characteristic attitude of the Cold War era, has likewise dissipated. Periods of instability resulting from political upheavals or uncontrolled regional conflict which could lead to prolonged oil production cutoffs, however, are easily conceivable. But the nature of such disruptions would be difficult to predict, and serious contingency planning for dealing with them on a single-nation basis is unlikely. Since such a development would constitute a threat to the world economy, the probability is that a major international effort would be made to restore oil production.

The third interest underlying United States policy in the Middle East, the security of the state of Israel, was largely independent of the Cold War and persists. But it would be difficult to make a case that this interest alone is sufficient to maintain a significant United States presence in the region. In apparent recognition of this point, the Bush administration has given top priority to a settlement of the Palestinian issue. The objective appears to be one of setting into motion a process which might result in an Israeli-Palestinian modus vivendi both peaceful and enduring. Unfortunately, the probabilities are clearly on the side of a continuing high-intensity conflict and of a continuing, although possibly diminishing, United States involvement.

A Lesson to Be Learned

Throughout this chapter, I have taken note of some strange, almost inexplicable patterns in Soviet-American relations in the Middle East. The most fundamental of these was the asymmetry of influence in favor of the United States. The geopolitical setting would have led one to predict a Soviet, not an American, influence advantage in the Middle East. This point is given emphasis by an associated pattern: willingness on the part of the Soviet government to acquiesce in U.S. political and military activities close to the Soviet southern border. The most conspicuous examples of this were the overthrow of Musaddiq in 1953, the triggering of a Kurdish rebellion in Iraq in 1974, and the vigorous support of Afghan rebels in the 1980s. These are not patterns to be expected from an ineluctably aggressive Soviet Union in an area in which it held a logistic advantage.

A common American explanation for this Soviet behavior was that it is a consequence of a successful containment strategy. The United States mustered not only the necessary resources but also the will and determination to deter and contain Soviet moves in the Middle East, including those of political subversion. However, as Russian and American scholars begin the process of reconsidering the nature of the Cold War, a competing proposition should be considered. That is that the Cold War, including its Middle Eastern manifestations, was for much of that era a classic example of a spiral conflict. A spiral conflict occurs when each party perceives the other as expansionist and responds with a strategy of containment and deterrence. Each party then interprets the defensive responses of the other as *offensive* and responds in kind. The conflict, grounded in mutual misperception, then proceeds to spiral into ever more lethal levels.

Georgy M. Korniyenko, in this volume, agrees that the Cold War in the Middle East fits this spiral-conflict model. He accepts the possibility that Soviet behavior in the Azerbaijan crisis in the mid-1940s was expansionist. But he paints an essentially reactive picture of subsequent Soviet policy, arguing that the primary interest of that policy was one of national security, a determination to defend the Soviet Union against perceived American aggressiveness. His analysis of basic Soviet intentions thus parallels that of this chapter concerning the primary U.S. interest. However, Korniyenko identifies another Soviet objective, advancing ideological interests, that does not have a U.S. parallel and could provide the motivational basis for an expansionist foreign policy. Indeed, a common Cold War assumption in the West was that Soviet expansionism was driven by ideological messianism. Korniyenko's meaning, though, is clear. He describes a dualism among Soviet decision makers. On the one hand are professional foreign policy bureaucrats, pragmatic and little concerned with Marxist ideology. On the other are the ideologically committed, who adopt a far more doctrinaire line. Since he sees a professional dominance, Korniyenko describes Soviet policy generally as reactive and defensive. But Korniyenko's description of Soviet policy in Afghanistan suggests that this was one area in which the ideologues had a major voice in the direction Soviet policy would take. But even there, they advocated polices that were consolidationist rather than expansionist. Korniyenko's conclusion that the Cold War was a spiral conflict is not really contradicted.

Given the course of events in Russia and the Commonwealth of Independent States, there is a likelihood that a documentary history of Soviet policy in the Middle East can be constructed in the coming years. Should the archives of the former Soviet Union yield material that supports Korniyenko's thesis, the conclusion would be defensible that the Soviet-American contest in the Middle East was a spiral conflict and therefore theoretically avoidable. The lesson to be learned then would be obvious and extraordinary. Translating that lesson into formulae for identifying and avoiding future spiral conflicts of similar dimension, however, would call for a major breakthrough in diplomatic theory.

References

British Foreign Office (1952). "Persia: United States Ideas for Settlement of the Oil Dispute," C.P. (52) 354, October 23.

Brzezinski, Zbigniew (1983). *Power and Principle: Memoirs of the National Security Adviser, 1977–1981.* New York: Farrar, Straus and Giroux.

Bush, George (1983). Excerpts of speech by Vice President Bush to the American Enterprise Institute. *The New York Times,* December 4 (I, 14: 1).

Carter, Jimmy (1982). *Keeping Faith: Memoirs of a President.* New York: Barton.

Copeland, Miles (1969). *The Game of Nations: The Amorality of Power Politics.* London: Weidenfeld and Nicolson.

Cottam, Richard W. (1967). *Competitive Interference and Twentieth Century Diplomacy.* Pittsburgh: University of Pittsburgh Press.

———— (1988). *Iran and the United States: A Cold War Case Study.* Pittsburgh: University of Pittsburgh Press.

Finer, Herman (1984). *Dulles over Suez: The Theory and Practice of His Diplomacy.* Chicago: Quadrangle Books.

Foreign Broadcast Information Service (1981). *Daily Report, Foreign Broadcast Information Service, Near East and South Asia,* 91–035 (February 21).

———— (1987). *Daily Report, Foreign Broadcast Information Service, Near East and South Asia,* 87–219 (November 13).

Gasiorowski, Mark J. (1987). "The 1953 Coup d'État in Iran." *International Journal of Middle East Studies* 19, no. 3 (August): 261–86.

George, Alexander, and Richard Smoke (1974). *Deterrence in American Foreign Policy*. New York: Columbia University Press.
Holsti, Ole (1967).. "Cognitive Dynamics and the Image of the Enemy: Dulles and Russia." In *Enemies in Politics*, ed. D. J. Finlay, Ole Holsti, and Richard R. Fagan. Chicago: Rand McNally, pp. 25–96.
Love, Kennett (1969). *Suez: the Twice-Fought War*. New York: McGraw Hill.
Morgenthau, Hans (1967). *Politics among Nations*. New York: Knopf.
Murphy, Richard (1984). Statement to Congress by Richard Murphy, Undersecretary of State. *The New York Times*, June 12 (1, 12: 5).
Quandt, William (1986). *Camp David: Peacemaking and Politics*. Washington, D.C.: Brookings Institution.
Roosevelt, Kermit (1979). *Countercoup: The Struggle for the Control of Iran*. New York: McGraw Hill.
Seale, Patrick (1965). *The Struggle for Syria*. New York: Oxford University Press.
Sick, Gary (1985). *All Fall Down: America's Tragic Encounter with Iran*. New York: Random House.
Tower Commission Report (1987). *Report of the President's Special Review Board, February 19, 1987*. Washington: Government Printing Office.
Treverton, Gregory F. (1987). *Covert Action: The Limits of Intervention in the Postwar World*. New York: Basic Books.
White, Ralph (1966). "Misperception and the Vietnam War," *Journal of Social Issues* 21: 103–22.
Village Voice (1976). February 16.

II

SOVIET POLICY IN THE MIDDLE EAST
A PRACTITIONER'S INTERPRETATION

Georgy M. Korniyenko

The Soviet Union's policy in the Middle East since the end of World War II was an integral part of the Cold War between the USSR and the United States. The policies of both countries for this region have been characterized by what might be considered the most typical feature of the Cold War: misperceptions of each other's intentions and actions. The result has been inappropriate counteractions, counter-counteractions, and so on. In other words, Soviet-American relations in the Middle East developed in accordance with the principle of a spiral conflict.

Misperceptions aggravated the different interests of the two countries and sometimes created unnecessary complications. Some were endogenous: one side assumed that the other's intentions were those it would have in the same situation. In other cases, actions by one side gave rise to misinterpretations of its intentions. In still other cases, perceptions that were initially correct hardened over the years and became misperceptions because the original causes ceased to exist.

U.S. policy during the post–World War II period was based, to a large extent, on the assumption that the main threat to the West came from the expansionist ambitions of the Soviet Union. This assumption was initially prompted by Stalin's attempts immediately after the war to install a pro-Soviet regime in Iranian Azerbaijan and to take back from Turkey territory that had belonged to imperial Russia. At least at the outset of the Cold War, Stalin's efforts to surround the Soviet Union with friendly neighbors in Eastern Europe were prompted by his wish to create a buffer between Communist USSR and capitalist Western Europe. However, his actions regarding Iranian Azerbaijan and Turkey probably qualify as territorial expansionism.

Strong opposition from the West and Stalin's unwillingness at that time to

spoil relations with the West forced him to step back. The attempt to Sovietize
Iranian Azerbaijan had been prompted by Soviet Azerbaijan's leaders and
probably was not especially important to Stalin himself, and this undoubtedly
played a role in his decision as well. At any rate, neither he nor his successors
ever tried it again. Territorial expansion was never a factor in Soviet policy in
the Middle East.

Many Western policymakers failed to understand this, yet it is an obvious
explanation for the lack of serious countermeasures on the part of the Soviet
Union following the overthrow of Iran's Muhammad Musaddiq in August
1953. Moscow's "weak" reaction in this case could also be attributed to its
being preoccupied with domestic issues, as the overthrow occurred very soon
after Stalin's death. However, the main reason for the Soviet Union's behavior
was that it had no motive for active intervention in Iran in that period or later.

Once the perception of Soviet expansionism appeared in the West, however,
it became deeply rooted, both among statesmen and in public opinion—so
much so that many Western observers considered the 1979 introduction of
Soviet troops into Afghanistan as a case of Soviet territorial expansion, an
attempt to gain access to "warm seas," although this intent bore little relation
to the real motives of Soviet leaders in making the decision. I shall return to
this point later.

In its turn, the USSR, guided by the logic of the Cold War, tended to regard
U.S. presence in the Middle East as a threat to its security. Although some U.S.
actions gave reason for such an interpretation, I think that, on the whole, this
was also a misperception.

Western fear of "Soviet expansionism" and USSR fear of "American aggressiveness" were the two major misperceptions which determined the confron-
tational nature of Soviet and American policies in the Middle East. Ridding
ourselves of these misperceptions, at least partially, has been instrumental in
moving our two countries from confrontation to cooperation in the region.

Underlying Interests in Soviet Middle East Policy

Soviet policy in the Middle East, like USSR foreign policy as a whole, was
determined by three considerations: national-security interests, economic interests, and ideological considerations. These categories of interests are obviously
paramount for any state in any region. I would argue, for instance, that American
attempts to strengthen freedom and democracy, always an important part of
U.S. policy, is an ideological consideration. But it is questionable whether any
of these interests has been defined correctly and, what is no less important,
whether there has been an appropriate correlation between these interests.

I admit that Soviet policy in the Middle East was sometimes lacking in both
respects. The most harmful has been the disproportionate role assigned to
ideological considerations, often at the expense of interests more important to

the Soviet Union itself. Ideological considerations in Soviet foreign policy with regard to the Middle East were basically of two kinds:

First, we thought it necessary to support any developments in this region if they were viewed as leading to the expansion and strengthening of socialism. One might even speak about this as "ideological proselytization." Second, all developments which could undermine imperialism in the region, especially American imperialism, were seen as favorable to the Soviet Union, even if the developments did not expand socialism. The 1979 Islamic revolution in Iran, for example, was in no way prosocialist or pro-Soviet, and the Iranian regime was hostile to both the Soviet Union and the United States, but since it was anti-imperialist in character, this was enough to persuade Soviet leaders that the course of events was favorable to the Soviet Union. (The revolution also abolished the U.S. military intelligence presence in Iran, an equally persuasive reason for Soviet support.)

An example of a different kind derived from the national security interests of the Soviet state. The USSR was never interested in preserving such a hotbed of tension so close to its border as the Arab-Israeli conflict. This has always been so, despite the assumptions sometimes made in the West that the Soviet Union was interested in prolonging the conflict. And the Soviet Union has never departed from its 1947 position favoring the existence of the state of Israel. However, due to ideological considerations (for example, solidarity with the Arab national liberation struggle), its publicly stated positions on issues concerning the Arab-Israeli conflict could not always be perceived as impartial. We worked hard behind the scenes to make Arab positions more flexible and realistic. And it must be said that the positions of the majority of Arabs have undergone a positive evolution since 1967, when practically all Arab states rejected Security Council Resolution 242 and only a few were prepared to resign themselves to the fact of Israel's existence. Until we succeeded in changing this or that element of Arab policies, however, we publicly supported their positions, which undoubtedly did not contribute positively to a settlement of the conflicts in the Middle East. The same thing applies—perhaps even more so—to U.S. policy, which has supported Israel just as strongly and much less successfully, at least until recently, in making Israel's positions more flexible.

Afghanistan is the most tragic example of Soviet policy being too ideologically oriented. Contrary to speculations in the West about Moscow's involvement in the Kabul coup d'état in April 1978, we in Moscow learned of the coup from reports by foreign-press agencies. Nur Muhammad Taraki, the leader of the coup, told me in 1979 that the coup leaders had decided not to inform Soviet representatives in Kabul about their decision to act because they suspected that Moscow would try to dissuade them, arguing that conditions had not sufficiently "matured." They were probably correct in this assumption.

As soon as the coup had taken place, Soviet party ideologists regarded Afghanistan as a future socialist country. Moscow sent increasing numbers of advisers to teach Afghans the Soviet model of socialism—something Afghans undoubtedly needed least of all, since, even by orthodox Marxist views, Afghan society was ages from any brand of socialism. But Russian party ideologists saw in Afghanistan another Mongolia leaping directly from feudalism to socialism. From this point of view, the December 1979 introduction of Soviet forces into Afghanistan was the culmination, rather than the beginning, of our erroneous course with regard to this country.

I do not mean to imply that the interests of the Soviet Union's national security were not involved in Afghanistan. They were. For instance, Moscow was reliably informed that since 1974 Washington had been actively pushing the Shah of Iran to involve Afghanistan in the Western-oriented sphere of economic and military cooperation, tempting it with $2 billion in assistance, conditional on the cessation of its cooperation with the Soviet Union. We also knew about the Central Intelligence Agency's subversive activities in Afghanistan long before the Soviet troops arrived and even before the April 1978 coup. All this was real, and all of it infringed on our security interests.

I am convinced, however, that national security concerns alone, even if they were exaggerated, would not have been sufficient to justify sending Soviet troops to Afghanistan if the Soviet leadership had not mistakenly seen Afghanistan as a prospective socialist state about to be "lost" to the West. I am speaking of those who made the decision to introduce military forces. This does not mean that all Russians agreed. None of the diplomatic and military professionals with whom I am acquainted considered the introduction of forces reasonable, and none welcomed the action. The price Soviet society had to pay for this adventure, largely if not wholly caused by ideological misperceptions, is well known.

The economic aspects of Soviet policy in the Middle East were no better reasoned and balanced than the ideological ones. On the one hand, the Soviet Union often offered economic aid based on ideological preferences, without taking account of purely economic reasons, let alone the mismanagement of economic assistance. On the other hand, there were cases when, for the sake of hard currency (which the USSR needed), some of our leaders were prepared to undertake commercial deals which threatened the security interests of the Soviet Union. For example, Nikolay Tikhonov, then our prime minister, without consulting either the Ministry of Foreign Affairs or the Ministry of Defense, agreed in principle with his Libyan colleague to provide Libya—for a good amount of money, of course—with nuclear-powered equipment for water purification. There would have been nothing wrong with the sale if the Libyans had not also been promised a plant for producing heavy water. This water is indeed necessary for the purification equipment, but at the same time it could also be used for entirely different purposes which are contrary to our own security interests and to our position on the nonproliferation of nuclear weapons. Fortunately, the Inter-Ministerial Commission on the Non-Proliferation of Nuclear Weapons, of which I was the chair in the early 1980s, learned about this blunder and managed to halt the implementation of Tikhonov's promise.

Another example is a situation where, for the sake of economic interests, we waived our precious ideological criteria. Thus, despite the fact that Saddam Hussein's regime brutally persecuted (among others) opposition people of the same faith as ours—Iraqi Communists—we maintained friendly relations with him for years. One reason was that Iraq was a major source of hard currency for the USSR. The same reason partially accounts for the fact that the USSR, which stopped arms supplies to Iraq in 1980 because of its aggression against Iran, later resumed them. Of course there was another serious motivation involved: discontinuance of arms supplies to Iraq after it attacked Iran was necessitated not only by moral considerations but also by the fact that the defeat of either Iran or Iraq did not correspond to Soviet geopolitical interests. That was another reason why, when the Iranian troops reached the Iraqi border, arms supplies to Iraq were resumed.

Such was roughly the Soviet policy in the Middle East before our "new political thinking" emerged.

The Final Years of Soviet Policy in the Middle East

Although the factors which initially determined Soviet policy remained the same—national-security interests, economic interests, and ideological considerations—through the late 1980s, over time the perception of these interests began to correspond to standards generally accepted in international life. The most important change consisted of insuring a more correct and more proportionate correlation of the three factors, while increasing the significance of national-security interests, on the one hand, and reducing the weight of ideological considerations on the other. Soviet approaches to the settlement of conflict situations, which are abundant in this region, became more consistent and systematic, but they remained flexible and favored compromise.

What does this mean practically, and what were the initial results of the new Soviet policy in the Middle East? The most important and evident result was the withdrawal of Soviet troops from Afghanistan in 1988–89. The reconsideration of our military involvement in that country dates to a much earlier time. By 1981, most of our leaders realized that Afghanistan's problems could not be solved by military means. When Diego Cordóvez, representative of the U.N. Secretary General, first visited Moscow in April 1982, he concluded that those Soviet officials who advocated withdrawal from Afghanistan would prevail in the long run. He had adequate grounds for drawing such a conclusion. When, in April 1983, after a round of indirect talks between Afghanistan and Pakistan, Cordóvez said that draft documents concerning the settlement in Afghanistan were "95 percent ready," he was right again. The remaining 5 percent was, of course, of critical importance: it was concerned primarily with the timing of the Soviet withdrawal of troops from Afghanistan.

But for Yuri Andropov's illness and death, the remaining problems might have been solved in 1983. However, as was justly noted by Selig Harrison, a leading American expert on Afghanistan, the "bleeders"—people who believed that Western interests were served in having Soviet troops remain as long as possible—determined U.S. policy on Afghanistan. According to Harrison (1988), only after the late 1985 U.S.-Soviet summit in Geneva did the "dealers"—those ready to assist in the withdrawal of Soviet troops with an eye to the improvement of U.S.-Soviet relations—gradually gain influence in the U.S. administration. It was not until the end of 1987 that they gained the upper hand. Efforts on the part of the Soviet Union became more persistent and creative after Gorbachev came to power, and attitudes in Washington had to change to allow progress toward a settlement of the Afghanistan issue.

This example shows the need not only for "new thinking" in Moscow but also for new approaches on both sides if any serious results are to be attained in international affairs. The Iraqi aggression against Kuwait, an issue to be separately dealt with, made this task harder for both the USSR and the United States, while adding urgency. The same type of change is required to advance a settlement of the Arab-Israeli conflict. A more balanced course by Russia and the Commonwealth of Independent States, along with recent changes in the United States' pro-Israeli stance, has created better conditions for joint efforts on the part of our two countries to promote a settlement of this conflict.

A number of changes have already taken place and will undoubtedly continue in the sphere of economic relations between Russia and the countries of the Middle East as well. These relations are more economically sound and more advantageous. They are also less influenced by ideological prejudice. Not all the changes in Russian policy toward the Middle East are welcome in every country of the region, however. Far from it. But the fact that we are now guided by wider political and moral considerations as well as by our national interests, rather than by a desire to please our partners, is one of the characteristic features of the "new thinking."

How Soviet Policy in the Middle East Was Made: Strategy and Tactics

A notion prevalent in the West of the Kremlin's having a sinister "master plan" or "grand scheme" and pursuing a Middle East policy based on it is yet another misperception. The weakest point of USSR policy in the Middle East was, in my opinion, the absence of a well-considered concept or doctrine, whether sinister or not—unless, of course, one was to take for such a doctrine a set of general guidelines: (1) to seek a settlement of the Arab-Israeli conflict, thereby liquidating a dangerous hotbed of tension; (2) to defend the right of the Palestinian people to an independent state of their own; and (3) to counter the expansion and strengthening of U.S. positions while at the same time seizing any possibility to increase Soviet influence in the region.

The absence of a strategic plan of action in the Middle East can be explained primarily by the existence of two irreconcilable tendencies in Soviet foreign policy, one defined by state interests and the other by ideological considerations. This was especially true with regard to regions with a preponderance of developing countries, the subject of a particularly keen interest on the part of our ideologists. In these circumstances, any attempts to create something like a "Soviet Middle East doctrine" produced papers too general in character and evasive in wording. That is why those papers could not be considered practical guidelines for feasible and action-oriented measures. As a rule, they soon fell into oblivion.

In reality, Soviet—and now Russian—policy in the Middle East provided for isolated, poorly coordinated, and sometimes contradictory action, which could—to my surprise—be perceived as solid when viewed from the outside and taken together. Without a sound strategic concept, tactics acquire paramount importance, and at this level we could find quite a number of actors (for example, heads of concerned regional and functional departments of foreign affairs and other ministries, ambassadors and representatives of other organizations in a particular country). Such people often find themselves in a difficult situation and have to act according to their own judgment. Hence the importance that such individuals have excellent qualifications and sound views.

Unfortunately, this is not always the case, and if it is, they are sometimes unaware of a strategic concept and may make serious mistakes. As an example, one could refer to a development during the Arab-Israeli conflict of 1973. The Soviet leadership was not interested in an armed conflict and did not give Syrian and Egyptian leaders its encouragement to engage in military action, as some in the West believe. However, as became clear afterwards, the Soviet ambassador to Syria made remarks to Syrian leaders which could have been interpreted as an endorsement of their plans. While strategically the elaboration of a coherent Soviet policy in the Middle East was impeded by the existence of two very different factors—state and ideological interests—on a tactical level a unified approach was further undermined by the conflicting interests of the organizations concerned.

Although in recent years Soviet—now Russian—policy in the Middle East has become more conceptually sound and better coordinated, inherent chronic illnesses persisted. Afghanistan again can be cited as the most typical example in this respect. We were able to correct the most tragic mistake of our policy in Afghanistan—Soviet troops were withdrawn—but it took considerably longer to reach a reconciliation within the framework of the previous Kabul regime.

Soviet Middle East Policy and the Gulf Crisis

The Gulf crisis, among other things, was a good test for Soviet and American policies in the area, and I begin with a brief discussion of the causes of the crisis.

Why did Saddam Hussein undertake such an irrational step—from a commonsense point of view—as the occupation and annexation of Kuwait? In my opinion, there were two primary reasons. The first and most important had to do with the general instability in the Middle East as a result of the protracted Arab-Israeli conflict. Had Hussein succeeded in provoking an Israeli military response, his goal to annex Kuwait would have been achieved without serious resistance on the part of other Arab states.

A second reason Hussein dared to take this military gamble was his failure to comprehend the profound changes that had taken place in recent years in the relations between East and West, especially between the USSR and the United States. I have a different view than Richard W. Cottam, who believes that Hussein's hopes for success were based on generally correct conclusions about the end of the Cold War, which gave grounds for hope that, when the Middle East ceased to be an arena of Soviet-American confrontation, the United States would not involve itself in an inter-Arab conflict. In my view, because Hussein failed to understand changes in Soviet-American relations as well as in Soviet foreign policy in general, he could not assume that the USSR and the United States would act in concert against Iraq's invasion in Kuwait. One Western military attaché in Moscow was correct when he said that Hussein lost his battle for Kuwait on August 3, 1990—the day the joint Soviet-American statement on Iraq's aggression against Kuwait was issued.

New features of both Soviet and American policies were displayed in the course of the Gulf crisis. The most important was that this time, unlike the case of Iraq's aggression against Iran in 1980, both countries took the position that the aggressor should immediately withdraw from Kuwait, thereby restoring its independence and territorial integrity. Even more important was the fact that the USSR and the United States, together with a majority of other states, took practical measures—unilaterally and collectively through the U.N. Security Council—aimed at compelling Iraq to submit to the will of the world community. In the past there had been situations when the USSR and the United States had acted jointly—for instance, in October 1973, to put an end to the war between the Arabs and Israel—but this time the two countries acted on a new level of mutual understanding and cooperation.

With regard to how to compel Iraq to withdraw from Kuwait, not all decisions were, in my opinion, in accord with new-thinking criteria. There were no doubts concerning economic and other nonmilitary sanctions mandated by the Security Council. Had those sanctions been employed for a long enough period and had they been supplemented with the threat of military action, there would have been a real possibility of getting Iraq out of Kuwait without war. If, at the same time, parallel steps had been taken toward a settlement of other Middle East problems (simultaneously, but not necessarily in linkage) this would have been even more beneficial. However, this chance was missed when the Security Council adopted Resolution 678, which permitted the use of military force against Iraq after January 15, 1991.

I do not consider this a document of "new thinking," first, because as soon as the resolution—in the form the United States wished—was adopted, war against Iraq became not just possible but unavoidable. Secondly, Resolution 678 gave the United States and its allies unrestricted and absolute freedom in choosing the means and methods of waging war. In adopting that kind of mandate, Security Council members—including the Soviet Union—rendered ill service to peace and to the United States. Given carte blanche, the U.S. administration could only be tempted to use it in the interests of a much broader goal than that of forcing Iraq to withdraw from Kuwait. In the opinion of Soviet military specialists—and some Western ones as well—the scale and character of the cooperative military actions, which resulted in inappropriately large casualties and material losses in Iraq, were unjustified. In addition to liberating Kuwait, they were prompted by a wish to punish the aggressor and to instigate the Iraqi people to rebel against their ruler. Simultaneous with crushing Iraq, the coalition used the war for purposes having nothing to do with liberating Kuwait—for example, to check some operational NATO plans, prepared in the past, for a possible war in Europe and to test new weapons systems.

The outcome of the Gulf crisis must become a lesson to potential aggressors as well as to those who currently occupy another country's lands. They were given a demonstration that the world community is ready to defend a victim of aggression and to punish an aggressor. That is fine. It is something new in world affairs. However, in the course of getting through this crisis, it became clear that even those states which were defending the right cause did not act completely in accordance with "new-thinking" criteria. Some things that were done were in the worst traditions of the past. This is bad not only in itself but also from the point of view of future developments in the Middle East.

Conclusion

Soviet-American relations with regard to the Middle East after World War II developed in accordance with the classical scheme of a spiral conflict. Although the policies of the two countries proceeded from substantially different assumptions, they had much in common, and their actions were often merely reactions based on interpretations of the other's intentions that were not always correct. Relations between the USSR and the United States were in many cases further complicated in the Middle East because their respective client-states sometimes used their patrons for purposes which were not in accord with the national interests of either of the two countries. As can be seen from recent Middle Eastern events, however, both the Soviet Union and the United States have learned from the past. Unfortunately, they may still not have learned all the necessary lessons.

Reference

Harrison, Selig S. (1988). "Inside the Afghan Talks." *Foreign Policy* 72 (Fall): 31–60.

Part II
Central Asia

III

CENTRAL ASIA'S POLITICAL CRISIS

Martha Brill Olcott

Prelude to Collapse

The collapse of the Communist Party and the subsequent dissolution of the USSR came as an unpleasant shock to Central Asia's leaders. Today, when they are technically the heads of sovereign and independent states, Central Asia's leaders are pushing for the survival and expansion of the Commonwealth of Independent States that serves as a successor to the USSR. They believe that the Central Asian republics are unprepared economically, politically, and culturally for independence. Although their caution is partly the product of fears that they may lose their jobs, the obstacles that the Central Asian republics face in their transition to independent states are substantial.

Central Asia is home to 50 million people, 12 million of them the European descendants of nineteenth- and twentieth-century settlers. The remainder of the population are Muslim descendants of the Turko-Mongol and Persian peoples who have always lived in Central Asia. Since the creation of the Turkestan and Steppe territories in 1867 and 1868 respectively, the area has been under Russian rule. Its replacement by Soviet power has left Central Asians with little opportunity to figure out who they are and how they would like to live.

It has also meant increasing numbers of Europeans in their territory. The Russians and Ukrainians who live in the region descend from homesteaders who came to Central Asia at the turn of the century, from kulaks[1] and other deportees of the 1920s and 1930s, and from Virgin Land enthusiasts of the post–World War II period. Europeans who came to the region saw themselves as living in a distant Russian or Soviet outpost, since no fixed boundary separated Russia from Central Asia or the Central Asian republics from one another. Divisions in the Russian and Soviet states were administrative demar-

---

1. Kulaks were farmers whose holdings were deemed "exploitative." The classification included anyone whose lands were extensive enough to warrant the use of hired labor.

cations: people and goods were free to move between and within republics. The Russians see themselves as citizens of a remote part of a Russian-dominated state. This is particularly true for northern Kazakhstan, whose five northern oblasts are undifferentiated in population, landscape, and economy from the Russian Federation oblasts of western Siberia that they abut.[2]

The Russians see native Central Asians as a superstitious and disease-ridden people. Moscow must pay to feed their large families. Many Russian nationalists share Solzhenitsyn's view (*Komsomol'skaia pravda*, September 19, 1990): absorb the Slavic northern part of Kazakhstan into Russia, resettle the Russian settlers, and cut Central Asia free (*Vremia*, February 20, 1991).

Central Asians are equally scornful of the Russians. They see Central Asian civilization as older and richer, the legacy of Genghis Khan and the Golden Horde, who ruled the Russians for 250 years. They snickered when Gorbachev incorrectly referred to the "thousand-year-old" Russian state (*Vremia*, February 20, 1991). To them the Russians are invaders who colonized their lands and subjected them to Communism. They have looked forward to a time when Russia's hold over them would end.

The consolidation of Central Asian peoples was in its earliest stages at the time of the Russian Empire's collapse (1917). The three nomadic peoples—the Kazakhs, the Kyrghyz, and the Turkmen—recognized themselves as distinct from one another and from the city-dwelling and farming communities of Turkestan. There was a small national movement among the Kazakhs and somewhat larger Pan-Turkic and Islamic reformist (*Jadidi*) movements in Turkestan, but the majority of the population in the Turkestan and Steppe regions identified with their clan or tribe if they were rural and with their place of residence if they were not. All considered themselves Muslims as well (Bennigsen and Lermercier-Quelquejay 1967).

Stalin set up the current five republics with an eye toward encouraging interethnic conflicts, and each is to some degree an artificial creation.[3] The Kazakhs are a bare plurality in their republic.[4] Kazakhstan's current demographic makeup is the direct result of Soviet economic schemes, which wiped out millions of Kazakhs and settled Russians and other Europeans in their place. The majority of Kazakhs, who live in ethnically homogeneous regions

---

2. Tselinograd, North Kazakhstan, East Kazakhstan, Karaganda, and Kokchetav are overwhelmingly Russian in composition (*Ekonomika i zhizn'* 1990: 66).

3. Initially the Bolshevik government kept the Russian colonial division, creating an autonomous republic from the Turkestan territory and an autonomous oblast from the Kazakh steppe territory. In 1924, Turkestan was divided into three union republics: Uzbekistan, Kyrghyzia, and Turkmenistan. Tajikistan, initially an autonomous republic within Uzbekistan, became a "union republic" in its own right in 1929. The Kyrghyz autonomous oblast became an autonomous republic (part of the Russian federative republic) and received full union republic status in 1936.

4. Kazakhs comprise 38 percent of the republic's population. Another 36 percent is made up of Russians. Russian-speakers outnumber Kazakh-speakers by three to two (*Soiuz* 8, 1990).

of southern Kazakhstan, enjoy better transportation links to Uzbekistan's capital of Tashkent than to their republic center of Alma Ata.

Kyrghyzstan, as Kyrghyzia was renamed in 1990, has a bare majority of Kyrghyz, but the large Russian population has made no territorial claims. The Uzbeks, however, have challenged Kyrghyzstan's control of agriculture and the cotton-rich Osh oblast, which is close to Tashkent but linked to its republic capital of Bishkek only by air.[5]

Tajikistan is the region's only Persian republic, although its population has been cut off from Central Asia's Persian cities of Samarkand and Bukhara by the way the republic's boundaries were drawn. In addition to boundary claims on Uzbekistan, Tajikistan's leaders also have pretensions to a small piece of Kyrghyzstan as well. Turkmenistan has a small and largely homogeneous population, but its leaders fear both Uzbekistani and Iranian territorial claims.

Uzbekistan is the most populous of the Central Asian republics and relatively homogeneous.[6] Uzbeks consider their republic the heart of Central Asia, as it borders all the others. In addition to Tamerlane's capital city of Samarkand, Uzbekistan is the site of the medieval city-states of Khorezm, Khiva, and Bukhara, and of today's Islamic centers of Marghilan and Namangan. Uzbeks also lay claim to the city of Turkestan, now in Kazakhstan, where the tomb of the twelfth-century Sufi poet Ahmed Yasavi draws thousands of pilgrims annually.

As long as the Communist Party was in control in Moscow, the artificiality of Central Asia's boundaries was irrelevant. The political autonomy granted these republics was limited. The USSR accepted only "international" interests as legitimate.

Moscow and Central Asia

For Leonid Brezhnev, it was enough to declare that internationalism had been achieved. He was willing to accept the praise of Central Asia's leaders for the "fraternal assistance" rendered by the Russians (Kunaev 1981). The Brezhnev years were a time of general stability and relative prosperity in the region. The conditions of *zastoi* (stagnation), as Gorbachev later dubbed the period, were well suited to Central Asia's party elite. They ruled like feudal overlords, free to steal and spend as they wished, once they had dispatched the required tribute to Moscow.

---

5. According to the 1989 census, there were 4.25 million people in Kyrghyzia, including 2.2 million Kyrghyz, 0.92 million Russians, and 0.56 million Uzbeks ("Financy i statistike" 1989: 87).

6. According to the 1989 census, 14.1 million of Uzbekistan's 19.8 million people were Uzbeks ("Financy i statistike" 1989: 64).

New university buildings, schools, and hospitals went up throughout Central Asia. Unfortunately, most government development projects were short on substance. Most rural hospitals, for example, lacked indoor plumbing. Preferential admission programs filled local universities with Central Asians, but curricular reforms were neglected, and new graduates were left without useful technical skills and little knowledge of their national pasts (Olcott and Fierman 1988).

After Brezhnev's death in November 1982, Central Asia's political leaders became a target for Yuri Andropov and "young" reformers like Mikhail Gorbachev and Yegor Ligachev, who came to power with him. The premise of Moscow's new leaders was a simple one: economic recovery was impossible unless corrupt practices were curtailed and the geographic regions of the country made to function as an integrated economic unit. Andropov had been wary of attacking the entrenched political elite in Central Asia. Gorbachev and Ligachev were less attuned to the political realities of the region, and they targeted the party elite of the five republics in a campaign that began with public humiliation and culminated in dismissal (Olcott 1988).

Rashidov's death in 1983 (just months before Andropov's) made it easier for Ligachev and Gorbachev to launch a campaign against Uzbekistan's scandal-ridden cotton industry, which led to a purge of that republic's political elite (Critchlow 1991). The dismissal of Turkmenistan's Muhammadnazar Gapurov, Tajikistan's Rahmon Nabiev, and Kyrghyzia's Usubaliev[7] in fall 1985 were quieter affairs, as was the subsequent "cleansing" of those republics' Communist Parties. In December 1986, Dinmuhammad Kunaev, a fifteen-year CPSU Politburo member, was forced into retirement to make way for Gennadi Kolbin, a Russian from outside the republic. Kolbin's appointment was designed to test a recently announced Communist Party policy of shifting personnel throughout the country (*Kazakhstanskaia pravda*, December 18, 1986). Demonstrators who took to the streets in the republic's capital city of Alma Ata were dispersed by force, leaving between two and 168 dead (the number of dead varies with the source of the information).

The events in Alma Ata were an introduction to the difficulties of introducing political and economic reforms in the non-Russian regions of the country. They had repercussions that extended far beyond Kazakhstan. For one thing, they caused Gorbachev and his advisors in Moscow to rethink the premises upon which their policies were based. The practice of dispatching cadres from region to region was cut back. More importantly, Moscow began to allow republics to exercise control of their own cultural policies. At first, this took the form of legislation making national languages state languages (Olcott 1989). This began in the Baltic republics in 1987 and culminated in Central Asia in 1989. These efforts coincided with Gorbachev's implementation of *glasnost*, which

---

7. All three were first secretaries (heads) of their respective republic Communist Parties.

allowed for new freedom of expression. The Baltic republics were the most aggressive about using these new freedoms in an effort designed to popularize the goals of the nascent pronationalist popular-front movements. National song festivals were held, long-suppressed plays staged, and forbidden literary and historical works were reprinted (Nahaylo and Swoboda 1990, esp. chap. 18). Nationalist-minded political activists demanded that the rights granted in the cultural sphere be expanded to the economic and political sectors as well. Baltic national-front leaders demanded economic autonomy, then political sovereignty, and finally, full independence for their republics. Ukrainian, Moldavian, Georgian, Armenian, and Azerbaijani opposition leaders began to press for the same rights and concessions that had been granted to the Baltic republics (Olcott 1991).

Central Asia was the only area where Moscow's Communist Party agenda remained almost entirely unchallenged. After the Alma Ata riots demonstrated the local response that Moscow's meddling could provoke, the political-boss system typical of Central Asian republican party politics received new life. The leaders of Central Asia's Communist Parties became loyal defenders of Gorbachev's reform politics. The one area where the Central Asian leadership diverged from the party elite in Moscow, however, was that of the role of Islam.

In the mid-1980s, Moscow mounted a campaign to identify Islam as the cause of Central Asia's "backwardness." Most of Central Asia's leaders voiced support for Moscow's new policy but did little to restrict local religious practices (*Kommunist Tajikistana*, August 4, 1986). A more aggressive anti-religious campaign was launched in parts of Uzbekistan by party leaders eager to reduce Moscow's pressure on them. However, the creation of the Congress of People's Deputies and the advent of "electoral politics" in the USSR gave Central Asia's leaders the necessary power to break with this policy. In its place, they sought to publicly identify themselves with what they termed Islam's "progressive trends" (Rorlich 1991).

The republics' leaders backed General Secretary-turned-President Gorbachev on every other issue of importance that came before them, however. The most vocal defender of these pro-Gorbachev positions was Nursultan Nazarbaev, who took over as head of Kazakhstan in June 1989 (*Narodnye deputaty SSSR* 1991: 337), but all the Central Asian leaders did their part to advance Gorbachev's cause. They echoed Gorbachev's call for the preservation of the USSR as a single economic zone. They called for the creation of sovereign republics in June 1990, only after Gorbachev did himself. They went along with the partial shift in power from the Communist Party to popularly elected republic and all-union legislatures and made sure that handpicked party activists filled the posts, guaranteeing Gorbachev his only predictable voting bloc (Olcott 1991b). They turned out their populations to vote for continuation of the Union of Soviet Socialist Republics in the March 1991 referendum (*Radio Rossiia*, March 21, 1991).

It was only at the time of the August 1991 coup that the loyalty of some of these men was called into question. But since the party hardliners who seized power thought that they had Gorbachev's support, the confusion Central Asia's leaders displayed was not surprising.[8] After the coup failed and the CPSU was banned, Central Asia's leaders declared their republics' independence.[9] Even then, however, they railed against the prospect of Ukrainian secession, predicting that it would destroy the union they sought to preserve.

Central Asia's Economic Crisis

While Central Asia's leaders complained privately of Russian exploitation, they all supported the gradual shift of control from Moscow to the republics. They failed to foresee, however, that the dissolution of the formal governmental structures of the USSR on December 21, 1991, also meant an end to Moscow's subsidies to Central Asia. The basic problem is that, despite the region's natural mineral wealth—oil and gas in Turkmenistan; oil, aluminum, coal, and chrome in Kazakhstan; gold in Uzbekistan; and uranium in Tajikistan—Central Asia has been the most impoverished region in the former Soviet Union.[10]

Even before the current economic crisis, nearly half the population existed on a diet of flat bread and tea, unable to afford the fresh fruits and vegetables, meat, and milk products, cheap by Soviet standards, on sale in the peasant market. Local economists blamed the over-centralized Soviet economic system, which set low purchase prices for cotton and other agricultural commodities (Nasyrov 1990).

Russians see the cause as the region's high birth rate.[11] Central Asians defend their right to large families on religious grounds and because they are necessary in the labor-intensive cotton-monoculture economy that dominates the region (Poliakov 1992: esp. chaps. 4–6). Two decades of official pressure to reduce family size has had minimal effect, however (*Soiuz* 20, 1990)—the 1989 census revealed only a slight drop in birth rate, despite the fact that Central Asia's infant mortality rate is the highest in the USSR, more than 100 per 1,000 in some places (Bohr 1989). Pregnant almost every year, a country woman may bury five or six children in her lifetime, and women are as unhealthy as the children they bear. About half of all women and children suffer from chronic illnesses, but most local physicians have only rudimentary medical training,

---

8. Askar Akaev, Kyrghyzstan's president and the region's sole leader who was not head of a republic Communist Party, was the only Central Asian president to immediately oppose the coup (*Slovo Kyrghyzstana*, August 20, 1991).

9. Kazakhstan did not declare its independence until December 1991 (*Izvestiia*, December 18, 1991).

10. The per capita distribution of national income is between 2 and 2.5 percent of the USSR average (*Izvestiia*, January 7, 1992).

11. The local Muslim population has nearly doubled over the past twenty years. Over 60 percent of Central Asia's population is under twenty-five years of age.

and most hospitals lack elementary sanitary facilities (*Komsomol'skaia pravda*, October 14, 1988).

The high birth rate of the Central Asians compounds the region's unemployment problem. Uneven industrial investment in the 1960s and 1970s created an economic depression in most of Central Asia that was exacerbated by Gorbachev's economic reforms. Factories lack skilled laborers, although nearly half of Central Asia's rural youths are unemployed (Rumer 1990: chap. 6). Even Russian analysts admit that much of the blame lies with former USSR state policy, which locked non-Russian-speaking Central Asians out of skilled employment (Poliakov 1992). Central Asia's shortage of skilled workers is sure to worsen in the next few years, as there is an out-migration of ethnic Russians, and other native Russian-speakers are moving out of the Soviet Central Asian republics. Over a quarter-million people per year for the past two years have relocated in Russia and other republics (*Literaturnaia gazeta* 40, October 7, 1991), leaving cities like Tashkent and Dushanbe critically short of trained medical personnel (Zolotukhin 1990).

Water is the region's greatest problem. Ten million residents are without potable drinking water, and there is little safe water for irrigation. Seen from the air, the region resembles a snowbelt because of the miles of salt deposits left by the evaporating Aral Sea and Kazakhstan's Lake Balkash. Local rivers are contaminated from the toxic chemicals used in the cotton and tobacco fields (Gleason 1991).

Central Asia's Current Political Crisis[12]

Central Asia's political elite has survived past economic and political crises. The same leadership has been in charge since the end of the purges of the late 1930s. It is determined to retain power and, with it, control of the powerful, family-based patronage networks that still dominate the economy.

While the Communist Party was the only legal political organization, it served as a regulating mechanism for intra-group conflict. Now that its control has been broken or forced underground, intra-elite rivalries have been stimulated, and new groups have demanded access to political power. Kyrghyzstan's "democratic revolution" of autumn 1990 is an example of the struggles that are developing throughout the region (Brown 1991). Three major political groups dominate Kyrghyzstan. They correspond to clan-based geographic divisions: those from Naryn (including longtime party boss Turdakun Usubaliev and President Askar Akaev), those from Talas (deposed Communist Party leader Absamat Masaliev), and the Kyrghyz from Osh (tied to the Ferghana Valley Uzbek party organization).

---

12. For a much expanded version of this argument, see Olcott (1992).

The Osh riots in June-July 1990 gave Masaliev's opposition an issue on which to attack him. Masaliev, who was born in Osh and spent his career in Talas, displaced the Naryn-based political organization of Turdakun Usubaliev when the latter was removed from office in 1985. The Naryn group constituted themselves as a "Democratic Bloc" within the legislature and championed the political rights of the non-Communist "Democratic Movement for Kyrghyzia," a collection of disaffected intellectuals and Muslim moderates whose goal was to break the CPSU's monopoly on power. Working in concert, they pushed Masaliev out, and the Supreme Soviet of the republic elected Askar Akaev, an academician, as president (*Slovo Kyrghyzstana*, October 28, 1990). Akaev has provided a visible but restricted role for the political opposition and won an unopposed popular election as president.[13]

There are two major groupings in Tajikistan: the Leninabad (now renamed Khojent) group, and the less powerful Kuliab faction. The Leninabad group suffered a serious defeat in 1985, when Rakhmon Nabiev was deposed as Communist Party first secretary. His replacement, Khakhar Makhamov, was a strong but unpopular figure, who was seen as more loyal to Moscow than to the Tajiks. Three major nonparty groups opposed him: the secular "Democratic Movement," the Rastokhez (Muslim moderate), and the Islamic Renaissance (Muslim fundamentalist) movements.

As their popularity increased, Rahmon Nabiev began to court them, promising to endorse some of their goals if they helped him defeat Makhkamov for the republic presidency; but the August coup made Nabiev superfluous to the nonparty reformers. Taking to the streets, they overthrew Makhkamov, only to have Nabiev lead a palace coup against the interim president after the latter demanded nationalization of Communist Party property. Tajik demonstrators, led by fasting *qazi*s (Islamic law judges), persuaded Nabiev to step down, but he returned to power with nearly 60 percent of the vote in the November 24, 1991, presidential election. Although the "democratic opposition" candidate, filmmaker Davlat Khudonazarov, charged fraud, Nabiev's election provoked no major disturbances in the republic. Nabiev may have had an understanding with some of the republic's religious leaders, for soon after his election, he declared the principal Islamic feast days state holidays (*Daily Report, Central Eurasia*, FBIS-SOV-92–009, January 14, 1992: 66).

The situation in Uzbekistan is more complicated. Separate coalitions represent the Ferghana Valley, Bukhara, Samarkand, Jizzak, and Tashkent oblasts. The "cotton scandal" of the mid-1980s seriously crippled the Communist Party's ability to regulate local conflicts, and the "cotton mafia" of the Ferghana Valley suffered disproportionately. This left the region's party organization relatively headless.

The weakening of the Communist Party sparked the development of several

---

13. He banned the former head of the Communist Party from running against him.

opposition groups. The first, Erk (Independence), is largely a legislative caucus. Its head, the well-known poet and former USSR Supreme Soviet Deputy Muhamed Salikh, ran against Uzbekistan's president, Islam Karimov, in the December 1991 election.[14] Birlik (Unity) is viewed as a more serious threat, and until October 1991 it was barred from the republic. At that time it was registered as a "movement," not a political party, and its cochair, Abdurahmin Pulatov, was unable to get on the presidential ballot. Its program (August 1990) is a potpourri of democratic ideals rather than a coherent set of policy recommendations. The Islamic Renaissance Party is also banned in Uzbekistan, but it is a powerful force throughout the Ferghana Valley and has a perceptible influence among young people in Tashkent as well.

Despite growing opposition, Uzbekistan's president, Islam Karimov, rules his republic with a strong hand. He has been able to use the dissolution of the Communist Party and his popular election as president to push out political opponents from within the party. In October 1991 he bested an effort by the prime minister, Shukrullah Mirsaidov, to defeat him in the republic's Supreme Soviet (*Daily Report, Soviet Union*, FBIS-SOV-91-193, October 4, 1991).

The situation in Kazakhstan is equally complex, in large part because of the republic's peculiar demographic situation. Kazakhstan's Communist Party was dominated by descendants of the Great Horde, the tribal group that ruled southern Kazakhstan (the area least affected by Russian and then Soviet rule). There were also party elites corresponding to the Small Horde in western Kazakhstan and the Middle Horde territories. Russians active in the republic's Communist Party typically allied themselves with one of the Kazakh groups.

Kazakhstan's president, Nursultan Nazarbaev, is very popular,[15] but he fears the secession of the republic's northern, Russian oblasts. He has tried to minimize this threat by supplanting local legislatures with his personal representatives. He has also promoted a Socialist Party (predominantly Russian in character) to succeed the Communist Party, hoping to create a rift between the Ural Cossack secessionists and the Russian-speaking population.

To avoid charges of Russian favoritism, he has sponsored the Popular Consolidation of Kazakhstan (a party headed by the poets Olzhas Suleimenov and Mukhtar Shakhanov), which is likely to remain overwhelmingly Kazakh in composition (*Izvestiia*, October 8, 1991). Nazarbaev's hope is that a Kazakh national party will defuse the appeal of the legally recognized party, Azat (Freedom), and that of the illegal Muslim party, Alash.[16] Nazarbaev has managed so far to keep the Islamic Revolutionary Party from gaining a foothold in the republic. Hoping to keep Islam under state supervision, he cut

---

14. Karimov got 86 percent of the vote (*Financial Times*, December 31, 1991).
15. Nazarbaev won over 98 percent of the vote in the presidential election (*Daily Report, Soviet Union*, FBIS-SOV-91-207, October 25, 1991).
16. Named for the Kazakhs' legendary founder.

Kazakhstan off from SADUM (the Spiritual Directorate of the Muslims of Central Asia and Kazakhstan) in 1990 and created a separate "muftiate" for Kazakhstan (*Kazakhstanskaia pravda*, September 6, 1990).

After the Kazakh *qazi*, Ratbek Nysanbaev, publicly opposed the creation of an Islamic party in Kazakhstan, a group of religious believers attacked him. Nazarbaev intervened and sustained the *qazi*'s rule (*Komsomol'skaia pravda*, December 17, 1991). Uzbekistan's Karimov has also had to intervene to protect SADUM's head mufti, Muhammad Sadyk Muhammad Yusuf (*Daily Report, Central Eurasia*, FBIS-SOV-92–009, January 14, 1992: 9).

Turkmenistan is the least turbulent of the Central Asian republics. The Turkmen are divided into two tribes, and there have always been two competing groups of party leaders. The opposition group within Turkmenistan's Communist Party has been out of power so long, however, that they are not as skilled at political infighting as President Sapurmarad Niazov and his coterie. Islam is a powerful force in the countryside, but Turkmenistan's clerics do not represent an organized opposition group, and Niazov's "democratic" opponents have been easy to isolate.[17]

The former party bosses who run Central Asia have an enormous advantage. Until recently, the Communist Party was the only arena for people to gain political experience, but the political advantage of the existing party elite is not indefinite. As one Birlik leader privately warned, "We will grow smarter, but they will become no more honest" (interview, July 15, 1990).

The Future

Many of Central Asia's leaders fear that they are running out of time. The economic situation in their republics is growing worse. They may continue to blame Moscow for their problems, but Moscow is no longer able to aid or protect them.

Central Asia's leaders have tried to fill the power vacuum by pressing for increased regional initiatives. In Alma Ata in June 1990, the heads of the five republics signed an agreement of economic, technical, and cultural cooperation (*Kazakhstanskaia pravda*, June 24, 1990). The goals of the council were reaffirmed in Tashkent just before the August 1991 coup (*Pravda Vostoka*, August 16, 1991), and the commitment to a regional network was renewed in Ashkhabad, Turkmenistan, before they joined the Confederation of Independent States in December 1991 (*Izvestiia*, December 19, 1991).

Despite this affirmation, none of Central Asia's leaders sees regional coop-

---

17. Opposition groups in the republic are so restricted that Turkmenistan's Democratic Party held its founding meeting in Moscow (*Daily Report, Soviet Union*, FBIS-SOV-91–204, October 22, 1991: 75).

eration as a way to solve their republics' developmental problems. All recognize that the challenges that each republic faces are beyond the group's common resources. Moreover, two of the region's leaders, Akaev of Kyrghyzstan and Nazarbaev of Kazakhstan, wish to project an image of their republics as secular, multinational states. This is particularly important in the case of Kazakhstan, which has a larger European population than an Asian one. Thus, despite the virtual ban on political parties that are not state-organized, Nazarbaev has devoted considerable time and resources to convince the world in general and foreign investors in particular that Kazakhstan is a pluralistic, multinational society.[18]

Nazarbaev is shrewd enough to recognize that public relations efforts may work abroad, but they cannot substitute for a stable political base at home. For this reason, he has been a strong supporter of Olzhas Suleimenov's idea of Russian-Slavic dualism. Suleimenov has been a hero to many Turkic intellectuals since the mid-1970s, when he published *Az i Ia* (1976), which retold the Russian epic *Lay of Igor's Campaign* from a Turkic viewpoint. The book was banned shortly after its publication, but it was reissued in 1989 and has become an important work for Muslim intellectuals in the USSR. As part of his ongoing and diverse political activities,[19] Suleimenov has tried to popularize the idea that Turks and Slavs can create a great secular state or confederation of republics based on their common history and cultural heritage. The pan-Turkic vision, however, has two crippling flaws: it is secular, and it is predicated on Russians and Turks functioning as equals within a single state. It is hard to imagine either community endorsing this. The Russians have never been tolerant of non-Russians, and now that Central Asia's Russians are experiencing a cultural revival, they are less tolerant still, protesting against laws which mandate learning Central Asian languages and having their children educated in local-language schools.

Central Asians, on the other hand, are determined to press for a revival of their national cultures, and they expect their national languages and religion to be favored in their republics. Even a moderate like Kazakhstan's Sabitzhan Aqataev, Azat's founder and former cochair, stated in an interview, "I would rather join forces with the Uzbeks, even if they swallow us, if that's what it takes to get free of Russia and Russians. Because a free people shows respect for its past, and so we must honor Islam and not the Russian ways" (interview, August 6, 1990). It is unlikely that moderates like Aqataev will succeed in speaking for the population, however. In 1991, when Azat began to attract

<hr>

18. It is reported that Nazarbaev has retained public relations firms in London and Washington to help popularize this picture of the republic.

19. Suleimenov has been a USSR Supreme Soviet, a president of the Nevada-Semipalatinsk Anti-Nuclear Movement, and the behind-the-scenes force in a short-lived Assembly of the Peoples of the East.

widespread popular support, Aqataev lost his leadership role to former Communist Party members who had recently joined the movement.

Aqataev's point about Islam and its role in Central Asia's future is extremely critical. Central Asian leaders must show themselves to be "on the side of Islam" if they expect to remain in power. Over the past few years, they have moved from attacking religion as a pernicious influence to advocating a partnership between religious and secular forces. Some, like Nazarbaev, still maintain that they are not believers (*Kazakhstanskaia pravda*, October 2, 1991), but others, like Karimov, claim to have become fully observant Muslims (*Nezavisimaia gazeta*, January 7, 1991). The religious leaders most willing to work with them are the clerics of the Muslim Religious Board of Central Asia (SADUM), whose activities, although officially approved, were restricted by Soviet authorities until the late 1980s.

Public manifestations of support for Islam by political leaders have not always been sufficient to convince Central Asians of their worthiness to rule. Although Khakhar Makhkamov of Tajikistan participated in a public blessing of Tajik pilgrims setting off for Mecca (*Kommunist Tajikistana*, June 13, 1991), he was driven from power by a group of secular and religious opponents three months later. The religious elite is also compromised by its ties to the political establishment. Despite the fact that the number of mosques, religious schools, and seminaries is increasing, many religious Central Asians still consider SADUM the handmaiden of the official elite.

The situation in Central Asia is both volatile and fluid. The relaxation of political tensions in recent years is making it possible for Central Asians to begin to come to grips with their national identities and with their Islamic past. However, it has also created difficult economic and political conditions under which to do so.

The end of Soviet power was unnatural—the Communist Party simply collapsed and brought the structures of government down with it. However, the political elite has remained in power. This is particularly true of Central Asia, where new democratic institutions were adapted to help the elite perpetuate its power. Leaders previously ruled in the name of an ideology to which no one subscribed; they now rule in defense of nationalism and the faith of their forefathers.

The current elite hopes to remain in power long enough for their political descendants to take over. Members of the next generation are more worldly; they have traveled and studied in the West and in the Muslim East. The current elite and their children are seriously disadvantaged as well, however. They have been educated in Russia or in local Russian-language schools, and, for all their invocation of religious themes, they are advocating secular visions of nationalism.

In the long run, their fate is likely to be that of "liberation" intellectuals everywhere. Trained in the colonizer's universities, their experiences have given them the clarity of vision necessary to understand their people's problems, but it has also distanced them from the population, and they are unable to modify their goals to meet popular aims. Central Asia's leaders may speak native languages, but they are talking in a political language people do not or wish not to understand. The people in Central Asia still have a minimal role in public life, but their voices will have to be heard.

References

Bennigsen, Alexandre, and Chantal Lermercier-Quelquejay (1967). *Islam in the Soviet Union*. London: Pall Mall Press.

Bohr, Annette (1989). "Health Catastrophe in Karakalpakistan." *Radio Liberty* (July 11).

Brown, Bess (1991). "The Fall of Masaliev: Kyrghyzstan's 'Silk Revolution' Advances." *Radio Liberty* (April 19): 12–15.

Critchlow, James (1991). "Prelude to 'Independence': How the Uzbek Party Apparatus Broke the Grip on Elite Recruitment." In *Soviet Central Asia: The Failed Transformation*, ed. William Fierman, pp. 131–58. Boulder: Westview Press.

Ekonomika i zhizn' [Economics and Life], no. 5 (1990).

Foreign Broadcast Information Service Daily Report, Soviet Union (1989–91). Renamed FBIS Daily Report, Central Eurasia, January 1992.

Gleason, Gregory (1991). "The Struggle for Control over Water in Central Asia: Republican Sovereignty and Collective Action." *Radio Liberty* (June 22): 11–13.

Izvestiia [News]. Moscow.

Kazakhstanskaia pravda [Kazakhstan Truth]. Alma Ata.

Kommunist Tajikistana [Tajikistan Communist]. Dushanbe.

Komsomol'skaia pravda [Komsomol Truth]. Moscow.

Kunaev, Dinmuhammad A. (1981). *Leninskaia national'naia politika KPSS v deistvii* [Leninist Nationality Policy of the CPSU in Action]. Moscow: Politizdat.

Literaturnaia gazeta [Literary Gazette]. Moscow.

Nahaylo, Bohdan, and Victor Swoboda (1990). *Soviet Disunion*. New York: The Free Press.

Narodnye deputaty SSSR [Peoples Deputies of the USSR] (1990). Moscow: Izdanie Verkhovnogo Soveta SSSR (Publisher of the Supreme Soviet).

Narodnye deputaty SSSR (1991).

Nasyrov, Pulat (1990). Interview. Institute of Economics, Uzbekistan's Academy of Sciences (July).

Natsionalnyi sostav naseleniia [National Composition of the Population] (1989). Moscow: Financy i statistike [Finances and Statistics].

Nezavisimaia gazeta [Independent Newspaper].

Olcott, Martha Brill (1988). "Gorbachev, the National Problem, and Party Politics in Central Asia." In *Assessing Soviet Power*, ed. Dan Nelson and Raj Menon, pp. 63–84. Lexington, Ky.: Lexington Books.

——— (1989). "Linking Gorbachev's Foreign and Domestic Policies: Nationality Relations." *Journal of International Affairs* 42, no. 2 (January): 399–422.

——— (1991a). "The Soviet (Dis)union." *Foreign Policy* 82 (Spring): 118–36.

——— (1991b). "The Slide to Disunion." *Current History* (October): 338–44.

——— (1992). "Central Asia's Post-Empire Politics," *Orbis* (Spring): 269–84.

Olcott, Martha Brill, and William Fierman (1988). "Soviet Youth: The View from the Komsomol Press." U.S. Department of State Contract 1724–620117.

Poliakov, Sergei P. (1992). *Everyday Lives: Religion and Tradition in Soviet Central Asia*. Armonk, N.Y.: M. E. Sharpe.

Pravda Vostoka [Truth of the East].

Radio Rossiia.

Rorlich, Azade-Ayse (1991). "Islam and Atheism: Dynamic Tension in Soviet Central Asia." In *Soviet Central Asia: The Failed Transformation*, ed. William Fierman, pp. 186–218. Boulder: Westview Press.

Rumer, Boris (1990). *Soviet Central Asia: A Tragic Experiment*. Boston: Unwin Hyman.

Slovo Kyrghyzstana [Word of Kyrghyzstan]. Bishkek.

Soiuz [Union]. Moscow.

Vremia [Time]. Soviet television news.

Zolotukhin, Vladimir (1990). Interview, October 30.

IV

ISLAM VERSUS COMMUNISM
THE EXPERIENCE OF COEXISTENCE

Alexei V. Malashenko

Did Islam manage to remain Islam under Communism, or did Muslim societies within the former Soviet Union lose their religiosity? I would argue that Islamic society, despite persecution, preserved its worldview and moral values, even in the political context of the Soviet Union. Comparing the position of Islam with that of, say, Russian Orthodoxy, the latter was essentially destroyed in the years of Communist rule while Islam was able to preserve its influence at all levels of society.

In some Muslim regions, a "ferment of opposition" allowed believers to preserve an Islamic form of life. This was possible because Communist ideology has features parallel to the egalitarian concepts of Islam: collective values are more important than individual ones, for example, and both define the individual in terms of his or her service to society as a whole. In both systems power is personified by a strong political figure who is also an ideological or spiritual leader. Communists did not have to teach Muslims to respect charisma.

Several Russian economists and sociologists have noted the harmoniousness of Communism and Islam. The work of the ethnographer Sergei P. Poliakov (1989; English translation, 1992) is particularly noteworthy. Work commissioned by the press agency Postfactum shows that the socialist system was easily incorporated into the traditional system; many institutions simply exchanged their Islamic "signs" for Soviet and socialist ones (Postfactum 1991: 14–16).

Another factor that lessened the pressure on Muslim identity was that the Bolsheviks—including V. I. Lenin—always showed caution in matters concerning the Muslim East in the postrevolutionary years. Lenin wrote to one worker: "It is devilishly important for our whole *Weltpolitik* to conquer the trust of

This chapter was translated by Anthony Olcott.

people from those parts. . . . We have to be scrupulously severe here. This will affect India and the East, so there can be no joking here; we have to be 1000 percent careful in these matters" (Lenin 1970: 190). Commander M. V. Frunze, sent to establish Soviet power in Turkestan, understood local traditions, knew Eastern languages, and was familiar with the Qur'an. One of his first orders was to proclaim Friday a day of rest.

A final circumstance that encouraged the "salvation" of Islam had to do with the isolation of many settlements and the severities of local climate. Moreover, the security services, including the Cheka and its subsequent incarnations—the NKVD, the MGB, and the KGB—were not in a position to establish absolute control over the lives of Muslims. A system of informants was not always effective in the face of strong kinship and clan ties.

The fact that Muslim traditional society survived the Communist regime does not mean that Islam and Communism coexisted peacefully throughout this seventy-year period. Indeed, there was a continuing struggle for the right to preserve or impose their respective ways of life. In the end, Islam was the victor.

The first stage of this relationship came immediately after the October 1917 revolution. The Bolsheviks initially respected the power and influence of Islam and did not come out openly against it.[1] Some Communist ideologists portrayed Islam as a revolutionary doctrine which did not contradict Communism. A second stage, from 1920 to 1923, might be characterized as the first attempt to persecute Islam and the Muslim clergy. It coincided with a general sharpening of the political struggle and an attempt by the Bolsheviks to rid themselves of their most serious rival.

The third stage—1923/24 to the late 1930s—was initially characterized by a compromise between the new power and old traditions, followed by an effort to eradicate the old structures of belief and authority. The authority of the clergy grew in the 1920s, and they began to take a more active role in public life. In the 1930s, however, the Soviet state turned to the building of socialism by force and collectivization. In the unconditionally totalitarian system that became established in the USSR, there was no place for a religious worldview—especially for Islam, which was a total way of life. Islam, however, was less the target of persecution than Russian Orthodoxy.

Just prior to World War II, the situation again changed, and repression of religion and the clergy almost ceased. Officially appointed Muslim functionaries spoke of the "just character" of the war, collected contributions, and made significant contributions to the war effort themselves. During the war years, the Spiritual Directorate of Muslims of Central Asia and Kazakhstan was created. It became the nucleus for the officially recognized Muslim clergy, as well as an intermediary between Muslims and the government. Like other

1. The historical summary which follows is based on T. S. Saidbaev (1978).

official religious structures, the Spiritual Directorate became an adjunct of government administration. Directorate employees often had offices in the same buildings as Soviet administrators.

This symbiosis continued until the mid-1950s. By then the effects of the war had been almost entirely overcome, and Soviet authorities no longer needed religious support. This is when the fifth stage began. The All-Union Communist Party leadership turned its attention to religious structures, including mosques, and began to close them. They even struggled against religious holidays and rituals. Religion became subject to attack by the higher authorities of both the Communist Party of the Soviet Union and the government.

"Communist education proposes the liberation of consciousness from the religious prejudices and superstitions which still hamper some Soviet people from the full demonstration of their creative powers," said Nikita S. Khrushchev. "The spiritual development of a man cannot proceed successfully if his head is chock full of mysticism, superstition, and false conceptions" (Khrushchev 1961: 193). This official line, with various modifications, was applied to religion until the beginning of *perestroika*. It limited the role of religion and the clergy as much as possible.

This was also the line taken in regard to Islam. One of the frankest expressions of this policy came from the Secretary of the Central Committee of the Communist Party of Tajikistan, E. B. Bobosadykova (1983: 193), who wrote that "our class enemies still are painting ideological diversions with religious paints." The general aggressiveness against Islam was consistent with the recognition of its influence on society. Many publications noted how ordinary Muslims, especially those in the countryside, observed the rites of Islam (see, for example, Abrarov 1961; Bazarov 1971; Vagabov 1974; Madzhidov 1973; Religiia v planakh antikommunizma 1970). The journal *Voprosy nauchnogo ateizma* [Questions of Scientific Atheism] wrote about the existence of underground Qur'anic schools and the activities of "wandering mullahs" (*Voprosy nauchnogo ateizma* 1983: 183, 200).

Ironically, public criticism of Islam by highly placed party officials was accompanied by covert efforts to protect it. Many officials openly voiced their adherence to Islam and demonstrated their religiosity after their retirement. Indeed, party members and bureaucrats were often direct conduits of the traditional social relations sanctified by Islam. The reports of the success of atheistic agitation sent to Moscow were fiction, as the local authorities who drew them up knew perfectly well—but so did the administrators and party ideologues who read the reports in Moscow.

With the exception of Tataristan and, to a lesser extent, Azerbaijan, no fundamental changes occurred in Muslim society. Most Muslims continued to work in the traditional economic sector. In the industrial plants created during the years of Soviet rule, the workers were predominantly Slavs who had moved into Muslim lands. The Europeanized intelligentsia was extremely small, and, as discussed below, its influence on society was insignificant.

It was common knowledge that educated mullahs could only gain entrance to the upper levels of the clergy with the sanction of the secular authorities. There were also instances when a bureaucrat aspiring to a high post in the administrative apparatus appealed to the elders and the clerical authorities for assistance. In a word, while Islam was not visible on the formal surface of social life, it was the implicit regulator, a fact which all government officials, even those at the highest level, had to take into account.

It is natural to ask whether one can speak at this time of an Islamic opposition to the official political line. The answer is no. Islam and the official political structures were so tightly interwoven that there was no possibility of opposition. Formal Islamic structures became the monopoly of the party and the state *apparat* (some demonstrations in Tashkent used Muslim slogans, but these were exceptions).

Despite the general socioeconomic and cultural stagnation of traditional society in the Russian East, particularly in Turkestan, the eve of the 1917 Revolution saw the development of tendencies common to the whole Muslim world—especially Muslim enlightenment and reformist impulses from abroad.[2] In adjoining countries, reform and education were the basis for introducing a generation of Muslims to advanced science and raising economic and cultural standards. They also affirmed Islam as a great civilization whose potential was yet to be fully realized.

Within the Soviet Union, proponents of reform or enlightenment suffered cruel persecution. Those who did not emigrate were destroyed by the repression which began in 1930, and the process of religious renewal was cut short. On an everyday level, Islam was limited to traditional rituals and the routines that regulate the life of Muslim families.

The status of the Sufi brotherhoods, which were based on folk Islam, was different. Indeed, it could be argued that these Muslim orders consolidated opposition to the secular administration, since they continued to exercise enormous influence on the Muslim population, especially in the countryside.

Continuities in Soviet Islam

It is clear that the "Islamic line" was never broken in Soviet society. Despite the ambiguity of its position, Islam remained the preserver of spirituality, the framework for a worldview, and, to a significant extent, the regulator of relations between people. What many politicians and scholars saw as the

---

2. The Tajik scholar R. Shukurov wrote vividly about this: "At the end of the nineteenth century and the beginning of the twentieth, Bukhara and Maverannakhr were in deep decline, . . . but this was a crisis of a great ancient culture and not a return to savagery on the part of recently cultured peoples" (Shukurov 1990: 76).

sudden appearance of Islam in the political arena was in fact an inevitable development. The renaissance of "Soviet Islam" was merely a continuation of processes which had been interrupted in the 1920s.

Perestroika activated political life in the Muslim republics of the USSR to an unprecedented degree. Islam appeared alongside nationalism. Initially the appearance of Islamic slogans and propaganda was seen as something new in Soviet political practice, but by 1991 no one was surprised by the hoisting of green flags. Today there is scarcely a demonstration in any city of the Muslim regions of the Commonwealth of Independent States which does not fly the banner of Islam.

The beginning of the Islamic renaissance is connected with the growth of nationalism and a slowly growing awareness among the intelligentsia that was reflected in the rebirth of Islamic traditions. This was most apparent in Central Asia. By the end of the 1980s, Muslim enlightenment had penetrated Tatar Muslim circles, in Tataristan and in Moscow, Leningrad (now St. Petersburg), and other non-Muslim cities.[3] The enlightenment movement has proven remarkably viable, and its adherents continue to work actively today.

The primary goal of Muslim religious leaders after *perestroika* was to familiarize ordinary Muslims with the history and philosophy of their religion, to improve morals, and so forth. Muslim educators continued, in different circumstances and on a higher level, the underground Qur'anic schools and illegal circles for the study of the Qur'an and Islamic tradition which had existed before *perestroika*. They also transmitted the traditions of the Islamic enlightenment that had appeared at the end of the nineteenth century in the Middle East and spread to the Russian Empire.

These educators included students in the humanities, journalists, and some Muslim clergy. Most were comparatively young. During the day, they worked for the government; and in the evening, they pursued their Islamic work. I have found the majority to be without political ambition or religious fanaticism.

With the coming of *perestroika*, they began to condemn Communism, holding it the cause of the troubles that had befallen Muslim peoples and others. The first issue of Islamskie novosti [Islamic News], published in Makhachkala, Dagestan, proclaimed:

> In April 1985 [the beginning of *perestroika* in the USSR] the Almighty finally heard the tireless prayers of believers and the groans of the tormented innocent and sent down to us liberation from this evil spirit. . . . *Perestroika* became the true banner of Allah. . . . On the pages of our newspaper you will find, first and foremost, the Word of God. . . . The newspaper will print articles by famous Soviet and foreign scholars, Arabists, and theologians. You will also receive

---

3. Muslim leaders claim there are 800,000 Muslims in Moscow and Moscow oblast alone (*Vecherniaia Moskva* [Evening Moscow], September 12, 1991).

explanation of the bases of Islam and become familiar with various translations
and interpretations of the Qur'an. (*Islamskie novosti* November 19, 1991)

The Tatar newspaper, *Musul'manskii vestnik* [Muslim Herald], published since
the end of 1990 in Saratov, takes a similar position. Its first issue contained an
article entitled "Kak stat' musul'maninom" [How to Become a Muslim], which
explained in detail all the formalities for converting to Islam.[4]

As enlightenment is interwoven with nationalism, so too the idea of national
renaissance is interwoven with Islam. This has been noted both by scholars of
Islam and by Sovietologists. Yaacov Roi writes that "Central Asians, and
particularly the intellectual elites among them, . . . are rediscovering the region's
traditional culture. This attaches them further to Islam, which is the *leitmotiv*
in traditional Central Asian literature and philosophy" (Roi 1990: 59).

Educational tendencies are present as well in the programs of the Islamic
political parties created at the end of the 1980s, especially the Dagestan-based
Islamic Democratic party (IDP) and the Islamic Party of Turkestan. Point 22
of the Islamic Renaissance Party (IRP) program states that the party "will
organize Islamic schools, *madrasas*, lecture series, special-interest circles, and
supply them with the necessary literature and instructors" (Islamskaia partia
vozrozhdeniia 1991: 8).

The Muslim clergy are also becoming more active in education. In newly
created Islamic universities and institutes, the course of study is conducted by
members of the clergy and by teachers invited from secular educational institutions. The Imam al-Bukhara Islamic University in Tashkent has special
courses for women, attended by several hundred young Uzbeks. Even programs
and activities of the secular organizations and parties created in recent years,
such as Birlik in Uzbekistan and Rastokhez in Tajikistan, now have religious
elements.

Secular authorities are forced to support the educational work undertaken
by the officially recognized clergy with whom they are associated. On the other
hand, they interfere as much as possible with independent religious educators
in an attempt to establish a monopoly on Islamic education and related
activities.

There is nothing unusual about Islamic political activism. It is, after all, one
of the world's most politicized religions, and the connection between religion
and politics in the Muslim world has long been recognized. Nevertheless,
Islamic political activism in the USSR was unexpected in official party and
government circles. The domination of the Communist Party and the limited

---

4. Among the Tatars, educational work had a nationalist character as well, as can be seen from
an appeal in the same issue, "K vozrozhdeniiu tatarskoi natsii" [Toward the Rebirth of the Tatar
Nation] (*Musul'manskii vestnik* [Muslim Herald], December 1990).

social and cultural bases for democratic forces seemed to preclude significant Islamic political activity.

The official Muslim clergy has continued to speak against political participation. Their stance is occasioned by concern for their authority, but it also reflects the fact that most of these functionaries were educated in a spirit of secular principles. For their generation, secularism was a "natural habitat." They have actively cooperated with the authorities, participated in quasi-political campaigns, taken part in international functions for the Soviet government, and run for elected posts, including the Congress of People's Deputies of the USSR.

Of course, the official clergy are not the religious activists unfurling Islamic flags. The fundamentalists who appeared on the political map of the Soviet Union in the late 1970s rapidly made their way from illegal gatherings to mass meetings, created political parties, and participated in efforts to form new power structures. The influence of those I am calling fundamentalists (as applied in the Commonwealth of Independent States, this term is somewhat artificial) and the nature of the fundamentalist movement varies with the situation in each republic. In Tajikistan, the fundamentalists were part of the coalition that made an open bid for power in October 1991. In Azerbaijan, after a brief appearance in 1989–90, the fundamentalists lost political influence.

Islamic Fundamentalism in the Former USSR

The first sparks of the fundamentalist movement appeared at the end of the 1970s in Tajikistan, where local Islamic groups began to call themselves Wahhabis, after Ibn ʿAbd al-Wahhab (1703/4–1792), the founder of an eighteenth-century movement for the revival of Islam in the Arabian Peninsula.[5] The social foundation for Wahhabism was the peasantry, those who had recently moved from the countryside and those who resided in small towns.[6] Members subscribed to a peculiar synthesis of folk and doctrinal Islam. They demanded that Muslims be allowed to observe the tenets prescribed by Islam; they fought for the preservation and reopening of mosques and for independence in contacts with foreign brethren. The period of the Afghan War saw an

---

5. Editor's Note: Abduvakhitov (this volume) contradicts Malashenko's claim that "Wahhabi" is used by Islamic activists themselves, and instead traces the term's apparent origin to reports commissioned by Moscow officials. It might be further noted that the term is not used as self-designation in the Arabian peninsula, where adherents to the doctrines of Ibn ʿAbd al-Wahhab prefer to call themselves the "unitarians" (*al-muwahhidun*).

6. The French scholar Oliver Roy holds that these appearances, which the Soviet press termed "wahhabite," were "not connected to the traditionalistic fundamentalists, but rather with members of the intelligentsia, or in other words, the local nomenclatura" (Roy 1991: 150).

increase in their activism, but it was also at that time that the *Wahhabi*s began to suffer official repression.

The heightened activity of religious forces after 1985 was related to the worsening of the economic situation. Another factor was nationalism.[7] Fundamentalist tendencies began to appear in the first three years of *perestroika* (1985–88). Fundamentalism was far from a consolidated movement: one can speak only of fundamentalist "strands" in the developing political struggle of that time. The fundamentalists had no political leaders, and they made no radical demands, which suggests that they might not have possessed a precisely formulated political program. Fundamentalist attitudes were, on the one hand, a continuation of revivalist and educational tendencies extrapolated to political life. On the other hand, they reflected the efforts of various groups and individuals to form mafia-like structures that used Islam for self-interested ends.

These timid appearances of fundamentalism provoked a stormy reaction from the authorities and the clergy who worked with them. Both the secular authorities and the clergy recognized the danger of this swelling political tide. Fearing fundamentalism, but knowing that attacks on its adherents would have a negative effect on the administration and its allies, the government tried to "hush the problem up." At the same time, representatives of the party *apparat* and intellectuals who collaborated with them became increasingly convinced of the necessity for a more flexible approach to the Muslim opposition and even of limited cooperation with it. The opposition included both the Sufi orders and the fundamentalists (see Makhatov 1990: 64, 65).

It is difficult to pinpoint the social groups that support fundamentalism, since there are no statistics. To judge by newspaper and magazine articles, as well as from information provided by those who support the revival of Islam and its "political presence," fundamentalism is most popular among university students, especially those in the humanities; young people as a whole, especially young men who have recently moved to the cities and are trying to come to grips with their adherence to Islam; members of the intelligentsia with a traditionalist bent;[8] and middle- and lower-level religious officials, who are trying to distance themselves from the higher echelons of state-recognized religious functionaries.

---

7. Nationalism was a factor primarily in Kazakhstan, where Islam is much weaker than in neighboring Central Asia. The Communist Party of the Soviet Union's dictatorial government, copied by the local administration subordinate to it, was also a factor. In the Muslim regions, there were no dissidents, much less a democratic movement.

8. The younger generation is the traditionally inclined part of the Muslim intelligentsia, which formed in the 1970s and 1980s. These young intellectuals do not share their elders' piety for European culture, including Russian and Soviet culture, which they see as alien to their national and religious spirit. While their predecessors were drawn to the natural sciences, younger intellectuals tend more toward the humanities. A similar tendency was seen in Arab countries in the 1970s and 1980s. An interesting analysis of the subject is provided by Olimova and Olimov (1991: 95–104).

Fundamentalism is attractive to broad levels of the population, especially those unconnected to the modern industrial sector. Workers, engineers, and technicians have seldom taken part in fundamentalist demonstrations. It may be for this reason that fundamentalist activism has been so limited in Azerbaijan, where there are so many large industrial enterprises and scientific research institutes employing members of the native population. At the same time, there is a high percentage of service-sector people, "people from the bazaar," among the adherents of fundamentalism. It may be that a significant part of the population, which is, in principle, indifferent to politics, is disposed to support fundamentalism to a greater or lesser degree.

The popularity of fundamentalist slogans is a result of disillusionment with Communist policies that did not improve the standard of living. Socialism in the USSR evoked more disappointment than hope among Soviet Muslims, and the war in Afghanistan dealt the authority of Communist rulers a dreadful blow. Faith in the construction of a socialist society also suffered during *glasnost*, when Soviet Muslims began to learn about the lives of believers abroad. Many came to understand that the socialist idea and its Soviet variant was bankrupt, and they began search for an alternative model. This search was inescapably associated with Islam and the principles of Muslim civilization.

By the end of the 1970s, the Muslim world had also become disillusioned with Western models of social and economic development. The failure of the Western version of progress led to the Islamic Revolution in Iran, while the degradation of Arab socialism pushed hordes of dissatisfied Muslims into the streets. Millions of people concluded that they could be saved neither by European capitalism nor by European socialism. Salvation would come from Islam. This same disillusionment stimulated fundamentalist support in Tajikistan, Uzbekistan, and other Muslim regions.

In Russia and most of the Commonwealth of Independent States, however, Islam is opposed by Communism, which has long existed on ideas which resonate with Islamic ones: "social justice," "collectivism," and "firm authority." It is even possible to speak of a repetition—in a limited way, of course—of the standoff between Communism and Islam from 1920 to 1940, when Marxism tried to dislodge Islam from its ideological and psychological niches of collectivism, social justice, and authoritarianism.

What is occurring today is a similar process, save in the opposite direction. Islamic fundamentalists have argued that Communism exploited the norms and values of Islam while trying to destroy Islamic culture. The struggle is for the same "ideological territory," and it is taking place, in part, under similar banners and slogans. Communists are trying to frighten local supporters of democracy by saying they will be replaced by Muslim fanatics.

The struggle between Islam and Communism became sharper once religious political parties began to appear, especially the Islamic Renaissance Party (IRP). The IRP was formed in June 1990 in Astrakhan. Its leaders were mostly Tatars and Avars (a people living in Dagestan) from Muslim societies. An Avar physician, Akhmedkadi Akhtaev, was elected president, and the party press secretary (who is also the party's chief ideologist) is a Tatar scientist from Moscow, Valiahmed Sadur.

The IRP's program states that it "is a religious and political organization which unites Muslims who are actively disseminating Islam, who fulfill the prescriptions of Islam, who participate in religious, cultural, social, political, and economic life on the basis of Islam's principles." Point 27 says that the party will "regulat[e] the excessive accumulation of wealth in single hands, on the basis of the *shariᶜa*." The document also asserts that "invented schemes of social development have brought mankind to complete crisis in all spheres of life. We see salvation only in following the way of Allah" (Islamskaia partiia vozrozhdeniia [Program and Statutes of the Islamic Renaissance Party] 1991: 6, 8).

The IRP is unique to the political map of the Commonwealth of Independent States. It is the only religious party that calls itself a party for all Muslims living within the borders of the former Soviet Union. It was initially denied official registration in Tajikistan and Uzbekistan, although that position may soon be reversed. The party has also drawn the ire of the local religious functionaries. The head of the Spiritual Directorate of Muslims of Central Asia and Kazakhstan, Mukhammed Sodik Mukhammed-Yusef, denounced the IRP on the grounds that "we [the official religious functionaries] hold that Islam is itself a party which has been in existence now for more than 1400 years" (Sodik 1990).[9]

Refused official registration in the Muslim regions, the IRP finally registered in the Oktiabr district of Moscow.[10] In Uzbekistan and Tajikistan the authorities did everything possible to prevent organizational meetings of local IRP chapters. In Tashkent, delegates to the January 1991 meeting were arrested (and later released) by the militia. In Tajikistan, the first meeting was held illegally in a small village near Dushanbe. Despite such harassment, the IRP was able to establish local chapters, although they were not recognized by the official administration.

Uzbekistan's president, Islam Karimov, and his Tajik colleague, Kakhar Makhamov, spoke against the IRP. A typical (and cynical) official opinion was expressed by N. Ovezov, a highly placed bureaucrat in the Council of Ministers of Turkmenistan: "I would say, and I am probably expressing the opinion of the absolute majority of Turkmen, that we don't need any kind of party of Muslim revival" (Ovezov 1991). Dagestan authorities were more receptive to the IRP and did little to interfere with the party's activities in their territory.

---

9. Editor's Note: In September 1990 a separate Spiritual Directorate was created for Kazakhstan. See Olcott (this volume).

10. Ironically, the chair of this region is Ilya Zaslavskii, a Jew whom Russian nationalists consider a Zionist.

A second political party appeared at about the same time, the Islamic Party of Turkestan, and its ideology was noticeably influenced by fundamentalism. It claimed the right to speak for all Turkic people living in the USSR. Another group was the Turkmenistan Sunna Society. Among other things, it demanded the restriction or banning of certain television programs because they "make people spiritually and physically ill" (Madzhilov 1991). The group called Jamaʿat, headed by Ali Aliev, holds that the main things of value for a Muslim are the Qurʾan and *shariʿa*. There are organizations with similar orientations in Azerbaijan, Checheno-Ingushetia, and Tataristan.

The independent information center called Tavkhid (Arabic, *tawhid* [unity]) is based in Moscow. Oriented primarily to the city's Tatar population, the center presents itself as expressing the common interests of the Muslim population. The wording used by Tavkhid's leaders, including Jamal Geidar, is extremely suggestive. Geidar writes of "the mortal crisis" of mankind, "the first and primary proof" of which is "the general global stupidity which rages across the planet as it never has before." The fault, argues Geidar and his supporters, lies with "the bureaucratic government," the "progressives," and the "enlighteners, utopians, and revolutionary satirists" (*at-Tawhid* 1990: 1–2).

On the whole, no monolithic fundamentalist movement has formed among Muslims in the former Soviet Union. Despite the IRP's claim to be an all-union fundamentalist party, it has no real political power. Local chapters of the IRP, however, are becoming increasingly influential. This is particularly true in Tajikistan, where Davlat Usmon, head of the local IRP chapter, has emerged as an independent political actor.

IRP leaders understand that the 30,000 Muslims who have declared allegiance to the party are not necessarily loyal to the party's central leadership. Islamic activists of Central Asia, the Caucasus, and Russia are primarily concerned with their own interests, and most do not cede even a nominal governing role to the IRP. Leaders are considering the idea of turning the party into an Islamic movement that would include all Muslims, not just fundamentalists. It could prove a decisive factor in the restructuring of traditional society.

"The Red Flag of Communism or the Green Flag of Islam" was the title of an article published recently in *Izvestiia* (Vyzhutovich 1991). Valerii Vladimir Vyzhutovich maintained that the struggle between Communism and Islam would be the main arena for the political spectacle unfolding in the Muslim portion of the USSR, including Central Asia. "We must keep in mind that it is not so much religious fanaticism which speaks with the Qurʾan in its hand as much as it is a natural protest against ossified Communist ways. This is a political struggle, not a religious one" (Vyzhutovich 1991). At first glance, the point is unarguable, because the forces which speak from beneath the banner of Islam are opposed to old Communist structures.

But how correct is this opinion? Is the relationship between Communism and Islam to be defined solely as opposition? While Muslim regions oppose Communism, Islamic activists make no effort to weaken relations with Communist structures, their successors, or their agents. The struggle with the Communist Party of the Soviet Union (until it collapsed) was essentially a battle of slogans. In addition, the outlines of an implicit consensus can be made out between the surviving Communist bureaucracy and a significant portion of Muslim fundamentalists, who share skepticism on the prospects for democracy in the Muslim republics. We should also note the IRP's negative attitude toward Boris Yeltsin, whom the party's leaders see as a Russian chauvinist.[11]

The natural tendency for fundamentalists is to search for an Islamic alternative for structuring society, and this makes fundamentalism an enemy of democratic movements, which fundamentalists see as incompatible with the traditions of Islam. An article in the IRP newspaper *Al'-Vakhdat* confirms this view. Entitled "Demokratiia—demokratam, Islam-musul'manam" [Democracy for Democrats, Islam for Muslims], the article asks: "Can we Muslims follow the various secularist systems which are based on teachings, whether they are about the dictatorship of the proletariat and class warfare or about nationalism and racial exclusivity or about Western democracy and absolute freedom, which leave God's teachings to the side, the teachings which raised us to a high level of civilization?" ("Demokratiia—demokratam, Islam-musul'manam," 1991).

The fact that Muslim fundamentalism, the Native Soil movement—a Russian version of fundamentalism—and Communism have been able to find a common language is not accidental. Neither is it simply a political coalition. There are deeper causes (see Malashenko 1991). Muslim fundamentalists are in complete solidarity with the pro-Communist wing of the Russian *pochvennichestvo* or Native Soil movement, pseudonationalists who reject democracy, which they consider alien to a Russian Orthodox people. While relations between Muslim and Russian fundamentalists were initially strained, today Russian "patriotic" newspapers enthusiastically publish materials written by proponents of an Islamic way of life. In January 1991, the conservative Communist newspaper *Den'* [Day] wrote of fundamentalist Islam as one of the forces working to undermine the government; but the tone had begun to change by summer, and in October the paper published an interview with Jamal Geidar, one of the leaders of the Moscow-based information center, Tavkhid. Geidar urged the immediate foundation in Tajikistan of a government based on principles of Islamic democracy. In the same issue were excerpts from the teachings of Ayatollah Khomeini (*Den'*, October 25–November 8, 1991). Just prior to this, *Den'* had published an article about the Azerbaijani Pan-Turkist, Gamid Kherishchi.

The most distinct unification of nationalist religious forces and the former Communist administrative *apparat* is in Tataristan, where the former ruling

---

11. See the interview with Valiahmed Sadur, Press Secretary of the IRP (Sadur 1991: 24). I have also heard this opinion of Yeltsin at press conferences held by the IRP and from representatives of other Muslim organizations that cooperate with the IRP.

class has been able to use nationalistic moods against the democratic wing of Russia. Tataristan, which journalists have ironically dubbed "an island of Communism" (*Argumenty i fakty* [Arguments and Facts], September 20, 1991), has become an arena for political cooperation of such forces—for example, the president of Tataristan, Mintimer Shaimiev, a Communist official, and Fawzia Bairamova, head of the nationalist party Ittifak. They have been assisted by the Tatar Civic Center and the Muslim clergy. The Islamic banner flies during mass meetings organized by these groups, and mass prayer meetings are frequent.

In Uzbekistan, in contrast, practical cooperation between the Islamists and the Communists, who renamed the local party, has been absent. To judge from the official press, the Uzbek administration tries to resist unsanctioned missionary activity by nonconformist Muslims affiliated with opposition forces. At the same time, the leaders continue to support the official religious functionaries, who in turn support official policies.[12]

Three types of relations have evolved in the Muslim regions between the fundamentalists and the local authorities who have inherited the Communist structures of authority:

In the first situation, former Communists preserve their hegemony and exploit the nationalist and fundamentalist moods of a significant part of the Muslims, giving their struggle against local democratic forces and the new Russian leadership a national and religious character. Tataristan is the most obvious example.

Characteristic of the second type of relationship is a continuation of an Islamic-Communist confrontation, combined with a growing awareness of the need for compromise. Both sides have a common enemy in the national liberals and democrats. This is roughly the situation in Uzbekistan, Turkmenistan, and Dagestan. Fundamentalists play the role of opposition in the present administration, but both sides strive to avoid open clashes, although they do not always succeed. In June 1991, for example, the Dagestani authorities used armed force to disperse a Muslim demonstration led by the radical fundamentalist group Zhaamatul Muslimi; thirty-five people were killed.

The third type of relationship between the two political forces holds in Tajikistan, where a change in the general situation led to a wholly unexpected clash. In September 1991, as a result of the emergence of democratic forces, the former Communists were removed from power. They tried to reestablish

---

12. In the summer of 1991, before Uzbekistan declared its independence, members of the official clergy assisted in the draft call-up for the Soviet army and helped to capture deserters (*Pravda Vostoka* [Truth of the East], June 7, 1991). In April 1991 the Central Asian Spiritual Directorate of Muslims promulgated a decree (*fatwa*) to draftees and servicemen: avoiding military service "is in Islam considered a sin; the religion demands the defense of one's own land" (*Pravda Vostoka* [Truth of the East], April 27, 1991). On April 25, 1991, the same newspaper reported that the *imam* of a mosque had persuaded a deserter to return to the ranks.

their positions but were opposed by a coalition of all non-Communist forces. The democrats, composed of Europeanized local intelligentsia and nonnative Slavs, were supported by Muslim politicians and some of the clergy. The contradiction between democracy and traditional Islamic values proved weaker than a general hatred of Communism.

In the conflict between the former Communists and the other political groups, one of the IRP's ideologists, Jamal Geidar, came to Dushanbe, the capital of Tajikistan, to support the presidential candidacy of Rakhmon Nabiev, who represented the Communist Party. The support of Moscow's fundamentalists testifies to their desire not to allow forces sympathetic to Boris Yeltsin to grow stronger in the republic. As a result, the local IRP chapter created an independent Party for the Islamic Revival of Tajikistan. Its head, Davlat Usmon, had been a key figure in the IRP. He insists that the party, which numbers between 15,000 and 20,000 members, will support democratic forces (*Islamskie novosti* [Islamic News], September 1991).

Events in the Muslim republics of the Commonwealth of Independent States are developing so rapidly that it is not possible to provide a "complete" and "final" analysis. Undoubtedly, we shall see completely unexpected turns. For example, in November 1991, Jakhar Dudaev, a major general in the Soviet Air Force, was elected president of Checheno-Ingushenia. He has declared a *jihad* [struggle *or* holy war] against both the former pro-Communist administration and the Yeltsin government.

The third variant described above may calm a significant part of the intelligentsia, which is concerned about the growing strength of Islamic forces. Only a few members of the intelligentsia openly express their opinions on this score. One was the Dagestan democrat Aivaz Meilanov, who characterized the Islamic government as totalitarian (*Drugoie nebo* [Other Sky], August 20, 1991). The present disposition of forces suggests that at this stage of government formation, fundamentalist and democratic, non-Islamic forces can work together, for all the contradictions between them, and that a consensus can be reached. Even in the heat of the Russian presidential election campaign in May 1991, Muslims in the capital of the Karachaevo-Cherkess Autonomous Region gathered to pray, asking Allah to help Boris Yeltsin.

To all appearances, 1991 has been a pivotal year of political development for the former Soviet Union's Muslim republics. By the end of the 1980s, specialists had begun to speak of the basic tendencies of the Islamic revival, especially culture and education. Political Islam was in the process of formation. Early in 1990, for example, IRP leaders announced that they would like to play a role analogous to that of the Muslim faction in the prerevolutionary Russian Imperial Duma. The fundamentalists were not in favor of leaving the USSR and creating Islamic governments.

The Communist Party of the Soviet Union's primary opponents were nationalists and national democrats, who grouped around organizations like Birlik in Uzbekistan, Rastokhez in Tajikistan, and so on. Nationalism predominated over

Islamic ideas, as can be seen from Central Asian conflicts, where Muslims fought among themselves. Fundamentalists and the official Islamic functionaries who sympathized with them tried to maintain peace between fellow believers.

Until the August 1991 coup, the Communist administration had the upper hand, although Islam's political influence was growing. At the same time, there was a conviction in the ruling circles that it would be possible to make the fundamentalists a "pocket opposition" and use them as they had the official clergy. With the collapse of the USSR, the position of the fundamentalists grew firmer. In Tajikistan and parts of the North Caucasus, where the political initiative passed to opponents of Communism, the fundamentalists have moved into the leading roles. The idea of forming an Islamic state is being posed openly, and its popularity is growing.

References

Abrarov, M. (1961). *Shariat i ego sotsial'naia sushchnost'* [Shariat and Its Social Essence]. Tashkent: Fan.

Argumenty i fakty [Arguments and Facts]. Moscow.

Bazarov, A. (1971). *Nekotorye osobennosti i puti formirovaniia ateisticheskogo mirovozzreniia tadzhiksogo dekkhanstva* [Some Peculiarities and the Methods of Formation of an Atheistic World]. Dushanbe: Irfon.

Bobosadykova, E. B. (1983). "O Sovershenstvovanii Form i Meteodov Ateistitcheskoi raboti" [On the Improvement of the Forms and Methods of Atheistic Work]. *Voprosy nauchnogo ateizma* [Questions of Scientific Atheism] 35: 193–205.

Den' [Day]. Moscow.

Drugoie nebo [Other Sky]. Newspaper. Makhachkala.

Islamskaia partiia vozrozhdeniia (1991). "Programma i Ustav Islamskoi partii vozrozhdeniia" [Program and Statutes of the Islamic Renaissance Party]. *Izvestiia*. Moscow, June 13.

Islamskie novosti [Islamic News]. Makhachkala.

Izvestiia.

Kebedov, A. (1991). "Demokratiia—demokratam, Islam-musul'manam" [Democracy for Democrats, Islam for Muslims]. *Al'-Vakhdat* (March).

Khrushchev, Nikita S. (1961). *Materialy 22 s"ezda KPSS* [Materials of the XXII Congress of the CPSU]. Moscow: Izdatelstvo politicheskoi literaturi.

Lenin, V. I. (1970). *Polnoe sobranie sochinenii* [Complete Collected Works], vol. 53. Moscow: Izdatelstvo politicheskoi literaturi.

Madzhidov, R. M. (1973). *Preodolenie religioznosti v usloviiakh perekhoda k sotsializmu minuia kapitalizm* [Overcoming Religiosity in the Conditions of the Transition to Socialism Bypassing Capitalism]. Dushanbe.

Madzhilov, Ishankuli (1991). *Nezavisimaia gazeta* [Independent Gazette]. Moscow, May 18.

Makatov, I. (1990). "Uskorit' perestroiku ateisticheskogo vospitaniia" [Accelerating Perestroika of Atheist Education]. *Kommunist Uzbekistana* 11. Tashkent.

Malashenko, Aleksei (1991). "Fundamentalizm—musul'manskii, russkii, sovetskii" [Fundamentalism—Muslim, Russian, and Soviet]. *Nezavisimaia gazeta* [Independent Gazette], May 18.

Musul'manskii vestnik [Muslim Herald]. Saratov.

Olimova, Saodat, and Muzaffar Olimov (1991). "Obrazovannyi klass Tadzhikistana" [The Educated Class in Tajikistan]. *Vostok* [The East] 5.

Ovezov, N. (1991). *Nezavisimaia gazeta* [Independent Gazette]. Moscow, July 6.

Poliakov, Sergei P. (1989; English translation, 1992). *Traditsionalizm v sredneaziatskom obshchestve* [Traditionalism in Central Asian Society]. Moscow: Znanit.

——— (1992). *Everyday Islam: Religion and Tradition in Soviet Central Asia.* New York: M. E. Sharpe.

Postfactum (1991). "Sredniaia Aziia: islamskii faktor?" [Central Asia: The Islamic Factor?], *Analiticheskie vestniki informatsionnogo agentsva Postfactum* [Analytic Heralds of the Postfactum Information Agency] 6 (April).

Pravda Vostoka [Truth of the East]. Tashkent.

Religiia v planakh antikommunizma [Religion in the Plans of the Anti-Communists] (1970). Moscow: Izdatelstvo politicheskoi literaturi.

Roi, Yaacov (1990). "The Islamic Influence on Nationalism in Soviet Central Asia." *Problems of Communism* (July–August).

Roy, Oliver (1991). "Geopolitique de l'Asie Centrale." *Cahiers du monde russe et soviétique* 32, no. 1 (January–March).

Sadur, Valichmed (1991). "Sredniaia Aziia: Islamskii faktor?" [Central Asia: The Islamic Factor?]. *Analiticheskie vestniki informatsionnogo agentsva Postfactum* [Analytic Heralds of the Postfactum Information Agency] 6 (April).

Saidbaev, T. S. (1978). *Islam i obshchestvo* [Islam and Society]. Moscow: Nauka.

Shukurov, R. (1990). "Bukhara. Sentiabr' 1920 Neobkhodimost' novogo videniia" [Bukhara: September 1920—The Need for New Vision]. *Izvestiia Akademii nauk Tadzhikskoi SSR* [News of the Academy of Sciences of the Tajik SSR] 4 (20).

Sodik, Mukhammed, Mukhammed-Iusef (1990). *Komsomolets Tadzhikistana* [Young Communist of Tajikistan]. Dushanbe, December 14.

Vagabov, V. B. (1974). *Islam i sem'ia* [Islam and the Family]. Moscow: Nauka.

Vecherniaia Moskva [Evening Moscow].

Voprosy nauchnogo ateizma [Questions of Scientific Atheism] 31 (1973).

Vyzhutovich, Valerii V. (1991). *Izvestiia.* Moscow, September 5.

V

ISLAMIC REVIVALISM IN UZBEKISTAN

Abdujabar Abduvakhitov

The Early Twentieth Century

When asked if the Islamist movement in Uzbekistan would try to take power in the republic, Abit-qari, one of its current leaders, answered that they have such a purpose but that the task is only for the future.[1] "Now," he said, "we are acting to educate people, enabling them to create a society based on the principles of Islam, where all matters would be regulated by the *ulama* according to the Qur'an. For us at this time, education is *jihad*."

Education is often the first step for many social movements. Muslim intellectuals in the early decades of this century, including Jamal al-Din al-Afghani (1838–97), Rashid Rida (1865–1935), Muhammad 'Abduh (1849–1905), Muhammad Iqbal (1875–1938), and others, show that the educational activity of those advocating a renewal of Islamic religious thought in Central Asia is an important part of this process. The reform movement in Central Asia, which I shall call "Jadidism," from the Arabic *jadid* [new], included both secular and Islamic elements. In Central Asia, the current Islamic activism grew out of an earlier concern for the renewal of religious ideas. Central Asian religious activism was, however, homegrown, although influenced by other parts of the Islamic world.

The history of political movements in the Muslim world provides an opportunity to consider some regularities in the experiences and ideologies of contemporary Islamic renewal movements. At the same time, we should bear in mind that activities and ideologies in any specific context are the result of many factors: tradition, tribalism, sectarianism, national and cultural identity, and the level of political awareness of different groups of people in the society.

---

1. The article was prepared in December 1991, prior to the creation of the Commonwealth of Independent States.

As a means of solving political, social, and economic problems, Islam unites people in contemporary Muslim societies as effectively as did the *sufi* brotherhoods of medieval times. Revivalism appeared as a part of the anticolonial movement and took political, economic, and cultural hold in urban areas. Throughout the Muslim world, the aim of Islamic renewal has been to rebuild the fundamental social principles of Islam. In Central Asia, the movement has united people of the urban middle and lower strata, but members of the intelligentsia, who are often socially and politically influential, frequently join the revivalists.

All the necessary conditions for the development of Islamic revivalism are present in Central Asia. In the past, there were many *sufi* brotherhoods there, and political and social movements usually claimed that they were acting on religious principles. The resistance movement against Russian expansion in the late nineteenth and early twentieth centuries, for example, saw itself as defending Islam. Had Central Asian Jadidism of the early 1900s not included political activism, it would have disappeared from the political and cultural scene as a transient phenomenon. Reformers like Munawwar Qari (1880–1933), Mahmud Khoja Behbudi (1874–1919), Abdalrauf Fitrat (1886–1938), Usmon Nasir, Tolegan Khojani Arov Tavallah, and others could not have acted in any other way. Qari and Behbudi were *ulama*; Tavallah wrote a book of poems, *Rawnaq al-Islam* [The Wealth of Islam], which emphasized the need to study the experience of European countries and spoke of the benefits of secular education. Jadidism was, in fact, part of a national liberation movement in the early twentieth century.

Some Islamic reformers sympathized with the Qorbashis, who offered armed resistance to the new Bolshevik state and thus formed part of the national liberation movement.[2] Qorbashi leaders included heads of *sufi* orders, so this movement found many supporters in the *sufi* brotherhoods.

By the 1930s, Qorbashi activity had become severely limited. Nasir-khan Tora Atantay's group was the last. Its members came from one *sufi* brotherhood. All were subsequently executed. With the group's defeat and Stalin's continued repression, the national and Islamic movement was forced underground, but the idea of a national and Islamic identity did not disappear.

The establishment of a Spiritual Directorate of the Muslims of Central Asia and Kazakhstan (SADUM) in 1943 was intended to mobilize the people to support the actions of the Communist Party, to control and regulate the thinking of the Muslim people, and to advance the party's foreign policy goals in the growing Islamic world. Although an artificial creation, this state-con-

---

2. Editor's Note: "Qorbashi," together with *mujahid*, or "struggler for the faith," were terms of self-reference considered so sensitive that they were until recently deleted from Uzbek dictionaries (Allworth 1990: 174–76). Benningsen and Wimbush (1979: 26), as is common in Western usage, refer to the movement only by the term Basmachi, or "bandit," coined by the movement's Soviet detractors.

trolled Spiritual Directorate, the largest of the four in the Soviet Union, was intended to unite all Muslims. The officials of the Spiritual Directorate controlled the Bukhara *madrasa* and the Islamic Institute in Tashkent, the main official center for Islamic education in Central Asia, although these schools produced few graduates.

This effort to exert official control over Islam was unsuccessful. The militant atheism which was propagated by Communist cadres in the years of Soviet rule was ineffective because a parallel Islamic practice continued underground. At the same time, the Spiritual Directorate and its mosques and cadres became a kind of base for the growing Islamic revival because it was difficult to insulate it from the influence of the parallel movément.

The Late 1970s

An Islamic revitalization took place in the Muslim parts of the Soviet Union in the late 1970s. At the time, Central Asia was characterized by a low standard of living, and the policies of the Communist Party resulted in major economic and social disparities. Social differentiation was accelerated and eventually corrupted the Communist Party, demoralizing some of its cadres. Some of the administrative elite became like the upper class in the Western world, and people in the middle and lower classes became increasingly poor. Young people of the urban middle and lower class felt that the situation was disastrous. The majority of the people who lived in rural areas felt the same, for Central Asia's emphasis on cotton production, to the exclusion of the cultivation of food crops, caused hardship for them. The number of unemployed grew alarmingly.

The Soviet Union's policy toward Central Asia aimed to destroy traditional social bonds. Lack of confidence in the future prompted the people, especially the youth, who did not fear state repression, to seek solutions to their problems. Some appealed to Islam, which they saw as providing a possibility for self-determination.

The new stage of activism at the end of 1970s focused on education. Small groups of youth began to be taught by older persons who had been educated before the revolution. Many came from religious families and had been educated at home. The basic subjects of study were Arabic language and script (the Turkic languages of the region were written in Arabic script until the 1920s) and Islam. Lessons were not oriented to politics; the teachers themselves had always remained aloof from politics, and oppression had made them fearful.

This education began a political process which was irreversible. Hundreds of young people began to study illegally under elder religious teachers, few of whom were related to the officials of SADUM. Students began with *Adib-i Awwal* [The First Teacher, ca. 1901], an Uzbek-language primer in Arabic script with an introduction to Islamic basics and excerpts from the Qur'an in Arabic. Next they studied *Adib-i Thani* [The Second Teacher, ca. 1903], which contained more Islamic themes. Both these Turkic-language pamphlets—the second was forty-four pages long—were written by Munawwar Qari (see Allworth 1990: 133).

The Rise of Rakhmatullah: 1950–1981

One of the leaders of the "parallel" Islam of those years, Hakim Qari (b. 1896 or 1898), lived in Marghilan. At times he enjoyed more influence than the officeholders of the Spiritual Directorate or the city's Communist authorities. Among his students in 1978 were Rakhmatullah (b. 1950) and Abduwali, who studied in his home for six months and then continued their studies independently.[3] Less than a year later, at a 1979 meeting attended by older religious people and by Hakim Qari and his supporters, Rakhmatullah condemned the position of his teacher and his followers, calling them "collaborators." Rakhmatullah spoke about their inability to preserve Islam and how Communist rule had destroyed the Islamic system. People were not only deprived of their right to pray but also of other human rights, he said. He demanded the printing and distribution of Islamic literature among the people. He said that Islamic leaders must stimulate people to seek knowledge, so that people could understand and defend their religion, their homeland, their families, and themselves according to Islamic principles. This knowledge would make them ready to revive the Islamic community and establish a new state, which he called Musulmanabad. His speech was a political bombshell.

Although, as Rakhmatullah's teacher, Hakim Qari had helped to form these views, Hakim Qari and his supporters were frightened by such words. Brezhnev and the Communists remained strong, and Rakhmatullah's condemnation of Hakim Qari as cowardly and subservient to authorities was insulting. In addition, Rakhmatullah demanded that Central Asian Islam be purged of what he regarded as compromising elements, such as permitting young believers to cut their hair so their appearance conformed to that of other people and allowing them to study at secular schools. He conceded that young believers had to be able to read books, newspapers, and journals and to watch television and keep informed about the political and social order from which they were defecting. Rakhmatullah himself had studied the doctrines of Marx and Lenin, and this helped him to understand the politics of the Communist state toward Muslims and others.

---

3. Here I follow Uzbek usage and refer to these leaders by their personal names only, to which Uzbeks add honorifics such as "the learned one" (*'allama*) or "one who has memorized the Qur'an" (*qari*). This usage follows the preference of the persons discussed.

Rakhmatullah was condemned by traditionalists, including Hakim Qari, as a fundamentalist and a modernist. Thus a split developed within "parallel" Islam in Uzbekistan which spread to other Islamic communities in Central Asia.

Rakhmatullah and Abduwali, together with their followers, opened clandestine schools and printed books and pamphlets. Each school had only five or ten students, who came from many cities and villages. Missionaries traveled to other cities and rural areas, where they recruited students from devout Muslim families. These students studied Islam and Rakhmatullah's political ideas. They were also taught the views of foreign activists, including Abu-l-ʿAla' Mawdudi (India and Pakistan, 1903–79), Hasan al-Banna' (Egypt, 1906–49), and Sayyid Qutb (Egypt, 1906–66), and they became teachers for others.

Because this educational process required literature on Islam, small printing houses were established and their publications spread in secret. I have seen, for example, one of Mawdudi's books bound in the cover of a book entitled *Materials of the XXVth Conference of CPSU*. Most of the literature was distributed free.

It is only in the last year that we have been able to ask how this educational activity was financed. It is the "way of Islam," I was told. The source of financing was not from abroad, because activists had no contact with foreigners or foreign Islamic countries until very recently. Activists claim that their main financial resource was their own income from crafts and trades.

Some activists were imprisoned and others encountered other difficulties, but the number of schools and small printing houses and adherents continued to grow. The late 1970s and early 1980s was the time of the Soviet invasion of Afghanistan. Activists expressed their solidarity with Afghans struggling for independence, but the solidarity did not take the shape of visible political action.

In the early 1980s, state and party officials founded some schools and printing houses in Central Asia as profit-making enterprises, but often they were taken over by the militia. One example of such militia-funded activities from that period is the efforts of the Institute of Atheism, which in 1989 changed its name to the Institute of Religion. It considered these educational and printing activities as a way to exploit Islam and make a profit at the same time.

Communist Party countermeasures in Uzbekistan against revivalist groups were unsuccessful. One arm of the party was hampered by tribalism, regionalism, and kinship ties and thus was uninterested in activities going on around them. Another group of party activists, mostly those occupying lower positions in the party apparatus, sensed their instability as a people and as a nation and realized how much their status depended on support from the Soviet center. Some were well informed about Islamic activism and considered it a way of gaining national independence and self-determination in the future. They sympathized with the Islamic activists but remained silent observers.

At the beginning of 1981, Rakhmatullah died in a traffic accident at the age of thirty-one. Some concluded that traditionalists had staged this accident. Others inferred that Moscow had played a role in the assassination of the activist leader. Perhaps sometime later, when archives are made public, the real reason for Rakhmatullah's death will become clear. It was clear from the beginning, however, that the growing activist movement and its leader, Rakhmatullah, were dangerous to the authorities, especially those in Moscow.

With Rakhmatullah's death, the process of reviving Islam slowed, but there was no observable lessening in educational activity or the printing of Islamic literature. It continued in the Ferghana Valley, the region of the greatest social, economic, and ethnic inequality.

Islamic activism in Central Asia should not be considered an import from abroad, although it is influenced by a growing Islamic activism elsewhere. Activists are assuming the previously vacant role of opposition to Communist authorities in Central Asia and advocates of national and religious self-determination.

The Growing Popularity of Islamic Activism

After the death of Rakhmatullah, Islamic activism became more widespread throughout Central Asia. New groups appeared in the Ferghana Valley—and in Samarkand, Bukhara, and Osh—but their educational activity was not halted by the authorities. By 1986, many new schools began to operate in the cities and villages of Central Asian republics, especially in Uzbekistan and Tajikistan. The policy of the Communist Party of Uzbekistan against Islamic revivalism and expressions of national and religious identity was unsuccessful and only served to aggravate the situation. Sometimes it seemed that the Communists were working against themselves. For example, the authorities outlawed the national Uzbek hat, the *dobba*, as a mark of national or Islamic identity. This campaign was launched by a party ideologue, Ra'na Abdullaeva, and its ineffectiveness symbolized the party's weakness in 1986.

The followers of Rakhmatullah led the coalescence of the Islamic community in Central Asia. It was rumored that they were *wahhabi*s [unitarians, influenced by the strict Saudi sect of that name] or were financed by the *wahhabi*s. I searched for a tie between Uzbek activists and Saudi *wahhabi*s but found none. SADUM officials tried to persuade people that the *wahhabiyya* sect, especially its local adherents, were against Islam and its traditions. Some non-officials supported the idea too. Thus there was a growing split within the Islamic community, and it began in the time of Rakhmatullah.

A few years ago I met the leaders of a Muslim brotherhood group which was rumored to be *wahhabi*, and I asked about their attitude towards Wahhabism. They clearly sympathized with some *wahhabi* ideas, such as reviving and preserving the main principles of Islam, but those ideas alone do not make them *wahhabi*. Until 1990, Uzbek activists had no contact with foreign Muslim activists. In 1990, some Central Asian revivalists visited Saudi Arabia for the first time when they undertook the pilgrimage [*hajj*]. Although they had contact with some Saudi *wahhabi*s at that time, those ties were not maintained on their return.[4]

The policy of *perestroika* in the field of religion began with a liberalization in attitude toward the Russian Christian church. In the beginning of 1989, in Uzbekistan, the Namangan group of Rakhmatullah's followers, led by Ishanbaev Aqilbek, demanded that local authorities restore the Gumbaz mosque, one of the country's largest, as a place of worship. The building had been used as a warehouse for the state wine factory. The day the Namangan group informed authorities of their plans to hold a meeting, Aqilbek and some of his friends were arrested. They were released two days later and told that the mosque would not be restored. Aqilbek's group then planned a hunger strike. The alcohol vats were removed from the warehouse, and I later observed thousands of young men praying in this mosque on Fridays.

Groups of Rakhmatullah's followers in centers such as Namangan, Andijan, Osh, Tashkent, Marghilan, and in other cities and villages of Uzbekistan continued their educational activities, philanthropy, and the printing and distribution of books and pamphlets concerning different aspects of Islam. They used these centers to train people, gathering young men and women from all the Central Asian republics. They lived and studied free of charge in camps. They also took part in physical training programs, and some participated in karate or boxing clubs.[5] I have never obtained any evidence concerning military training.

In 1990, the Islamic Renaissance Party became the first activist party to receive official recognition, although not in Uzbekistan. It included members from all the Muslim republics in its organizing groups. Its First Constituent Conference was held on July 9, 1990, in Astrakhan. The Tajik group tried to register its own branch in Dushanbe, but the republic's parliament refused to allow this, declaring that the inspiration for creating an Islamic Party came from abroad and that *sunni* Muslims should not enter politics. Recently, however, the party was registered.

As for Uzbekistan, a request to hold the First Constituent Conference in Yangi-yol city in Tashkent was made to Tashkent executive authorities on December 20, 1990. Group members also informed the officials of their decision to hold a Republican Conference on January 26–27, 1991. The Tashkent

---

4. I tried to find the origin of the insinuation that Uzbek nationalists were *wahhabi*. During a Congress of Soviet Orientalists in Leningrad, I spoke with a Moscow colleague who said that in 1986 he was asked to report on Central Asian Islamic trends. He called this group *wahhabi*s because official documents suggested the prevalence of ideas which he considered close to Wahhabism. The claim that such Central Asian groups were Wahhabi-inspired was thus exploited by the authorities to discredit them.

5. Editor's Note: The activities described here, including karate clubs, parallel those of groups elsewhere in the Muslim world, including North Africa.

City Executive Committee refused to allow the conference, saying that it saw no need to interrupt the citizens of Tashkent and the people of Uzbekistan, then thought to be one of the most stable republics of the Soviet Union. At that time, of course, the Uzbekistan government linked "stability" to Communist Party rule, and it tried to stop the pressures for democratization coming from Moscow.

In January 1991, I was asked to study the documents, program, and charter of this Islamic Party (see Appendix). I received from the City Executive authorities all the documents provided by the party in its request to be registered (it is probable that I was not the only one asked to make a recommendation). In my report I noted that the experience of Arab countries shows that administrative and police repression of such organizations creates the image of martyrdom and instigates some activists to resort to terrorism. When activists have an opportunity to work legally, however, their efforts are usually concentrated on broadening their support. Allowing such movements to develop can often transform their character, and they will probably appeal to people who have a democratic orientation. Party recognition, I argued, might help to prevent violence. I recommended that city authorities attempt a dialogue with this party and that they register it.

When they received my recommendations, the officials told me that although they approved of them, they had a government order forbidding registration of the Islamic Renaissance Party. We knew that a branch of the party had been registered not long before in Tajikistan, where it has gained strength. But the IRP has still not been registered in Uzbekistan.

The party, existing illegally, is led by Abdullah Uta, leader of the organizing group in Tashkent. Abduwali, one of Rakhmatullah's closest friends, seems to be independent in Andijan. Aqilbek and Abdulahat lead the group in the city and region of Namangan. The authorities denounced all as *wahhabi* some years ago.

The Role of the Spiritual Directorate of Central Asia and Kazakhstan (Sadum)

Some years ago, at the beginning of *perestroika*, there was an upheaval in the administration. There were many meetings in which people demanded that the official *mufti*, or senior jurisconsult, be displaced because of his inactivity, and some people demanded that the Central Committee of the Communist Party replace the leader of the Spiritual Directorate. A party functionary replied that the government could not interfere in the problems of the Muslim community. Nonetheless, the *mufti* was replaced without serious incident, although people from the Ferghana Valley had intended to employ violent measures if necessary. The authorities probably knew of this and remained unobtrusively in the background, presuming that the new *mufti* would be as compliant as the previous one.

Muhammad Sadiq Muhammad Yusuf was elected the new *mufti* by a majority at one of three meetings. He was born in Namangan to a religious family and was educated in Bukhara, Tashkent, and Libya. Although relatively inactive in politics, he was elected as deputy to the Supreme Soviet of the USSR. I have known Sadiq for about ten years, and I think that he was close to earlier activists in his views and attitudes. On entering the system of official Islam, however, he changed and became part of the political elite. This group provided Sadiq and his clan with an opportunity to make money. Within a year, his group had forced out office-holders belonging to the clan of the previous *mufti*.

The Spiritual Directorate suffered a schism at about this time: the Kazakhstan branch announced its independence, and Tajikistan followed. Although the name of the Spiritual Directorate continued to be maintained as covering all of Central Asia, in practice it now controls only parts of Uzbekistan.

Because Sadiq has contacts with Libyan authorities, relations between official Islam in Uzbekistan and the Muslim world elsewhere have became polarized. Although it is neither strong nor effective, the Spiritual Directorate of Central Asia has contacts with other countries and Islamic international organizations.[6] The directorate's schism was used by opposing clans to create an independent Spiritual Directorate in Tashkent city and its suburbs. Thus we see a growing "tribalization" of the "official" religious administration.

It is important to note here that Sadiq subsequently ran afoul of the Islamic Renaissance Party when he said that the Muslim community is a single party of Allah and had no need for other parties. His remark caused a new split between some activists and Sadiq's group. Since 1989, activist groups had coordinated their efforts to reopen closed and destroyed mosques, construct new *madrasas*, and print Islamic books and pamphlets. But at the beginning of 1991, when Sadiq came up against the Islamic Renaissance Party (and had probably made an agreement with the authorities), relations with other activists were marred.

On September 1, 1991, after the failure of the August coup d'état, the president of Uzbekistan declared the republic's independence. I later asked activist leaders about this declaration and was told that it was not real independence. In their view, it was an effort to preserve the government from the new trends emanating from Moscow because it was clear that Uzbekistan's government supported the *putchists*. About three days after the coup, activists told me that they were preparing for arrests and reprisals.

A new trend appeared after the proclamation of independence. In the middle

---

6. Editor's Note: For example, at the conclusion of an international Islamic conference held in Tashkent in September 1990, the Spiritual Directorate concluded an agreement with the Islamabad-based—and Saudi-financed—International Islamic University to exchange faculty and students, providing the Directorate with an important financial infusion and control over patronage ("Historical Opening" 1991: 4–5). Saudi Arabia is the principal donor, although funds are also provided by Egypt and the United Arab Emirates.

of September 1991, revivalists in Namangan and other cities of the Ferghana Valley agreed, along with Sadiq and his officials, to forget their disagreements and join together to struggle for power in the republic. Activists have confirmed that such an agreement existed.

In October 1991, I decided to study the situation in the Ferghana Valley, where the Islamic Renaissance Party is most active, and there I observed some new trends. There are many new mosques in the valley, each with special places to teach children. In small neighborhood mosques, I found ten or twenty pupils who came from different parts of Uzbekistan to study Islam; some came from outside the republic. In large mosques, the number of students was much greater. Some pupils had no experience of secular schooling; others attended secular school in the day and studied Islam in the evening. Each pupil attends voluntarily, undoubtedly on the advice of religiously oriented parents. There are also special *madrasas* where hundreds of young men and women study Islam. And, of course, these schools are well supported with the necessary literature.

Before 1917 there were 360 mosques and two madrasas in Namangan; now there are many more mosques, each with attached schools, and a large *madrasa*. This growth has occurred since 1989. Visiting bookstores, one can find large numbers of religious books and pamphlets printed by both the state publishing houses and new semiprivate cooperatives. There are also many small shops selling religious books in bazaars.

I have interviewed many people, including *imams* of the mosques. They have told me interesting things about Islamic revivalism in Namangan. More than 20,000 people have become members of Sabadi Aᶜzam, an Islamic foundation organized in 1991 in the region of Namangan to collect money for building mosques.[7] A manager of the Gumbaz mosque asked me to help him create an Islamic bank which would be independent from the state (unfortunately, neither of us had any banking experience). Thus I was able to observe firsthand the first steps in an arena which is completely new for Central Asia.

I asked how people are going to live with the Russians and was told that the Qur'an teaches how to live with other people in peace, provided that they respect Islam. As for the Communist Party, they said, "In Russia the party is prohibited, but in our republic it is not. Communism is still strong in Uzbekistan, and everything is being done to preserve it, even by changing the party's name." Religious people are against its preservation.

Some activists see the necessity of secular education and said it should be preserved; others saw no need for secular schooling—"We will take all knowledge from the Qur'an." On the status of women in society, some activists spoke of some insignificant changes and mentioned that they will dress in a more

---

7. I am grateful to Arthur Brenner (personal communication, Tashkent, October 1991), for sharing this information with me.

Islamic way; some were sure that women's status will change to accord with the Qur'an and that women will dress *hijab*, which in Uzbekistan means reversion to prerevolutionary Central Asian dress.

We spoke about the possibility of violence. All activists with whom I spoke invoked the Qur'an, saying that Islam is a religion of peace and humanism. And it really is. I have observed no militant activities. But political and economic life in Central Asia is gradually becoming more unstable, and this may lead to greater militancy. I had heard about the presence of Islamic militia in the suburbs and in the city of Namangan, which is intended to provide security, especially at night. When I met the leader of this Islamic militia, Hakimjan Satimov, he told me there are 8,000 young believers organized into patrol groups who deal with criminals, punishing them or allowing them an opportunity to "return to Islam." These vigilantes originally had no connection with Islamic groups, although they have since become incorporated into the Islamic movement.

In other cities of the Ferghana valley, I observed less activity, but Islamic activism is becoming pervasive everywhere. Thus I see the following trends:

- Islamic activism is gaining strength in Central Asia. The process of reviving Islam is growing in Central Asia. Many mosques and *madrasas* have been built, and many more are under construction. The number of adherents is growing. Young people with no established positions and uncertain about the future look to Islam as a solution to their problems and the problems of the republic as a whole.
- Religious education, the printing of religious literature, the propagation of religious thought, and the construction of mosques have all become legal activities. Attempts by local authorities to block these activities were ineffective.
- Namangan and its environs in the Ferghana valley is the most active center of Islamic activism.
- To a considerable extent, Islamic revival is stimulated by social and economic problems, especially in the cities, where the middle and lower classes are concentrated.
- The positions of officials and non-officials in the Islamic community are converging. This trend was stimulated by the political situation that followed the proclamation of the republic's independence. The first steps in this convergence have been made by the "official" clergy, who are seeking to retain their influence.
- Activists intend to create Islamic banks and will in the near future probably seek to elaborate their own concepts of Islamic economics.
- At the present time, with democratic structures undeveloped, revivalists cannot accept democratic methods of political activity; however, I have not observed any intent to solve problems by violence. There is no evidence to indicate that Islamic activists intend to engage in terrorism.
- The cooperation of different groups among Islamic activists is tactical and

temporary and may suffer setbacks because of such factors as tribalism, regionalism, and the strong interests of officials in retaining their authority by encouraging divisions.

- The transformation of Uzbekistan to a market economy will create a situation where some groups of people will quickly become more impoverished than they presently are. This situation may increase the potential for violence.

- The inability of authorities to solve effectively social and economic problems and their antagonism toward Islamic activists will aggravate the present situation, as will attempts to preserve the old regime under new names.

Political Development in Central Asia Today

The importance of the Central Asian republics is growing. Democratization, the weakening of the Communist Party's power, and the transformation to a market economy are all taking place. I had a conversation not long ago with an American businessman who hoped to deal with Uzbekistan. "We studied the situation here," he said, "but we cannot foretell what will happen. In unstable countries in Africa, we can estimate risk. Our predictions may not be entirely accurate, but they allow us to make business plans and prepare for contingencies for several years in advance. In Uzbekistan we felt we could predict the future only in terms of days, not years. The political situation is simply unknown."

I agreed with him. In business you must plan, and you expect your business to provide some kind of profit. I have great respect for people taking the first steps toward launching businesses in Central Asia. The region has a promising future because of its natural resources, its geographic position, and its importance as a center connecting Russia, China, Afghanistan, Iran, and the former Soviet Republics in Central Asia.

Since the nineteenth century, however, the history of Central Asia in general and Uzbekistan in particular has been one of dependence, first on Tsarist Russia and then on the Soviet state, which turned all the former republics, including those of Central Asia, into laboratories for experiments on building Communism. We must not forget that the idea of a permanent revolution and its export to other countries was vital to Communism. A song which was popular many years ago said: "We were born to turn the tale into the reality." I think that's what happened, but it was a terrible tale, and we got a terrible reality. It was time to change the policy, and these changes affected the foundations of our society.

The national policy of the former Communist Party included the delimitation of republics in the 1920s, the removal of peoples from their native lands to other places (often in Central Asia), and many other things which have been described in American studies of Soviet history. But the present situation has not yet been described.

At the beginning of 1980, I was asked to act as an interpreter for some Arab visitors. In a visit to the Uzbek Ministry of Health, the minister told us that the number of hospitals was growing rapidly and that Uzbekistan would soon be a world leader by virtue of the number of its hospitals. That was due to the efforts and the policy of the Communist Party, he said, which was doing everything it could to provide the people with necessary services. I later asked a ministry official to explain the minister's words. He said that the number of hospitals was evidence of a very different trend: Ubekistan is a world leader in the number of invalids, and we do not have enough hospitals for them. In countries where people are healthy, there is no need to open new hospitals. Because of the Communist Party, we have a great number of hospitals which are poorly equipped and do not solve the basic problem of preserving health. The infant mortality rate in the Central Asian republics is the highest in the world.

The Communist Party became an elite class in our society. The people who worked within the party system, including a large number of army officers, should be considered a single social class. At the beginning of *perestroika*, it was announced that the party system involved more then 18 million people. The Communist Party of Uzbekistan (CPUZ) included two groups of people: officials, and ordinary members of the party. We should pay attention to the party system because it held power; the Uzbek Communist Party, however, was limited, to a certain extent, by the All-Union Communist Party (CPSU).

Functionaries of the Uzbek Communist Party had never been firm Communists, but they enjoyed power in the republic and thereby gained extra privileges. In recent years, party functionaries have also begun to occupy key positions in new joint ventures and semiprivate companies, so they remain a significant force in society.

One way they infiltrated the economic system was to legalize small private enterprises which were actually part of the Central Asian "mafia." Some of their income went to party functionaries and police officers. The mafia grew rapidly in the decades before *perestroika*. It became part of the party's administrative system, to the point where it was difficult to distinguish between the mafia, the militia, and party functionaries. For this reason, I feel certain that the party was able to control the black market. A well-developed system of bribery, which became the usual way of solving problems, united the party and the mafia. And the policy of the Communist Party was directed toward preserving this cooperation with support for the different clans in the republics, each occupying its own niche in the system of corruption.

It is true that we were ruled by Moscow, but it is important to remember that local authorities played a very significant role. The policies of local authorities is a very real reason for Central Asia's present problems. Moscow turned Central Asia into its breadbasket and exploited it as much as possible. Local authorities often went further than Moscow ordered. Advisors from the CPSU—usually the second secretary of the local Communist Party—had little to do but observe and rest.

Until recently there was no overt hint of nationalism in the Central Asian republics, for the balance between national and ethnic entities had been destroyed. At the beginning of 1970, Leonid Brezhnev had proclaimed that nationalism had no place in a socialistic society, and this was developed by party ideologists as doctrine. The police and KGB did not officially recognize crimes based on nationalism. For this reason, most people imprisoned in the 1970s and 1980s who had in fact been protesting against national oppression were found guilty of different civil crimes.

At the same time, the imbalance continued to grow. In the first decade of the 1980s, for example, ruling positions in the government, the economy, and the trades in Uzbekistan were occupied by Armenians. The chief of the Uzbek KGB, the chief of the Department of Investigations, the chief of the mafia in the Republic, and many others enjoying the same kind of power were Armenians. According to documents on punitive operations against the national liberation movement, and especially against supporters of this movement in the rural areas, the Communist Party often used Armenian military units in the 1920s.

It became common practice for the Communists to rule the national republics with another national minority. According to unofficial sources, in 1984, tens of thousands of Armenian nationals went to live in Tashkent. At the time, people of other nationalities were not permitted even to register their passports in Tashkent because of limited living space. The same situation was true for the countryside of Tashkent, where ruling positions were held by Koreans. The Communists considered this the best way to rule the Central Asian republics— dividing each into small contradicting groups and provoking conflict between the groups when necessary.

There was no conflict between local and Korean peoples in Uzbekistan, even though there were attempts to provoke it two years ago after events in the Ferghana Valley, which I describe below. The possibility of conflict is ever present, however, and it demands that both sides be attentive, circumspect, and flexible toward each other. But conflict was unavoidable with Turk-Meskhetians and the Kyrghyz.

It became clear that party activists were unable to change the course of events. They strengthened army forces in the region and tried to turn people's attention to regional conflicts in Ferghana, Osh, and elsewhere.

It was preferable to provoke small conflicts and to keep the majority group unengaged. Small conflicts of course provided party activists with a reason to strengthen military forces, even as it enabled them to further exploit natural resources and to control the area.

I interviewed many party officials who had observed the Ferghana events of

1989. The conflict was based on inequalities among the ethnic groups in the region. The city of Marghilan and its environs in the Ferghana Valley had a tradition of well-developed trades and local crafts products. Even during the Soviet period, local merchants and craftsmen were able to preserve their positions. The region is home to people of many different nationalities: Uzbeks, Jews, Russians, and others. Crimean Tatars and Turk-Meskhetians were re-moved to this area, and they lived in both cities and suburbs. The Crimean Tatars were a well-organized community. They had never been involved in any conflict with local people, and it was not their actions that destroyed the balance.

The officials considered Turk-Meskhetians to be extremists, and any action against the authorities or the party in the 1970s was laid at the extremists' door. In the 1980s the Turk-Meskhetians had become very active in trades and other fields, displacing local people. At the same time, there was growing unemployment and a decline in living standards, a situation which stimulated people, especially the youth, to express their growing discontent.

All this was taken into consideration by the people who planned and organ-ized the subsequent conflict. The Turk-Meskhetians were chosen as a target. Among the plotters were party activists and army and militia officers of different nationalities.[8] A military unit that had taken part in the Afghan operations against the *mujahidin* was, for some unknown reason, withdrawn from the Ferghana region just before the conflict broke out.

When the trouble began, the militia and other local forces were paralyzed. The provocateurs, who came from outside the Ferghana Valley,[9] were equipped with maps, transportation, weapons, communications equipment, and other supplies. Observers noted that helicopters appeared wherever operations against the Turk-Meskhetians occurred. About 200 officers instigated the conflict. The operation began at a defined place and time, involved the local young people, and then seemed to "disappear." No one from the group appeared among those sentenced to imprisonment.

The media initially announced that Islamic activists had organized the con-flict. Later the report was corrected, and the local Uzbek mafia was said to be the organizing force. In fact, the local mafia was not even involved in the conflict. The CPSU was the most likely to take advantage of a tense situation and to use its results to strengthen the army and militia units in Central Asia to accelerate the export of gold and other material from the region. The equipment for gold production in Uzbek mines was later dismantled and removed to Russia. Since then they have exported mostly ore containing gold, and those exports have increased tremendously. Recent announcements in the

8. Details of the conflict are drawn from interviews with people who observed the events firsthand.
9. Differences in their accents and other characteristics made this evident.

Soviet media concerning the illegal export of hundreds of tons of gold closes the circuit.

The next conflict took place in Osh. There the conflict was bloodier and the consequences more serious. It allowed the Communist Party to take action against *perestroika*. It was a difficult time for democratic forces in our country.

Central Asia was chosen as the place to oppose *perestroika* because of its tense situation. It had become a place for exiled peoples. The traditional ethnic balance had been destroyed with the Russian invasion. Many Russians settled in the new colony, which was primarily agricultural. The greatest number of Russians came after the revolution. They brought with them factories and plants removed from other European Soviet republics and Russia. Central Asia quickly became populated with Russians, Ukrainians, Belorussians, Jews, Armenians, and others.

Many who came prior to the revolution settled in rural areas and small towns. They became assimilated to local traditions and often spoke local languages, but at the same time, they preserved their own traditions and relationships within the community. Paradoxically, these earlier settlers have fewer mixed marriages than Russian-speaking newcomers. Perhaps it is because they wish to preserve the religious and tribal traditions of a purely Russian community of "old believers." The relationship between this group of Russians and the local people demonstrates how difficult it is to provoke conflict in a stable situation. These people have never intended to go back to Russia, probably because they no longer have roots there. They are thus less chauvinistic than other groups.

Other Russian-speaking people who live in Central Asia were often negatively affected by the imperialist policies of the USSR Communist Party, which was closely connected to the Soviet Union's political, economic, and cultural expansion. This policy included a clearly defined role for new groups of migrants, some of whom saw themselves as superior to local people. Domination—often combined with Eurocentrism—in Central Asia gave birth to a nationalism which has never diminished. It has not been manifested overtly until recently because of fear and because people's level of political awareness was not sufficiently developed. *Perestroika* provided people with an opportunity to take the first steps toward this goal.

It is important to remember that Uzbekistan had no dissident movements, as was the case in Russia, prior to *perestroika*. Interfront, an informal group organized mostly by former members of the Communist Youth Organization, Komsomol, was intended to unite ethnic Russians and Uzbeks and form an alternative to the nationalist Birlik [Unity] Party, which was intended for Uzbeks only. Interfront was, however, short-lived, probably due to the strong role of former Communist leaders in its creation. Hence the secular Birlik Party and Islamic activism became the principal opposition to the Communist Party.

Because Islamic revivalists were initially preoccupied with educational activities, Birlik became the focal point of political opposition, although it was officially recognized as a political party only in December 1991. Basically it appealed to Uzbekistan's intelligentsia. Its platform, which includes democratization and proposed solutions to many of the country's social, economic, and cultural problems, is very popular among the elite. It began with meetings in Tashkent. One of its first successes was declaring Uzbek the state's official language. Since Birlik was unauthorized until late 1991, it is only beginning to gain wider influence. Up to the present time, it has remained an elite political party, secular and appealing to ethnic Uzbeks only.

In addition, there has already been a major split among the party's leaders, some of whom left to create the separate Erk [Freedom] Party. This breakaway group received official recognition in early 1991, well before the main group. I asked some Birlik Party members about the reasons for the split and the differences between the two parties. They suggested that the appearance of Erk had to do with the personal ambitions of its leaders. Doctrinal differences between the two parties seemed insignificant.

After the Erk Party was officially recognized, the differences between it and Birlik became more pronounced. Birlik looked to the Islamic Renaissance Party for support—I personally observed their close contacts—but as yet there is little coordination of activity between the two movements. The Erk Party, according to some Islamic leaders, became part of the official political structure after its legalization. They expect the party to be "obedient" to the power elite to preserve its status; if so, however, it will lose its popularity. Nevertheless, the leader of the Erk Party, Muhammad Salih, was a candidate for Uzbekistan's December 1991 presidential elections. Since opposition to the Communist Party was divided, it came to the elections significantly weakened. Moreover, Islamic activists planned to boycott the elections.

Perestroika stimulated the growing dilemma of pan-Islam and pan-Turkism in Central Asian society. On the one hand, Islamic activists in the Muslim community began their social activity with an appeal to a Muslim *umma*. Their appeal excluded the growing sense of nationalism. Pan-Islam, as practiced in the Muslim world, was not a power that could unite millions, and it has had no perceptible result in the political life of modern Uzbek society.

In the Central Asian republics, where people have for many years been united by the Muslim community, the national identity of the different peoples has limited this factor of pan-Islam. The activist movement, which includes Uzbeks, Tajiks, Turkmen, Kyrghyz, and others, must preserve itself from a growing nationalism. Tribalism and regionalism also remain strong in Central Asia. Thus it is difficult to see how pan-Islam can be a uniting factor in the political life of Central Asia.

Another possible unifying factor in Uzbekistan is pan-Turkism. Since the period of Communist rule, this factor has not been significant. Indeed, there is no example of pan-Turkism serving as a successful unifying mechanism anywhere outside of Turkey. In Uzbekistan, pan-Turkism has appealed only to the intelligentsia and has never been a widespread popular movement.

In conclusion, in Uzbek society we have the secular Birlik and Erk parties and the Islamic Renaissance Party as formal political organizations. They are supported by different social groups. At the same time, we should not forget the potential strength of Uzbek nationalism, which appeared late in the nineteenth century as a reaction to Russian imperial domination and colonization and developed in response to the nationalities policy of the Communist Party. Uzbek nationalism has its counterparts, of course, among the nationalist movements throughout the former Soviet Union.

It is safe to say that national independence movements set one ethnic group above others. Uzbek nationalism has not yet developed in this way, except among some of the intelligentsia. It is likely, however, that the appeal to an exclusionary nationalism will play a major role in new ethnic conflicts in Uzbekistan and elsewhere if there is no large-scale democratization of political life and economic liberalization in the near future.

Appendix

The Program of the Islamic Renaissance Party
of Uzbekistan Republic[10]
December 16, 1990

The Islamic Renaissance Party aims are as follows:

1. To explain to the people the real meaning of the holy Qur'an and *hadith* and to call the people to live and act according to the Qur'an and *hadith*.

2. To create its own publishing house.

3. To call to Islam by all means of mass media.

4. To fight national and racial discrimination, impudence, crime, alcoholism, and all other things which are forbidden by *shari'a* through understanding and appeal.

5. To educate young people on the principles of Islam and, for this purpose, to create instruction and training centers and *madrasa*s.

6. To insure that the rights of all Muslims are exercised according to the Qur'an.

7. To strengthen Islamic brotherhood, to develop religious relationships with the Muslim world, and to seek for the relationships equal rights with representatives of other religions.

8. To cooperate with other democratic parties and state organizations in all fields.

---

10. Taken from the new edition of the program, which differs in some points from the Moscow group edition.

9. To create philanthropic funds that will support anyone in need of help.

10. To support educational and scientific progress, which is to be independent and free from the commanding system and ideological restrictions.

11. To strengthen the family according to the principles of Islam and to insure the rights of women and children.

12. To insure the principles of an Islamic economy and regaining ecological purity.

13. To insure the distribution of food in the society according to the *sharicʿa*.

14. To solve the problems of people according to the Holy Qur'an and *hadith*.

References

Allworth, Edward A. (1990). *The Modern Uzbeks from the Fourteenth Century to the Present: A Cultural History*. Stanford: Hoover Institution Press.

Benningsen, Alexandre A., and S. Enders Wimbush (1979). *Muslim National Communism in the Soviet Union: A Revolutionary Strategy for the Colonial World*. Chicago: University of Chicago Press.

"Historical Opening" (1991). *Dacʿwah Highlights* 19:4–5. Islamabad: International Islamic University.

Part III
Afghanistan and Iran

VI

THE AFGHAN REVOLUTION
A FAILED EXPERIMENT

Victor G. Korgun

In the study of the dynamics and specifics of development in contemporary Eastern society, it is important to consider the mutual interaction of contemporary and traditional factors determining their development. In the case of Afghanistan, the research focus should be the mutual interaction between the new state and political structures that came into being after the April 1978 Revolution—the government, the ruling party, and public organizations—and traditional ethnic, religious, and tribal institutions.

The simplest course would be to regard the protracted social and political conflict in Afghanistan as a struggle between new and old; in fact, however, matters are somewhat more complex. To understand the role of contemporary and traditional factors in Afghan society today, it is necessary to look at the April 1978 Revolution—to examine its roots, what it meant to accomplish, and the basic reasons for its failure. This chapter discusses the unsuccessful April Revolution and its influence on traditional society. I begin by describing the social and political preconditions of the revolution.

In 1978, Afghanistan was in the fifth year of a republican regime headed by Muhammad Daud, who came to power in July 1973 by means of a coup d'état. This coup was the culmination of the general social, political, and economic crisis that had gripped the country through the late 1960s and early 1970s. The efforts of the monarchy to liberalize the social and political life of the country and to hasten economic development ("the democratic experiment") had proved unsuccessful.

The basis for economic development was a planned economy that relied heavily on a strong state sector. As a result, there had been a range of large-scale

This chapter was translated from the Russian by Anthony Olcott. The analysis of the Afghanistan Revolution offered here reflects the personal opinions of the author and does not necessarily reflect the position of the government.

102   Victor G. Korgun

projects in the 1950s and 1960s to create a social and political infrastructure: highways, hydroelectric plants, educational institutions, and irrigation complexes. Although this created conditions for accelerating economic development, these new possibilities were not realized because the system of government proved corrupt. By corruption, I mean that most civil servants purchased their positions through bribes and once in office took bribes themselves and abused their formal authority for private gain. When I was first in Afghanistan (1966–68), I personally witnessed these phenomena.

The five-year plans, financed primarily with foreign assistance, fell far short of their goals. Private investors preferred to put their capital into commerce, not industry, and rapid price increases led to a decline in the standard of living. At the end of the 1960s there was a wave of strikes across the country.

Efforts to democratize public life were stillborn. The 1964 constitution permitted political parties, but the king never ratified the law about political parties, so the few political groupings which emerged in the second half of the 1960s were left in a semilegal position. A privately held press had also emerged but functioned under the constant threat of closure. And despite the passage of a relatively democratic election law, the parliament was dominated by feudal landowners and clerics and was extraordinarily conservative.

Toward the end of the 1960s, there was a crisis in relations between the lawmakers and the executive branch; supported by the king, the parliament blocked all government efforts at reform. Frequent cabinet shuffles became common, because no minister could put even the most insignificant reforms into effect. The result was paralysis of state power and economic stagnation. A bad drought in 1971 and 1972 worsened the already complex political situation and made a political explosion unavoidable. At this point, the army entered the political arena. On July 17, 1973, the monarchy was overthrown and a republic announced, and a coalition of those favoring accelerated modernization came to power. It was headed by the king's cousin, Muhammad Daud, a former prime minister (1953–63).

Accusing his predecessor of despotism and an inability to solve important social and economic problems, Daud introduced a fairly strict regime. Various factions, including left-wing and democratic forces, were represented in the government, but all political parties and public organizations were forbidden, parliament was dissolved, and the private press was shut down. At the same time, Daud initiated the relatively democratic program of his government and planned to introduce a range of radical economic, social, and political reforms.

The Daud government realized some social and political changes, including new labor laws, nationalization of private banks and a number of trading and manufacturing concerns which had been involved in embezzlement and smuggling, and the creation of conditions favorable to the development of national entrepreneurs. The republican regime also destroyed the monopoly on commercial capital in both internal and external trade, which had been serving narrow and self-interested ends; these circles had provided the deposed king's primary base of support.

The government had great hopes for agricultural reform, which had been the basis of the national economy and was the most backward of all sectors of the economy. Antiquated forms of property rights and land use, as well as the system of social relations in the villages, seriously retarded development of the rural economy. Although Afghanistan is an agricultural country, it could not supply its own food needs. By the end of the 1960s, the trade deficit in grain was 200,000 metric tons (Davidov and Cherniakhovskaia 1973: 78).

A land-reform law adopted in 1975 placed a limit on large-scale landholdings, distributed seized lands to landless peasants and small landholders, settled pastoralists, and promised compensation to former owners. However, the opposition of large landowners meant that the reform was ineffective. Only 7,500 peasants ever received land, all from government holdings (Basov 1984: 121). On the whole, in the sphere of social and economic development, the republican regime strengthened the state sector by weakening the position of the large-scale trade and industrial bourgeoisie while simultaneously expanding the scope of private small- and middle-level enterprises.

Basic foreign policy goals remained unchanged. The republican regime tried to maintain an "equal distance" from both East and West while securing economic assistance from both sides. At the same time, the government's foreign policy was increasingly influenced by the balance of power within the ruling circles, where conservative elements of the regime were gaining power. Thus while Soviet-Afghan economic relations remained stable or grew slightly, there was a rapid rapprochement with Pahlavi Iran and with the conservative Arab regimes, as well as with Western countries, primarily the United States and West Germany.

Over time, major changes took place in the domestic policies of the Daud regime. In the second stage of the government a rightward leaning began to appear.[1] In his first years in power, Daud had dealt decisively with attempts by conservative elements and Islamic fundamentalists to undermine the policies of the republican government, but in later years he began to establish an authoritarian form of government by removing representatives of the People's Democratic Party of Afghanistan (PDPA) from positions of power. At the end of 1976, Daud introduced a one-party system with the creation of the Party of National Revolution. In February 1977, he was elected president of the republic, which gave him broad legislative and executive powers. Implementa-

---

1. In the context of the Daud period (1973–78), leftist forces led the country in the path of progress and democracy—or their programs included these goals, at any rate. Rightists tried to preserve the feudal system. "Rightward leaning," in this context, means the rapid transition from democratic government to authoritarian regime, with the support of conservative forces. Afghan Islamic forces were also politically and socially differentiated. In his reformist program, Daud used the support of progressive-minded clergy and suppressed the orthodox elements.

tion of important changes in the social and economic spheres came to a halt, beginning with land reform, and open repression of PDPA members began. In early 1978, it was obvious that a destabilization of the political situation was under way. Dissatisfaction with the authoritarian regime intensified.

On the whole, the policies of the Daud regime created the conditions necessary for the gradual elimination of the outdated feudal system and accelerated the transformation of society. In this respect the republican government may be considered progressive. However, the regime's reluctance to realize reform, the social character of the regime itself, the attempt to solve pressing problems with authoritarian methods, and the rejection of democratic principles in social and political life effectively undermined its objectives.

The April 1978 Revolution

It was under these conditions that the PDPA was reactivated.[2] In 1977 the party prepared to overthrow the Daud regime and seize power. Since it did not enjoy mass support, it directed its work to democratically inclined officers of the army. The army had already been used once for a coup d'état, and this time too it played its role successfully, although, as subsequent events demonstrated, the success was not unambiguous. Probably the PDPA was not in complete control of that part of the officer corps loyal to it, for the revolution of April 27, 1978, was achieved solely through the efforts of elements of the Kabul garrison: Hafizullah Amin organized party cells within army units, and many high-ranking officers who took part in the revolution, including Colonel Abdul Qadir, were not party members. The party leaders, headed by Nur Muhammad Taraki, had been imprisoned on the eve of the revolution. The leaders of the Khalq group, who subsequently came to power, published a detailed plan for an armed uprising (Political Department of the Armed Forces 1978: 38–55). They claimed that it had been elaborated in advance and that both Taraki and Hafizullah Amin had copies, but there is some question about its existence prior to the revolution.[3]

By the evening of April 27, 1978, Daud and some of his ministers had been killed and a new organ of state government created, a revolutionary council

---

2. After the 1973 *coup d'état*, the Parcham faction of the PDP actually legalized itself, and many of its members were absorbed by the Daud regime. Meanwhile, however, the Khalq faction went underground. As a result, the entire party became inactive. It revitalized its activity only in 1977, when it began the task of reunification and gaining state power.

3. A conversation between the author and a former PRP official is interesting in this regard. Toward the end of the day on April 27, when battles were still going on in Kabul and the outcome of the armed uprising was far from clear, the official told me that Taraki, who had been freed from prison and was in the headquarters of the Air Force, suddenly wavered. He even appeared ready to flee to Moscow. The officers who led the uprising persuaded him to wait until morning before making a final decision.

headed by Colonel Abdul Qadir, who had led the revolution. He announced that "the revolution had been made to defend the principles of Islam and democracy" (Taraki 1978: 63). The council was made up entirely of officers belonging to the People's Democratic Party, which meant that power in the country passed formally to the army, but since the army had no political organization of its own, the officers who led the uprising were forced to pass power to the party. On April 29, the Revolutionary Council of the Democratic Republic of Afghanistan (DRA) was announced. It was headed by Taraki and included all the members of the military revolutionary council.

Taraki revealed the government's program on May 9, 1978. It encompassed radical changes in the political, economic, and social spheres: land reforms to favor the poorest peasants, liquidation of feudal and prefeudal relations, democratization of public life, solution of the nationalities question, equality of men and women, and eradication of illiteracy. The government quickly began to put the program into effect. Decree 6 of the Revolutionary Council (RC), adopted in June 1978, freed 11 million peasants (according to official statistics) from debts to moneylenders and landowners. RC Decree 7, which was issued in October 1978, declared equal marriage rights for men and women. In January 1979, the government addressed land reform in RC Decree 8.

The Failure of the Revolution

The basic reforms of the revolutionary regime were doomed to fail, primarily because the country was unprepared for the revolution and its radical transformations. The revolution occurred without popular support. The PDPA, which had directed the armed uprising in Kabul, relied not on the support and participation of the masses but upon its reading of popular sentiment.

In fact, a significant part of the population was dissatisfied with Daud's authoritarian government. This is why, in the first months after the revolutionary regime seized power, there was no serious opposition until the reforms began. The lack of readiness of the populace to accept and support the revolutionary government's program of reform manifested itself from the beginning. It was not a case of mistakes made by the regime or of apologists for the regime attempting to present matters but the nature of the new government that caused the problem. It set an unreal goal in attempting to create in Afghanistan as rapidly as possible "a society free of exploitation of man by man" or a socialist society (Taraki 1978). The country was not yet ready to build such a society in terms of Afghan society itself, material conditions, the level of productive forces, and the political capabilities of the party leaders.

The experience of the former socialist countries in Eastern Europe and the Soviet Union showed that construction of such a society was impossible even for more developed societies, which also had longer periods in which to do it. The Afghan Marxist leadership tried to force the Soviet model of socialism—a model which subsequent events in the USSR have shown to be bankrupt—onto a traditional society. Thus the program of revolutionary transformation in Afghanistan was doomed to fail, particularly since the Soviet experience was introduced without consideration for the national specificity of Afghanistan and its traditions and customs.

In freeing the peasantry from debts to moneylenders and landowners, for example, no alternative to the moneylenders was introduced. As a result, peasants who needed money were forced to turn once again to the moneylenders and landowners. The leaders of the DRA committed a social and psychological error in overestimating the significance of social contradictions in the villages. They assumed that, freed of debt, the peasantry would support party policies and oppose the landlords. This did not occur—first, because the peasants were devout Muslims who respected *sharica* law, which dictates repayment of loans, and second, because the ethnic, religious, tribal, clan, and family ties in the villages proved much stronger than the contradictions between social strata. Thus the peasantry and the landowners in Afghanistan were not opposed as antagonistic classes.

Similarly, the reforms were introduced without taking account of such important factors as kinship ties in villages. Many peasants who rented land from a landowner were the owner's relatives. In contradiction to the Marxist understanding of the exploitation of peasants by landowners, these landowners often acted as protectors of the peasantry, providing them with material assistance.[4]

RC Decree 7, which declared the equality of men and women and banned the *mahr* (bride price), meant direct interference by secular authorities in the sphere of clerical influence and the violation of centuries-old traditions. The Muslim population and the mullahs did not support this law, and it remained an empty declaration.

Land reform was the single largest failure of the revolutionary regime. RC Decree 8 (December 1978) confiscated from landowners all holdings greater than six hectares and transferred them, free of charge, to small landholders and landless peasants. Once again, important economic and social factors were disregarded. The peasantry followed the lead of the mullahs, who declared the seizure of land illegal. According to the *sharica*, private property is inviolable. Many peasants refused to accept land from the state because it had been declared illegal by the mullahs. The power of Muslim belief and the authority of the rural mullahs proved stronger than the propaganda of the party which had introduced the reform.

The authorities also underestimated how much land the landowners pos-

---

4. When the author met peasants of Ningrahar and Qandahar provinces in the spring of 1979, he was told of landowners who loaned money for the weddings of sons or to pay for medical treatment in the capital or overseas. The peasants saw such assistance as paternal and had corresponding filial attitudes to such landowners.

sessed. It was only in the course of the reforms that it became clear that there was not enough land for all who needed it. In fact, when the DRA leaders announced the end of the reforms in July 1979, only 296,000 peasant families had received land—less than half of those in need. In addition, the government was unable to provide agricultural equipment, fertilizer, seed, or credit. The problem of water was also unresolved. Since most cultivated land is in the arid zone, water is a primary resource for agricultural production, and water was in the hands of large private landowners.

There is one more important factor. Even in its first program (1966), the PDPA intended land reform to proceed with the participation of the peasantry, and this principle was ignored. The peasants became passive objects of a reformist policy, an oversight that was generally true of the revolutionary regime's policies as a whole. Not only did the peasants fail to support land reform, they also opposed the revolutionary government. Introduction of the reforms was forced on the population without regard for the real conditions that exist in an Afghan village.

Land reform also became a point of dissatisfaction among those who had lost land, for they received no compensation for the land seized, and the government refused even the possibility of political compromise with the landowners. In addition, the reforms touched both the largest landowners and the rural petit bourgeoisie. It was these groups, supported by the clergy, who constituted the core of anti-government opposition.

The anti-illiteracy campaign also proved a failure, in part because it was conducted forcibly and in violation of national and religious traditions.[5]

Factions within the People's Democratic Party

The PDPA, as leader of the revolution, also played a role in the collapse of the reform policies and the failure of the revolution itself. The PDP was created in 1965. By 1967, it had split into two factions, which later became independent political entities with separate first secretaries, central committees, strategies, and supporters. These were (1) the Khalq (literally, masses)—radical Marxists, headed by Nur Muhammed Taraki, and (2) the Parcham (literally, banner) group, liberal Marxists headed by Babrak Karmal. The Khalq Party wanted a "socialist revolution" and a "dictatorship of the proletariat," while the Parcham Party supported a "national democratic revolution." The USSR embassy in Afghanistan, ideologically and materially, supported both groups, and

---

5. Accounts in the Afghan press in the summer of 1979 spoke of the death of scores of party activists who had shown excess zeal in bringing adults to anti-illiteracy courses. Accompanied by armed companions, they invaded harems and snatched the *chadurs* from Muslim women, in gross violation of Islamic law and custom.

both were armed with an ideology of "scientific socialism." Both groups were also only quasi-legal.

After the 1973 coup, in which members of the PDPA had taken part, leaders of Khalq and Parcham accepted posts in the Central Committee of the republic and in the Daud government. In addition, Parcham leaders cooperated fully with Daud and achieved legal recognition for their organization, while Khalq went underground. After the purge of left-wing forces in the central and local government got under way and the one-party system was introduced, the two factions of the PDPA rejoined (June 1977) and began to make preparations to overthrow the Daud regime.

The coup of April 27, 1978, was effected primarily by officers who were members of the Khalq group. Amin, who had taken upon himself leadership for the uprising, did not inform the Parcham people about preparations for the action, and this enabled the Khalq people to seize key posts in the new government bodies. The extreme radicalism of the Khalq leaders and their refusal to share power led to a new split in the party. In June 1978, Parcham leaders Babrak Karmal (the vice president of the Revolutionary Council and a deputy prime minister), Abdul Wakil (a Council member and General Secretary of the Ministry of Foreign Affairs), Anahita Ratebzad (a Council member and Minister of Social Problems), Dr. Najib (a Council member), and Mahmud Barialai (a Council member and Karmal's cousin) lost their posts and were sent abroad as ambassadors to Prague, London, Belgrade, Teheran, and Islamabad respectively.

In August, other important Parcham members were arrested and accused of an antigovernment conspiracy; these were Sultan ʿAli Keshtmand, Minister of Planning, Abdul Qadir, Minister of Defense, and Muhammed Rafi, Minister of Public Works. They were condemned to death, but the intercession of the Soviet embassy commuted the convictions to long prison sentences. A month later, Sulayman Layeq, Minister of Radio and Television, Dastegir Panjashiri, Minister of Public Works, Bariq Shafie, Minister of Information and Culture (in November 1978), and several other influential Parcham leaders were relieved of their posts. Having rid itself of the liberal wing of the party, Khalq consolidated power in its own hands and began its reforms in accordance with the party's main goal: accelerated formation of a socialist society.

However, the leaders were not satisfied even with this. In the fall of 1978, they declared war on all political forces and movements which opposed them, even those which had initially been loyal to the regime. In this way, Khalq rejected its own idea, advanced at the end of the 1960s, of creating a united front of national-democratic forces to unite all the left-wing and democratic parties and groups.

Without popular support, the PDPA—or, more precisely, the ruling Khalq group—began to initiate a revolution from above, in part by force. In the months following the revolution there were meetings, demonstrations, and marches all over the country expressing support for the revolutionary government "and condemning enemies of the revolution as agents of international imperialism." In this way, the leaders of the Democratic Republican of Afghanistan fed the populace and themselves disinformation, for they came to evaluate the situation in the country, as well as public feeling, on the basis of these acts of mass support organized by local party organs.

The Beginnings of Mass Resistance

As the reform programs advanced, however, mass discontent grew until it became armed resistance. The first outbreaks of open dissatisfaction came at the end of October 1978. The discontent was provoked by the raising of the new state flag, which was red and resembled the Soviet flag. While Kabul was celebrating this new flag, a crowd in Qandahar, incited by the local mullahs, stormed the governor's palace, tore down the red flag, and ran up a green Islamic flag. The governor and the secretary of the provincial party committee barely escaped. The uprising was suppressed by tanks sent into the city.

This was the first serious expression of growing opposition to the regime. However, party leaders were so certain of the success of their policies that they ignored the growing danger and instead made the reforms even more radical. The most important of these, land reform, demonstrated the party's theoretical and practical weakness and immaturity, demonstrating its inability to govern the country or to transform it.

The PDPA was a small urban party whose primary constituency was petit bourgeois intelligentsia, and it had no connection to the villages. The party had only a vague idea of what was going on in the villages. It misjudged the character of social relationships in rural localities and exaggerated the degree of social contradictions in the villages. On the whole, party leaders made use of preexisting Marxist concepts of class and class struggle, applying them to Afghanistan, but because Marxism considers the nature of class and class struggle in developed societies, such a policy could not have been successful. Afghanistan had not made the transition from feudalism to capitalism and had not yet formed the classes of modern society.

It is significant that PDPA leaders were unable to evaluate properly the social structure of their group, their party, and the revolution. Official propaganda termed the April coup a "national-democratic revolution" and the Democratic Republic of Afghanistan a state of "socialist orientation."[6] After Hafizullah Amin came to power in September 1979, these characterizations changed significantly; the only thing that remained unchanged was the main goal, the

---

6. There is evidence that in the spring of 1979 the leadership of the Democratic Republic of Afghanistan asked Leonid I. Brezhnev to accept Afghanistan into Comecon. The country was, however, offered only associate membership.

"building of a society free of exploitation of man by man." As early as 1978, Amin had announced that the "workers'" or "proletarian" revolution had been completed in Afghanistan. "Our revolution is a part of the world proletarian revolution," he said (Amin 1978: 25), and he called the PDPA a "proletarian party" (Amin 1978: 23). Under the leadership of this "new type" party, the country would "pass immediately from feudalism to socialism" (Amin 1979a: 24) without experiencing capitalism.

Once in power, Amin rejected what he considered the outmoded idea that Afghanistan belonged to countries with a socialist orientation, maintaining that "in the third quarter of the twentieth century the bourgeoisie and proletariat arose in Afghanistan in their classical form" (Amin 1979b: 7). Thus, as he concluded, "in Afghanistan the victory of the April revolution established not a regime with a socialist orientation, but a proletarian government on the basis of the complete dictatorship of the proletariat, thanks to the creative application of the epochal theory of the working class" (Amin 1979b: 12–13).

This inclination to race ahead characterized not only the ideology of the regime but its practical policies as well, which is what doomed the reforms to failure. The growing internal struggles within the PDPA increased the instability within the country. It was from this struggle that a new leader appeared in the political arena, Hafizullah Amin, who represented the extremist wing of the party. His rise to power had proceeded swiftly. After the April 27 coup, he was made Foreign Minister, and in the fall of 1978 he became a member of the Politburo of the Central Committee of the PDPA. In April 1979, he became Prime Minister; in July 1979, he in effect became Minister of Defense.[7]

When Amin took charge of the military, he began to repress democratically inclined officers. In August, the 32nd Paratroop Regiment mutinied because of mass arrests which had been made within the regiment. On August 5, I witnessed a terrible sight: the historical fortress of Bala Hisar in Kabul, where the mutinous regiment was being punished, was subjected to rocket and artillery bombardment. The battle raged for five hours, during which time loudspeaker trucks drove around the city announcing that the military action on the southern border of the capital was the result of another imperialist plot by international reactionaries against the "peoples' regime."

Meanwhile, the struggle within the party increased. By the end of August 1979, there were effectively two powers in the country. During this period, Amin and his supporters praised Taraki's services with the intention of lessening his vigilance. Taraki was given the unofficial title of "Baba" ("Father" of the

---

7. He was also able to advance his relatives and friends to influential posts. His brother, Abdullah Amin, became the president of a large textile company (Spinzar), which had been nationalized by the Daud regime; his nephew, Asadullah Amin, was made head of state security; his son, Abdul Rahman Amin, held the number-two post in the national youth organization; and one of his cousins was vice minister of health.

Nation), which had earlier been bestowed only upon the founder of the Afghan state, Ahmad Shah (1722–73). Taraki had clearly lost to his rival.

A typical Eastern ruler of the patriarchal type, a man of letters, a philosopher disposed to reflection, committed to the traditional way of life, with a predisposition to a sort of sybaritism, Taraki was opposed by a new sort of dictator. Amin had been educated in the United States. He was an energetic, sly, pragmatic man without the slightest trace of Eastern sybaritism. Upon taking up the post of Prime Minister and controlling the army and state security, he essentially left to his "teacher" only the function of "Father of the Nation," while carrying out his own political program behind Taraki's back.

The climax of the struggle for power came in September 1979, when Amin flew to Havana for a conference of heads of nonaligned states. On the way back he stopped in Moscow, where he met with Brezhnev and received assurances of firm support. He was greeted triumphantly in Kabul. Amin felt that he had reached the zenith of his power, that he was loved by his people, but subsequent events demonstrated that this was an illusion.

In spite of Amin's fame and glory, Taraki made an unsuccessful attempt on Amin's life, with the assistance of the Soviet embassy. This occurred on September 14. Relying on the army and security people loyal to him, Amin issued a secret order for the arrest of Taraki.

On September 16, Amin usurped power by assuming the highest posts in the government: General Secretary of the PDP Central Committee, President of the Revolutionary Council, and Prime Minister. Other than the efforts of one tank brigade, there was no resistance. The secret murder of Taraki, on October 8, did not even evoke a note of protest from the Soviet embassy, though in general the Soviet leadership was negatively disposed to the change of power in Kabul. Some accounts report a second unsuccessful attempt on Amin's life in November 1979, with the participation of Soviet agents. Plans for Soviet intervention in Afghanistan were already being discussed.

.The figure of Amin is ambiguous. On the one hand, it is not possible to take seriously subsequent Afghan propaganda that Amin was an agent of the CIA and that the coup was prepared in a secret plot with the leaders of the opposition. On the other hand, in propagating slogans about "building socialism in the shortest possible time," Amin caused rejection of even the most insignificant achievements of a revolution which had occurred before he came to power. Unleashing terror and repression of an unprecedented scale and cruelty, Amin was moving toward a personal dictatorship.

Soviet Military Intervention

With all power in the country concentrated in the hands of Amin and his closest circle, other governmental structures began to fall apart—the civil service, the army, the party, and social organizations—and the crisis of the

revolution came closer. The fragments of the traditional system of land own-
ership led to reduction in agricultural production. The mass exodus of various
categories of the population overseas caused noticeable harm to the functioning
of the national economy. A general lack of faith in the regime grew rapidly,
gradually isolating it from the people.

It was in this setting that the Soviet Union began its military intervention in
Afghanistan. Although Babrak Karmal, who came to power with the assistance
of Soviet troops, chose a more flexible and moderate course in internal and
foreign policy, he was unable to halt the rapid disintegration of the revolution.
The Karmal government (1980–86), enacted a temporary constitution which
outlined the basic rights and freedoms, halted the land reforms that had been
such a powerful catalyst for universal displeasure with the regime, achieved a
certain liberalization of the economy, enlarged the rights of the clergy and
believers, and created a National Fatherland Front. However, many of these
reforms had no more than a formal character.

President Najibullah announced in 1987, for example, that of the 350,000
peasants who had received land as a result of the land reform, only 80,000
had become landowners (28 percent). The National Fatherland Front, which
included women's groups, youth movements, and trade unions, was totally
controlled by the party.

On the whole, the one-party system continued to function in a severely
authoritarian form, and a process of Sovietization began. It affected all spheres
of the country's political, civic, and religious life and was based on the Soviet
model of social development. The model bore no relation to the national
specifics and traditions of Afghanistan.

Gorbachev's assumption of power in the USSR and the beginning of *perestroika* had a strong influence on Afghan political development. In 1986,
under pressure from the Kremlin, there was a change of leaders in Kabul, with
Najibullah replacing Karmal. The direction of the new political leadership of
Afghanistan included reconciliation of all warring sides and liberalization of
social and economic life. Some parties of the left were legalized and received
seats in the parliament, which began to function, and a private press emerged.
In 1989, Soviet troops were removed.

Afghanistan's new leadership renounced the policies of earlier regimes and
confessed that many political and economic actions had been mistaken. However, in the wartime conditions of the country, an authoritarian regime continues to function, with less than 10 percent of the country under its control. It
does not enjoy mass support and continues to exist basically because of Soviet
military and economic assistance.

The failure of the revolution in Afghanistan was caused by a series of
objective and subjective factors. Most important was the country's lack of
socioeconomic and psychological preparedness for this sort of social change.
The extremely rapid transformation of a traditional feudal society into a
socialist one proved to be an unrealizable task. The political leaders also proved

unprepared for such a task in trying to create a "revolution from above" without the support or participation of the masses.

A third important factor was the attempt to force the Soviet experience of socialism on Afghanistan when it had not succeeded in any of the former socialist countries and without regard for national specificity, the level of social development, or historical traditions. Finally, the policies of the USSR also had a destabilizing influence on the political processes of the country, with regard to both its military participation in the conflict and to its attempt to move Afghanistan along the path of Soviet-style social development.

The best outcome for Afghanistan would have been a gradual transition to the liberal-democratic model of development. However, even in the event of cessation of military activity, this seems impossible for the near future. The most likely path of development is a return to traditional structures, with the intention of gradually modernizing them and incorporating them into modern society.

References

Amin, Hafizullah (1978). "Doklad chlena politburo sekretariata tsentral'nogo komiteta Narodno-demokraticheskoi partii Afganistana zamestitelia premir-ministra i ministra inostrannikh del Khafizulli Amina na torzhestvennom zasedanii partii-nogo aktiva Kabula posviashchennom 61 godovshchine Velikoi Oktiabrskoi sotsialisticheskoi revolutsii." Speech delivered by Hafizullah Amin to Kabul party activists on the occasion of the 61st anniversary of the October socialist revolution. Kabul: Government Printing Press.

——— (1979a). "Matn-e baianie-ie Hafizullah Amin munshi-ie komite-ie markazi-ie hezb-e democratik-e khalq-e Afghanistan mo'aven-e sadr azam wa wazir-e omur-e khareje ba monasebat-e charoahomin salgard-e awwalin kongere-ie hezb-e democratik-e khalq-e Afghanistan." Speech delivered by Hafizullah Amin on the occasion of the 14th anniversary of the PDPA. Kabul: Government Printing Office.

——— (1979b). Speech delivered by Hafizullah Amin at the opening of the Institute of Social Sciences. Kabul: Government Printing Press.

Basov, Vladimir (1984). "Revolutsionnyi protsess v respublikanskom Afganistane" ["The revolutionary process in republican Afghanistan"]. In *Aktualnye problemi afganskoi revoliutsii* [Current problems of the Afghan revolution]. Moscow: Nauka Press.

Davidov, Alexander, and Neonila Cherniakhovskaia (1973). *Afganistan*. Moscow: Mysl Publishing House.

Political Department of the Armed Forces (1978). *Dar bare-ie inqilab-e saur* [About the Saur Revolution]. Kabul: Government Printing Press.

Taraki, Nur Muhammad (1978). "Khutut-i asasi-yi wazoev-i inqilabi-i jamhuri-yi demo-cratik-i Afghanistan" ["Basic lines of revolutionary goals of the Democratic Republic of Afghanistan"]. Speech delivered in Kabul, May 8. Kabul: Government Printing Press.

VII

WORDS IN THE BALANCE
THE POETICS OF POLITICAL DISSENT
IN AFGHANISTAN

David B. Edwards

Oh, ye sacred liberating and benevolent sun,
rise up, rise up. We have amid storms and
darkness found the outlet and light. Red is
the brave man's path and sacred is that of
friendship. This revolutionary land belongs
to the working class. This heritage of the dar-
ing people now belongs to peasants; the age
of tyranny is over now, the turn is that of
the laborer. We in the world long for peace
and friendship. We wish freedom for the oppressed. We want for them Bread, Clothing,
and Shelter.

Afghan National Anthem

When the flag of Islam is soon raised in
Kabul, my injured heart will again be at
peace in my breast. I am Rafiq Jan, and I
weigh my poems on a true scale; I will keep
reciting these [lines] even if my flesh is roast-
ing on the fire.

Rafiq Jan

Between April 1978, when the government of Nur Muhammad Taraki took
office, and December 1979, when the Soviet Union took control of the Afghan
government, a bold attempt was undertaken to transform the Afghan nation
into a different kind of social and political entity. Those responsible for this
transformation envisioned the establishment of a socialist nation in which

class oppression would be erased and the productive energies of the poor mobilized. Spearheading the new Afghan state would be the People's Democratic Party of Afghanistan (PDPA), which was seen as a vehicle for incorporating into the governing structure those previously excluded from power: women, low-ranking military officers and bureaucrats, and the younger generation of Afghan students. After training and indoctrination in the principles of scientific socialism, cadres would go into the countryside to bring literacy and an awareness of the economic and social conditions that confined the poor to lives of brutal poverty and limited the economic and social development of the nation.

There is little doubt that Taraki, Hafizullah Amin, and other leaders of the PDPA saw April 27, 1978, as the dawning of a new era, but the sun that rose that day brought instead a firestorm of protest. Those who flocked to the party standards were far fewer in number than the tens of thousands who took up arms against the new regime and the millions who chose exile in Pakistan and Iran to life in the new socialist paradise.

During the early 1980s, many observers offered explanations as to why the Marxist revolution failed in Afghanistan. Opponents of the regime—especially the exile resistance parties in Peshawar—argued that people saw through the regime's propaganda and raised the banner of *jihad* to preserve Islam and dislodge the infidel usurpers from power. One variant of this position—translated into the language of democratic individualism for Western consumption—was formulated under President Carter and embellished by the Reagan administration. This variant proclaimed that those resisting the Kabul regime were "freedom fighters" and "patriots," much like America's own "founding fathers," who threw off the chains of the British colonial tyrant.

Supporters of the regime, on the other hand, blamed the popular backlash on the machinations of the royal family, landowners, and religious clerics, who played on the "superstitions and prejudices" of the people in an effort to misrepresent the party's intentions (Male 1982). After the Soviet invasion in December 1979, which installed Babrak Karmal in power, Soviet analysts focused their criticism on the deposed leaders, especially former Prime Minister Hafizullah Amin, who was depicted as an opportunistic despot willing to pervert the principles of scientific socialism to preserve his own power. Following the Soviet withdrawal from Afghanistan and the subsequent collapse of Communism in the Soviet Union, new explanations have been offered, including the one presented in this volume by Victor Korgun. According to Korgun, there are two reasons for the failure of the revolution in Afghanistan:

The first has to do with the political schisms that split the Marxist factions in Kabul. Korgun is not oblivious to the situation in the countryside—he accurately describes some of the problems the government encountered in gaining popular support for its reform programs—but he is more concerned with the rivalry between the "sybaritic Eastern patriarch," Nur Muhammad

Taraki, and the "sly, cruel dictator," Hafizullah Amin, and less so with the relationship between government and people and the reasons for the government's failure to enlist popular support. This emphasis on the personalities of the leaders distances the Soviet policymakers and administrators who supported Afghanistan's Marxist regimes from the consequences of their actions and suggests that whatever abuses occurred were the result of the "immaturity" of the political personalities who led the revolution and not the fault of Soviet advisors.

A second reason cited by Korgun for the failure of the Afghan revolution relates to the unrealistic nature of the goals set by the Marxist leadership, given the primitive stage of economic and political advancement Afghanistan had attained. According to this line of reasoning, the socialist experiment was doomed to fail, and any mistakes committed by the regime and its advisors were irrelevant since the final outcome was "preordained."

Arguments such as these suggest a continuing faith in Marx and Engel's views on social evolution, but they also suggest a fundamental uncertainty as to why the socialist revolution—in Afghanistan and elsewhere—failed. This ambiguity revolves around the issue of whether the failure was the result of some feature of the situation within which the socialist program was to be implemented (for example, the unrealistic aspirations of the leaders or the fact that the country had not reached the requisite stage of social and economic development) or whether the socialist model itself was at fault. They also suggest a continuing unwillingness to consider the situation in its own specificity and to view the people involved as motivated by beliefs that might have coherence and value in and of themselves.

Instead of seeing the revolution as doomed to failure because of mistakes made by the PDPA leadership or because of the nature of Afghan society, I believe it is more useful to view the conflict as an unfolding set of actions and responses, at any stage of which alternative actions and responses would have led to different outcomes. The PDPA's decision to adopt a red flag as the national symbol, for example, was a choice made by the regime's leadership. Along with other actions and statements, it conveyed a message to the people about the nature of the regime's political ambitions and its relations to the Soviet Union. Because the action led to an unanticipated and undesirable outcome, it must be viewed as a mistake. However, we must also recognize that if the regime had acted otherwise, another outcome might have occurred.

My point is not simply that the Soviet-sponsored regimes that have ruled Afghanistan since 1978 have made errors in their efforts to win the people's support. It is also—and more fundamentally—that we cannot assume to know why the Afghan people acted as they did without attempting to discover their point of view. What is missing in Korgun's analysis—and in the analyses of most Western observers—is the testimony of Afghan people; and without that testimony, it is impossible to gain any real understanding of why the PDPA's call to popular revolution—a call that had found a sympathetic audience in the past—proved so unsuccessful on this occasion.

Poetry and the Afghan Revolution

The nature of the popular consensus that developed in Afghanistan in response to the Marxist revolution can be gleaned by considering the reactions of poets, a group not normally heard from in social-science analysis. For those who have grown up in the West, poetry might seem an inappropriate avenue for studying politics.[1] Poetry is about values and beliefs and the aesthetic and spiritual domains of life. To the extent that it is political, poetry is thought to be sullied, perhaps because political language has come in our era to represent a debased and deficient form of speech.

Recent scholarship on Middle Eastern societies has demonstrated, however, not only that poetry has retained a central place in the lives of the people in this region of the world but also that poetry and politics are integrally related. Meeker (1979), for example, has shown how poetry expresses and sustains the most fundamental features of political relations among pastoral tribes in North Arabia.[2] Abu Lughod's work among the Awlad ʿAli bedouin in Egypt (1986) supports Meeker's assertion as to the centrality of poetry as an expressive medium, but she provides additional insights on the role of poetry as a form of "resistance," mediating relations between men and women. Finally, Caton, in his study of North Yemeni tribal poetry (1990), demonstrates the multiple ways in which poetic composition and performance both structure social relations and provide Yemenis with their primary forms of political expression and persuasion.

In Afghanistan, as elsewhere in the Middle East, poetry expresses cultural values and norms and is one of the traditional channels for articulating political beliefs. Its role in Afghan culture has long been noted by scholars, beginning with Elphinstone (1815) and continuing with a number of late nineteenth-century writers such as H. G. Raverty (1864) and C. E. Biddulph. The preface of Biddulph's 1890 anthology of Afghan verse contains the following observation:

---

1. An alternative understanding of the relationship between poetry and politics in the West is contained in Paul Fussell's *The Great War and Modern Memory*, which traces the origins of the separation of poetry and political experience to the traumas of the First World War. Fussell's thesis is essentially that the brutalities of mechanized trench warfare rendered established poetic idioms obsolete. Following this experience, the only poetic trope that could express the experience of warfare—and the modern age in general—was irony.

2. As important as Meeker's work has been in making poetry a subject of concern for anthropologists working in the Middle East, it must be remembered (as Meeker is fully aware) that an earlier generation of Middle Eastern scholars had already tapped this rich vein of cultural material. These scholars include Ignaz Goldziher (*Muslim Studies* [1889-90]) and Alois Musil, especially *The Manners and Customs of the Rwala Bedouins* (1928).

Afghanistan has always been a country abounding in rustic poets, and amongst a people absolutely devoid of any other form of literature, the poetic has, as amongst most free and mountainous races, been ever the favorite mode of recording any forcible impression, whether of a sentimental, historical or moralistic description which may have occurred to the composer.[3]

The poems I consider in this chapter have been translated from Pakhtu-language tape cassettes recorded between 1978 and 1980 and offered for sale in the music bazaar in Peshawar and other market towns along the border.[4] The cassettes were produced by poets, musicians, and cassette shop owners on portable tape recorders, without the assistance or control of any political party or governmental agency. While the primary place of production and purchase of these cassettes was the North-West Frontier Province, the poets, musicians, and most purchasers came from the border provinces of eastern Afghanistan. Many of the cassettes were carried back to Afghanistan, where they were played with great frequency in the months following the Marxist coup d'état, when people in the border region were deciding to oppose the government. One individual who was with a segment of the Mohmand tribe when the decision was made to attack the government noted that the poetic exhortations contained on the tape cassettes played a significant role in galvanizing people to take up arms.

Anecdotal information such as this is, of course, insufficient to prove any causal connection between poetry and political action, but the poems provide an invaluable window onto the kind of political discourse that was produced in opposition to that emanating from Kabul.[5] Whatever their influence, they do provide a way of understanding, if not *the* Afghan perspective, at least one significant strand of popular rhetoric in the wake of the revolution.

---

3. In recent years, Afghan poetry has received critical attention from both historians and anthropologists. In the former category, I would note the work of Sir Evelyn Howell and Sir Olaf Caroe (1963) and D. M. K. Kamil Mohmand (1968). In the latter category, the notable contribution is Margaret Mills' study of storytelling and poetry in Herat (1991). Although Mills is primarily concerned with narratives and story-telling performance, her work is relevant, since it deals with the period prior to and including the current conflict and because it is concerned with the way in which political and social identities are negotiated and constructed through forms of oral expression.

4. Tape cassettes were purchased between 1980 and 1984 while I was conducting research on Afghan refugees sponsored by fellowships from the Fulbright-Hays Commission and the National Science Foundation. I would like to acknowledge the assistance of several people who helped me collect, translate, and make sense of this material: Sayyid Shahmahmood Miakhel, Naseem Stanazai, Sayyid Abdullah Tora, and Zalmai Ghazi Alam.

5. This is especially significant because few such sources exist. Thus, while written documents published during the period of the first uprisings do exist, they are mostly products of the exile resistance parties and, as such, biased in their representation of events. Contemporary oral accounts by participants in the early uprisings are also of limited value, since they too tend to be deeply influenced by the current political climate, especially the general polarization of political views between "Marxist" and "Muslim" extremes.

One of the chief characteristics of traditional Pakhtu tribal verse is the frequency of disparaging references to the state. This can be seen clearly in the verse of the great sixteenth-century warrior/poet, Khushhal Khan Khatak, who is often held up as an exemplar of Pakhtun cultural values. Khushhal Khan's poetry deals with a variety of subjects, but one topic that comes up repeatedly is the immorality of the state, particularly that of the Mughal emperor Aurangzeb. For Khushhal Khan, as for his successors, the state is responsible for sowing inequity, corruption, and division within the solidary moral universe of the tribe; and his verse exhorts his fellow Pakhtuns to defend their homeland and culture from the moral subversion of Mughal rule:

1. A year hath passed since Aurangzeb is encamped against us,
   Disordered and perplexed in appearance, and wounded in heart. . . .
2. Still Aurangzeb's malevolence hath not a whit diminished,
   Though the curses of his father it before drew down.
3. For this reason, also, no one can place dependence on him:
   He is malignant and perfidious, a breaker of his word.
4. For this state of things, no other termination can be seen
   Than that the Mughals be annihilated or the Afghans undone. (Raverty 1864: 151-52)

The April Revolution

The poetry written during the early days of the PDPA regime shows a continuity with traditional poetic representations of state power. Like Aurangzeb, Mur Muhammad Taraki and his comrades are seen as the harbingers of a new kind of moral disorder that seeks to transform the system that traditionally linked tribes and state in a consensual political arrangement. The order from which the Marxist regime was seen to deviate is based on a notion of hierarchy as an extension of tribal structure. Previous rulers of Afghanistan had been members of the Durrani Pakhtun tribe, which other Pakhtuns viewed as first among equals in the constellation of tribes. Durrani ascendancy was premised on being in the line of elder sons of the apical Pakhtun ancestor, Qais Abdul Rashid, and on the role of the eighteenth-century Durrani chief, Ahmad Shah, in forming the Kingdom of Kabul, from which the nation of Afghanistan later emerged.

The tribe's dominance is based on other social and economic factors as well, but it is important to emphasize here that the Durrani rulers inherited nobility as their birthright. Theirs was an exalted line which entitled them to occupy a singular position and receive the loyalty and allegiance of the other tribes. The fact that a ruler was entitled to loyalty did not mean that he would always get it or that the tribes would not pursue their own interests, even in the face of the ruler's opposition. It meant simply that the ruler had a right to rule, to pursue his interests, and to enter into mutually beneficial relationships with his tribal subjects (who were also, in a distant sense, his cousins).

To illustrate the way the Marxist state was viewed as altering the traditional political order, we can look at a verse by Rafiq Jan about the events of April 27, 1978, when the government of Muhammad Daud was overthrown in a coup led by Colonel Abdul Qadir, a tank commander in the Afghan army and member of the PDPA.[6] The central event described in the poem is the attack by Abdul Qadir's armored unit on the presidential palace, during which President Daud and his family were killed:

1. The tanks have besieged King Daud Shah.
   Qadir has laid siege to Daud Shah with his tanks.
2. He called on him to get his pen ready for signing.
   Daud Shah gave this answer to Qadir:
3. "Shepherd, don't boast so much of yourself."
   (The tanks have besieged King Daud Shah.)
4. "Shepherd, wait for me, I will fight you.
   I will either become a martyr or be disfigured.
5. My head is a sacrifice for the name and honor of Islam.
   I will not abandon my faith for you, even if someone gives me several countries."
   (The tanks have besieged King Daud Shah.)
6. "I will not abandon my faith for you even if you give me the world
   Or set all of my family on fire.
7. Oh Qadir, don't run away—show yourself to me.
   Then I will beat your mouth with my heavy fists."
   (The tanks have besieged King Daud Shah.)
8. The children of King Daud were killed in the battle.
   They were killed like the children in Karbala.
9. Daud was martyred by the will of God.
   Oh, Rafiq, all of the countries praise him!
   (The tanks have besieged King Daud Shah.)[7]

---

6. The name "Rafiq" refers to the poet whose pen name is "Rafiq Jan." Since Rafiq Jan was one of the best-known oppositional poets to emerge immediately after the coup d'état, it is worth noting a few relevant biographical facts about him. Unlike the great sixteenth-century poet Khushhal Khan Khatak, whose work he emulates, Rafiq Jan is not a chief of his tribe or a man of renown. Rather, he is the son of an itinerant mullah who served as prayer leader in various villages in eastern Afghanistan. Rafiq Jan's father owned a small amount of land, but not enough to survive on, and the patrimony was made more tenuous after it had been divided by inheritance among Rafiq Jan and his brothers. Rafiq Jan began earning a living by smuggling tea and cloth across the border at a young age. He also worked as a day laborer on construction sites in Peshawar and eventually earned enough to buy a small tea shop in the Peshawar bazaar. He is the kind of person who should have been attracted to the message of the Kabul regime, in the sense that he would have been likely to benefit from land redistribution and the general restructuring of the rural sector. Instead he chose to oppose the government's program and did so independently of any organized political opposition structure—in fact, before any of the major opposition parties had gained much influence and before most had even come into existence.

7. The full Pakhtu text of this and other poems will be included in a forthcoming study of the Afghan War.

The poem commemorates what is seen as the noble struggle by the deposed president, Muhammad Daud, against the attack of the ignoble tank commander, Abdul Qadir. What makes the poem interesting is the way in which historical fact has been submerged in the rhetoric and paradigmatic form of a political myth, a myth in which the hero is portrayed as "king" rather than "president," while his enemy is identified as a base "shepherd" instead of his actual position as a military officer. In this way, official ranks of state are set aside and replaced by what is more essential to the meaning of the events—the ancestry of the men involved. Regardless of his own choice of the title of "president," Muhammad Daud was a member of a noble lineage and, as such, entitled to rule. Abdul Qadir, for all his success as a military officer, was a "shepherd," the embodiment of humble ancestry.

For those who hear the poem, these titles reinforce the message of the narrative: that the attack against Daud was an act of usurpation by individuals devoid of the credentials necessary for legitimate rule. The fact that Daud was generally unpopular, that he had overthrown his cousin, the former king, or that he was largely responsible for increasing Soviet involvement in the country is overshadowed by the fact of his noble birth, and we see that nobility highlighted throughout the poem. Abdul Qadir's actions are especially despicable to Pakhtuns because he had been a follower of Daud. He is therefore both a usurper and a traitor. In contrast, Daud is wrapped in the mantle of the hero: it is Daud who wants to meet his attacker face-to-face, Abdul Qadir who attacks in his tank and then with bombs; it is Daud who is willing to sacrifice all for honor, Abdul Qadir who would run away.

The message of usurpation is sealed with the last image of the poem—the analogy between the death of Daud's children and the murder of the Prophet Muhammad's grandchildren by Yazid on the plains of Karbala. Alhough the Karbala story is encountered more often in Shi'i contexts than in Sunni ones such as this, it remains for many Muslims the preeminent example of injustice and political usurpation, and its use here demonstrates the poet's view that Daud and his line were the legitimate rulers of Afghanistan.

Invoking the Karbala myth has additional significance in relation to the message of the new government. The regime's claim to authority rested primarily on its sharing ties of class with the rural poor of Afghanistan. Through proclamations, radio propaganda, and organized marches, the Marxist government declared, in essence, that "we, like you, are of humble stock and, like you, we have experienced the oppression of the ruling class. Together we will end oppression and institute a government in which the people rule." In other parts of the world, this kind of message has met with overwhelming approval. In Afghanistan, however, it failed, and the poem suggests one of the reasons: if people understood the political conflict in Kabul as a reenactment of the Karbala story, they were unlikely to respond to the government's message of political oppression by the monarchic elite and economic exploitation by the rural land-owning class.[8]

"Great Leader" Taraki

A central feature of the PDPA's propaganda campaign was glorification of Nur Muhammad Taraki, the head of the PDPA and the president of the Democratic Republic of Afghanistan. According to official party biographers, Taraki was a man with whom millions of poor Afghans could identify, a man of impoverished background who had felt the lash of feudal oppression. Unlike his fellow countrymen, however, he had recognized his plight and had fought back through his writings and his efforts to organize a party of the working class. Taraki offered hope to peasants and workers because he had shown that it was possible to break the chains of poverty and despotism by embracing and broadcasting the message of revolutionary struggle.

That this vision of Taraki was not universally accepted by the Afghan people is seen in another poem written by Rafiq Jan, ostensibly about the eight decrees instituted by the Marxist government shortly after the coup.[9] The decrees were intended to mobilize a massive outpouring of support among the rural poor by improving their economic fortunes, but they became instead a target of popular outrage:

1. Either become a camel herder again, Uncle Taraki,
   Or issue your ninth decree, uncle.
2. Listen, the eight eggs that you laid have been lost.
   You held back your decrees, and because of this, you were dishonored.
3. You were boasting so much, but found you needed the (tribal) chiefs.
   Wherever there is a chief, you bribe him, uncle.
4. "Oh devil," you said, "I have brought thirty decrees."
   Twenty-two of these you have hidden, eight you have enforced.

---

8. The government's strategy of portraying Afghanistan as a nation of downtrodden peasants was misguided in other ways as well, for Pakhtuns, if not Afghans in general, do not tend to glory in the pitiableness of their life circumstances. To the contrary, they imagine that the poorest tenant farmer can maintain his honor as long as he acts in an honorable manner, and one sign that an individual's honor is intact is his willingness to stand up to the most powerful landlord if his rights are violated or his independence is in jeopardy. When local farmers were commandeered by the PDPA to march around the village square with shovels across their shoulders shouting "Hurrah! Death to the Feudals," "Long Live the Glorious Saur Revolution," they were perceived as violating the sense of self-determination that Pakhtuns value above all else. The imposed identity of "downtrodden peasant" was thus inimical to the Pakhtuns' self-professed identity as men of honor, men of family, men of tribe, and the insistence of PDPA officials that Pakhtun villagers play out this other identity in public performance before their peers induced shame rather than solidarity.

9. The most significant of these decrees were Number 6, which eliminated or drastically curtailed all existing debts; Number 7, which abolished the traditional custom of the groom's family giving monetary compensation to the bride's family; and Number 8, which attempted to redistribute land from wealthy landowners to tenant farmers and agricultural laborers.

5. Please resist now, you who were insulting the Quran.
   You claimed to be one *kharwar*, but you came out one *charak*, uncle.

An interesting feature of this poem is its disparaging portrayal of Taraki. Taraki proudly proclaimed his humble background in the hope of instilling a basis of common cause with the poorer classes of Afghans, but most Pakhtuns felt he had no right to install himself in power. This was even more evident when Taraki's background was used as the foundation for a government-or-chestrated personality cult exalting "Great Leader" Taraki. Among the more hubristic aspects of this tactic were the enshrinement of the Taraki family home in Ghazni as a national landmark and museum and the doctoring of newspaper photographs so that Taraki appeared to be larger than anyone else in the frame.

The Taraki cult was viewed by many Pakhtuns as an example of the government's attitude of self-importance. In a tribal setting, men deride and mock those who boast too much or show an exaggerated opinion of themselves, and Rafiq Jan, as a mouthpiece for Pakhtun values, takes it upon himself to put Taraki in his rightful place. This is what the poet is doing when he declares that "you claimed to be one *kharwar*, but you came out one *charak*, uncle." *Kharwar* and *charak* are units of weight, a *kharwar* being approximately 1,246 pounds and a *charak* 3.9 pounds.[10] The poet is saying that, despite Taraki's pretensions to being a man of importance, to being "heavy," he is in reality of little consequence (a reference which has much the same implication as Garry Trudeau's portrayal of Vice President Quayle as a feather in his "Doonesbury" cartoon strip).

Like Abdul Qadir in the previous poem, Taraki is called a "herder," in this case of camels. He is not referred to by any of the honorific titles the government bestowed on him (such as "Great Teacher"). Instead, the poet calls him *"mama,"* a term generally used to refer to one's maternal uncle. It is also the form of address for a house servant or a man who regularly shows up at his kinsmen's homes around mealtime.

Morality and Revolution

Although the PDPA regime that took power in 1978 was initially greeted with derision and satiric laughter—at least by the poets examined here—the government came to symbolize a kind of infidelity which forced Afghans to reassess their own priorities and categories. Consider a poem by Gul Sha'ir written after the Soviet invasion. It expresses in more detail than we have seen

---

10. It should be noted that while the terms *charak* and *kharwar* signify different units of weight in different parts of the country, the basic relationship of the *charak* being small and the *kharwar* large is uniform throughout Afghanistan.

before, not just the political threat represented by the government, but the moral threat as well:

1. In Moscow a dragon has risen up
    And grabbed the throat of every Muslim.
2. They trick some with jobs and some with salaries.
    This is a lesson for every Muslim.
3. They tell some to join the militia.
    They tell some to come to join the army.
4. They make one brother fight another.
5. Everyone is walking about, drunk with wine.
    They have a camel halter through the nose of many.
6. They give them Beirut shoes.
    They kill some people in the name of prisons.
7. They tell someone, "You are the chief of the [village] treasury."
8. They tell some to boldly take a salary.
    They give the lands of one brother to another.
9. Today two brothers have been made enemies like infidels.
10. They use a drawstring as a belt for their pants.
    They give the clerk the job of the minister.
11. They cannot leave their homes for fear.
    A kingdom is not like this—this is garbage.
12. Khalqis and Parchamis[11] are the slaves of the Russians.
    They are slavishly doing what they are told to do.
13. They are nothing but pimps.
14. Their sisters and brothers are serving the Russians.
    With their hairy heads, they are the number two infidels.

In poems such as this, composed after the Soviet invasion, the tone tends to be darker, as knowledge of the changes in Kabul began to spread from the center and the seriousness of the situation was more fully realized. One dimension of this change is the diminished use of satire. The author does include lines of ridicule—as when he mentions the clerk-cum-minister who holds up his pants with a drawstring instead of a belt; however, most of the verses reveal a tone of outrage, and one gets the sense that the government's infidelity has passed the point where satire can continue to operate as an adequate response to the situation.

In place of satire, we encounter a litany of every moral offense the poet can imagine, beginning with the accusation that the government has caused people to forget those aspects of life which are sacred and beyond objective considerations through the inducement of "jobs," "salaries," and petty goods ("Beirut shoes"). Under the influence of Soviet ideals and material blandishments, some Afghans have been led astray. The poet sees people "drunk with wine," people

---

11. "Khalqi" and "Parchami" refer to members of the two competing wings of the PDPA. The Khalq wing was initially led by Mur Muhammad Taraki and Hafizullah Amin. The Parchami wing, which took power after the Soviet invasion of December 1979, was led originally by Babrak Karmal, who was installed by the Soviets as the president of Afghanistan after the invasion.

who have forgotten their honor and allow themselves to be led around like a camel with "a halter through its nose."

This signifies a profound disruption in the normal social order, a turning upside down of the moral understandings upon which Afghans had heretofore based their acceptance of government rule. Under the new order, Soviets make the rules and tell people what to do. Where tribes and villages were previously able to negotiate with the central government over issues like conscription and the formation of militia units, the regime now forces people to join against their will. Those whom the government recruits are no longer the best and most able; they are opportunists who would betray their principles and become "slaves" to the Russians for immediate advantage.

Like Taraki himself, the local people who support the Khalqi government are viewed as petty tyrants whose absence of honor is evident in the fact that they have allowed themselves to be influenced and seduced by the trappings of power and prestige. It is this which creates the conditions for the moral disorder signalled by the sight of "brother fighting brother," "people afraid to leave their homes," and "sisters running in front of the Russians." These are the actions of individuals who have abandoned their sense of honor and self-respect, as can be seen by their acceptance of positions of subordination to the Russian invaders. In the eyes of the poet, any government that allows this kind of immorality to come about is not a proper "kingdom" but useless and corrupting "garbage."

"Feudal" Landowners

Those the government referred to as "feudal oppressors" were often lionized when they opposed the regime. This is seen in another poem by Gul Sha'ir which concerns a wealthy family that settled in the area of Behsud, near the eastern city of Jalalabad:

1. When the Khalqis took power in Kabul,
   The Sardars of Behsud have made *hijrat*.
2. Oh, Martyr Muhammad Rasul Sardar.
   He was attacking the English.
3. Sardar Faiz Muhammad Khan was very brave.
   The Sardars of Behsud have made *hijrat*.
4. Zemarai can be called martyr.
   In every activity, he was in the front.
5. He worked honestly for the *ghazian*.
   The Sardars of Behsud have made *hijrat*.
6. They left for the government much wealth,
   Full rooms and much property.
7. Oh, in Banghor they had good houses.
   There were beautiful gardens and good streams.
8. They had much wealth and countless farmers.
   The Sardars of Behsud have made *hijrat*.

9. One of them is secretary in Milli Jabha.
    Now he is a servant in a room.
10. Gul says, "It is important to admire this kind of youth."
    The Sardars of Behsud have made *hijrat*.

The poet honors the Sardars of Behsud for being exemplars of the Pakhtun ethos. The title *sardar* tells us that the family comes from the Durrani tribe, and their location in the vicinity of Jalalabad—rather than near the southern city of Kandahar, where the Durrani tribe is concentrated—indicates that they probably obtained their lands as an entitlement from the government rather than on the basis of local tribal attachments. Such people were the sort of "feudal oppressors" against which the Khalqis hoped to rally public indignation, but the poem gives some indications as to why these efforts generally failed.

In tribal society, being a man of wealth is cause for neither adulation nor scorn. On the contrary, it is generally believed that a man is entitled to his wealth, whether inherited or achieved, and, until proven otherwise, the possession of wealth is looked upon as a sign of an individual's worth and/or the superior ancestry of his family. Men of wealth are not necessarily honored, but if they live up to their heritage and act in accordance with the Pakhtun cultural ethos, then theirs is a special renown.

In the case of the Sardars of Behsud, several forebears proved their courage on the battlefield as *ghazian* [fighters in a religious struggle] against the British, and at least one member of the family has been martyred in the present fighting. The family has also demonstrated its mettle by leaving the country, thereby sacrificing homes, gardens, and property. What makes this commendable in the eyes of the poet and his listeners—most of whom have also gone into exile—is that they are following the example of the Prophet Muhammad, who "made *hijrat*" from Mecca to Medina rather than accept oppression at the hands of his enemies. Given the Prophet's example, the act of seeking asylum is not looked down upon or viewed as cowardly. Rather, if undertaken for the proper reasons, it is seen as an act of piety and assumed to connote a readiness to sacrifice all and accept continuing privation for the sake of religion. It is further assumed that those who make *hijrat* intend to go back eventually; flight merely facilitates the effort to recapture their homeland at a propitious moment. That this is the intention of the Sardars of Behsud is indicated by the fact that one member of the family, which had great wealth in Afghanistan, has become an ordinary official—a "servant"—working in a bare office for one of the resistance parties (*"mili jabhah"*) hoping to overthrow the Marxist regime.[12]

---

12. While the Marxists were condemned in the previous poem for becoming "slaves" of the Russians, the Sardars of Behsud are honored in this poem for their willingness to become "servants" of one of the resistance parties. The difference is that the latter represents an act of "service" (*khidmat*), in which the individual subordinates his own interests end ambitions for the common good, while the former reflects the individual's willingness to accept debasement to gain material advantage.

Conclusion

The poems examined here represent a small sample of the political discourse that arose in response to the Marxist revolution. I have included examples written by a few poets from a single region of a large and complex society, but they demonstrate the possibility of extricating meanings lying outside the controlling grasp of the political parties in Peshawar and Kabul (not to mention Moscow, Washington, and Islamabad). The presentation and analysis of these poems is an exercise in allowing (some) Afghans to speak to an audience that has gained what little information it has from ideologically interested sources. While poets like Rafiq Jan and Gul Shaʿir cannot necessarily be taken as representative of the Afghan people generally, their words are significant for having been directed at other Afghans. Their verses were written as an immediate and unpremeditated response to the revolutionary transformations of 1978 and 1979, and, given that fact, they can be taken to represent one perspective on those transformations from within the society itself.

Rafiq Jan's and Gul Shaʿir's responses to the Marxist takeover are in no way unusual or unrepresentative of those who chose to take up sides against the Kabul regime. Indeed, it would be difficult to find an individual who could be characterized as "unrepresentative," since the opposition has included, from the very beginning, individuals from virtually every ethnic group, economic stratum, occupational category, and level of educational attainment. To the extent that it is possible to calculate such matters, it appears that Rafiq Jan's and Gul Shaʿir's view of the April Revolution was very much like that of several million other Afghans. Even the men's status as poets does not place them outside the normal spectrum of Afghan citizenry, since poetry is a popular art form practiced by men and women, educated and uneducated, rich and poor. More than anything else then, the verse quoted here reflects the ubiquity of the cultural ethos binding Afghans of diverse backgrounds and histories and the potency of the moral outrage Afghans felt at the transformations initiated by the PDPA regime.

While the regime of Nur Muhammad Taraki and Hafizullah Amin styled itself as the defender of the oppressed "masses," they were perceived by those "masses" not as saviors, but rather as traitors to the moral principles that bound the society together and gave meaning to the impoverished existence most Afghans know. This perception was not preordained. The government of Muhammad Daud was generally unpopular with the people. Much of the credit President Daud received as a member of the Muhammadzai tribe had been dissipated, and toward the end of his reign, he was increasingly viewed as autocratic and oppressive. Even though many Afghans might have been ready to cheer when Daud was overthrown, however, the actions of those who accomplished it quickly alienated this potential base of support, and Muhammad Daud came to appear in death much more heroic and noble than he had in life.

The source of this alienation, I would contend, was not that Taraki and his followers subscribed to Marxist ideas. Rather, it was that they made a conscious and avoidable decision to *portray* themselves as Marxists and to follow a path of symbolic identification with their Soviet sponsors, which indicated to the Afghan population that the regime intended not just to reform inequities within the social and political system but also to transform Afghanistan into a copy of the Soviet Central Asian republics to the north. In following this path, the regime announced to the people that its actions were to be in accordance with the dictates of a foreign ideology and not with the customary cultural and religious norms to which the people themselves adhered. In making that decision and announcing it as they did, the Kabul government effectively severed its ties with the people and unleashed the tide of civil strife and ideological extremism that continues to inundate the country to this day.

Through their struggle to overthrow the Marxist regime, Afghans have taught us something about the requirements of freedom and the dangers of looking to universalistic creeds to bring about social change. Twelve years into the conflict, more than a million people have been killed. More than four million have been exiled. Many hundreds of thousands have lost arms and legs or have been disfigured. A generation of children has lost its opportunity for education. The achievements of several decades of social and economic development have been erased. The lessons have been costly, and we can only hope that an end is near. So too must we hope that the former domains of Soviet Communism learn the lessons taught them by their southern neighbor without paying the same terrible price.

References

Abu-Lughod, Lila (1986). *Veiled Sentiments: Honor and Poetry in a Bedouin Society*. Berkeley: University of California Press.

Biddulph, C. E. (1890). *Afghan Poetry of the Seventeenth Century*. London.

Caton, Steven (1990). *"Peaks of Yemen I Summon": Poetry as Cultural Practice in a North Yemeni Tribe*. Berkeley: University of California Press.

Elphinstone, Hon. Mountstuart (1815). *An Account of the Kingdom of Caubool*. 2 vols. London: John Murray.

Fussell, Paul (1975). *The Great War and Modern Memory*. Oxford: Oxford University Press.

Goldziher, Ignaz (1967). *Muslim Studies*. Chicago: Aldine (originally published as *Muhammedanische Studien* [Halle: Max Niemeyer, 1889–90]).

Howell, Sir Evelyn, and Sir Olaf Caroe (1963). *The Poems of Khushhal Khan Khatak*. Peshawar.

Male, Beverley (1982). *Revolutionary Afghanistan*. London: Croom Helm.

Meeker, Michael (1979). *Literature and Violence in North Arabia*. Cambridge: Cambridge University Press.

Mills, Margaret (1991). *Rhetoric and Politics in Afghan Traditional Storytelling*. Philadelphia: University of Pennsylvania Press.

Mohmand, D. M. K. Kamil (1968). *On A Foreign Approach to Khushhal*. Peshawar: Maktabah-i-Shaheen.

Musil, Alois (1928). *The Manners and Customs of the Rwala Bedouins*. New York: American Geographical Society (Oriental Explorations and Studies, no. 6).

Raverty, Major H. G. (1864). *Selections from the Poetry of the Afghans*. London.

VIII

REIMAGINED INTERNAL FRONTIERS
TRIBES AND NATIONALISM—
BAKHTIYARI AND KURDS

Gene R. Garthwaite

> In the Middle Ages . . . it was assumed that
> a people who, as some kind of political unit,
> shared common customs and law—and quite
> often a common language—. . . were there-
> fore of common descent. Nowadays, on the
> other hand, it is often thought that people of
> common descent share a common culture
> and therefore *ought* to form a separate politi-
> cal unit. The medieval assumption was an un-
> reasoned justification for the status quo; the
> modern belief is an often controversial justifi-
> cation for change.
>
> Susan Reynolds

> The individualism of the tribal scheme was
> predicated, and still is, on its infinite divisibil-
> ity. That of the nation-state, by contrast, is
> predicated on an absolute moral unity.
>
> Paul Dresch

Reynolds, a historian, is writing about medieval European society, but her
words apply equally well to people of the Middle East, for they face comparable
issues of identity in the nineteenth and twentieth centuries. Dresch, an anthropologist, highlights the polymorphic nature of tribal society, a problem for

I wish to thank Sekandar Amanolahi, Shiraz University; Pamela Crossley, Dartmouth College;
Lois Beck, Washington University in St. Louis; Dale Eickelman, Dartmouth College; Misagh Parsa,
Dartmouth College; Susan Reynolds, Lady Margaret Hall, Oxford; and Charles Wood, Dartmouth
College, for reading and commenting on all or part of this manuscript.

organization within the tribe and for its control by the state. He identifies the critical issue of political change and the problem posed to tribal societies by the centralization of new nation-states. In addition, Dresch's factor of "infinite divisibilty" opposes nationalism and the nature of the nation-state. Both Reynolds and Dresch deal with the critical historical issue of identity and representation in the face of change.

The emergence of nationalism in the late nineteenth century and of nation-states in the post–World War I Middle East has placed extraordinary demands on individuals' political loyalty and identity. Middle Eastern tribal peoples have been especially vulnerable to the centralization that accompanied the formation of nation-states. They are often viewed with antagonism because of the perceived conflict between tribal and national identity, fear of their military power, and because their way of life—pastoral nomadism—is seen by most nation-states as out of place in a modern society.

Tribally organized or identified peoples have responded in a variety of ways to the enormous changes of the twentieth century, but for those peoples who have maintained a pastoral nomadic life, the basic economic and social units have proven remarkably flexible. Many Middle Easterners continue to demonstrate a variety of identities, as they always have, despite the exclusive requirements of nationalism that nation-states have sought to impose.

In the case of Iran, Reynolds's and Dresch's quotations suggest a process in which some ethnic groups, including tribally organized ethnic groups, view themselves as nations. Some go further and represent themselves as nation-states. A comparison of the Bakhtiyari and the Kurds—the two groups discussed in this chapter—illustrates the complexity of such a process. The Bakhtiyari are an ethnic group that does not regard itself as a nation and accepts Iranian nationalism and their place in the Iranian nation-state. Many Kurds, on the other hand, regard themselves as a nation that ought to be a nation-state.

Pastoral nomadism and tribal organization are commonly associated with both the Kurds and the Bakhtiyari. Although aspects of their societies, cultures, and economies are comparable, however, significant differences have arisen between the two groups as a consequence of other factors, especially historical ones. In terms of identity, especially national identity, those differences illuminate critical historical processes.

The Kurdish population exceeds 11 million.[1] They are generally seen as peoples of common descent, values, and culture who have been denied a "land" and a political voice by the Iranian state—and the other states in which they are to be found—and by the great powers. Many have argued that the Kurds ought to have autonomy, if not a state. The Bakhtiyari are found only in Iran

---

1. There may be as many as 3,701,000 Kurds in Iran alone (Mostyn 1988: 464). Bates (1984: 421) estimates that the total Kurdish population is 11 million; Mostyn (1988: 464) calculates it as 16,320,000.

and are significantly smaller in number: a decade ago there were between 500,000 and 700,000 Bakhtiyari (Garthwaite 1984: 81); today they number about 1 million, of whom some 250,000 are pastoral nomads.[2] No one, including the Bakhtiyari, has called for autonomy for them, let alone a state. And they have never been identified with any nationalist movement other than the Iranian one.

It is common to associate the Bakhtiyari geopolitically with the central Iranian plateau and the Kurds with the periphery. The Bakhtiyari were part of organized tribal confederations in nineteenth-century Iran, which meant political representation in the state under the Qajar dynasty (1796–1925). These confederations persisted into the twentieth century. The Kurds were ruled indirectly, and they were regarded as separate in terms of culture and religion, since they were seen primarily as Sunni. With the possible exception of people in the Sanandaj region of Iran under the Vali of Ardalan, the Kurds were not represented as a unitary political grouping within the state, and they seem not to have regarded themselves as a people that ought to be recognized as a nation until relatively recently. Furthermore, the Kurds are spread across five states and thus have been influenced by local nationalist movements, especially in Turkey.

History: Tribe, Ethnic Group, and Nation

It was in the nineteenth century that Middle Eastern tribes first began to figure in government and military reports and travel accounts. The reports often corresponded with strategic interests. What was observed in late-nineteenth-century Iran, for example, were recently formed confederations (including that of the Bahktiyari), which were assumed to characterize all tribal peoples. Such assumptions continue to influence the way we look at Iran. In fact, these confederations were the consequence of particular historical circumstances.

The interest in tribes and confederations during the nineteenth century was accompanied by ethnic labels and categories, which assumed new significance for European states and Western observers and for Middle Eastern reformers of traditional states. The Kurds exemplify that process. Europeans especially perceived them as tribal—hence autonomous—with their own set of loyalties, and as an ethnic minority, with a significant political and national potential. The emergence of Kurdish nationalism has reinforced the nineteenth-century view of the Kurds as a single people, but it obscures the complexity of what is encompassed by the term "Kurdish."

During the late nineteenth and twentieth centuries, the history of the Middle

2. Sekandar Amanolahi (personal communication, May 1992).

East can be seen as a process of reorganizing society. For governments, especially after the development of nation-states, the problem was to encompass tribal economic and political structures within the state while accommodating cultural and social factors such as identity and loyalty. New ideologies, the concentration of power in new elites in new capitals, and new centralizing policies impinged on the autonomy and flexibility of tribally organized groups.

In these new ideologies, especially nationalism, the issue for nationalist leaders was politicizing tribal peoples. In the case of the Kurds, this meant the possibility of conflict with their respective state's nationalism. Furthermore, nationalism itself, whether Kurdish or Turkish or Iranian, could be seen as a threat to the social and economic order of tribally organized groups.

Part of the problem of tribe, ethnic group, and nationalism starts with terms and concepts, about which there is little general agreement and, until recently, limited critical analysis. Notions of "tribes," even among Middle East specialists (with exceptions—for example, Beck 1990: 187–198; Caton 1990; Eickelman 1989; Tapper 1983) have remained relatively unexamined and unchanged since the nineteenth century. Western social scientists have only recently begun to take account of historical factors; similarly, historians have become interested in anthropology (Caton 1990: 74–108). Soviet scholars have dealt with tribes in the context of metahistory, with Marxist-Leninist evolutionary assumptions, and only a few have gone beyond (Khazanov 1984). Soviet tribal specialists have also been hampered by limited access to field experience in the Middle East and in Soviet Central Asia and by the state's attitudes and political agenda.

In one sense, "tribe" and "nation" share common characteristics. Both employ the idea of a historical past that centers on a common land, language, and culture: both tribal and national identities are imagined (Anderson, 1983). In addition, both tribe and nation are essentially political, the result of internal and external factors. Self-definition, or representation, is especially important, but it occurs within specific and larger contexts. Similarly, Persian terminology for "tribe,"—*il, ʿashaʾir, tayafah*—like the English term, is general and depends on context for meaning when used by native speakers.

Specialists sometimes confuse "tribe" and ethnicity. "National minorities," especially as an analytical category,[3] is reductionist and ignores the complexity of Middle Eastern society, where people identify themselves contextually. Richard L. Tapper argues that "ethnic group" and "tribe" are not useful concepts in themselves:

> [The terms] "ethnic group" and "ethnicity" . . . serve rather to obscure than to illuminate the cultural complexity we are concerned to describe and interpret. . . .
> Ethnic group . . . is a poor translation of indigenous categories in Iran, Afghan-

---

3. The assumptions implicit in the use of language as a key determinant in "national minorities" are not supported by historical reality. The traditional and legal category of religion as the basis for identifying "national minorities" provides a better fit with history and society.

istan and elsewhere, and hinders the analysis of their subtleties and ambiguities. Worse, its usage betrays a scientistic and bureaucratic urge to impose order on an essentially fluid and negotiable reality. Ethnicity constitutes a theory of social organization. . . . I urge that "ethnic groups" be not allowed the concrete character that has already been rejected for "lineages" and "tribes." (Tapper 1988: 31)

Context—whether historical, social, or cultural—is critical for understanding tribe and Middle Eastern society.

Nationalism: Tribe and Representation in the Iranian State—The Bakhtiyari

The first part of Reynolds's observations about European medieval society in the epigraph appears to describe the Bakhtiyari within Iranian history; the second part could describe contemporary groups with nationalist aspirations, such as the Kurds. This is a significant distinction: why are the Bakhtiyari not regarded as a group with nationalist aspirations? We need to examine this question by analyzing identity, representation, and power in the Iranian historical context. I begin by briefly describing Bakhtiyari-state relations, including issues of identity and its symbols, representation, and power in the nineteenth century. I then analyze representation in the context of, first, Reza Shah's formation of the nation-state (r. 1925–41) and its continuation under his son, Muhammad Reza Shah (r. 1941–79), and, second, the Islamic Revolution and subsequent formation of the Islamic Republic in the 1980s.

Qajar representation of what we call their state was traditional, and its bases need to be examined in terms of ideology, identity, role and organization, and use of power. Qajar titles linked the shahs and their government to an Iranian political and cultural tradition, as well as to the Islamic one. The shahs' legitimacy derived from maintaining "right" religion by protecting it and allowing for its administration by the ʿulama. The Qajars used symbolic action in appointing religious functionaries such as imam-i jumah [leader of congregational prayer appointed by the shah in each major city], by patronizing taʿziyah [passion plays] and Husayniyah [centers of veneration of Shiʿi Imams], and in their attendance at public prayer, mosques, and shrines. Bast [sanctuary] was found in the mosque and at the throne.

The Qajars effectively overcame the Shiʿi political doctrine that questions the legitimacy of any rule save the Imam's (the successors of the Prophet Muhammad and the sole source of law for the Shiʿa), for they coopted or coexisted with the ʿulama, even in the constitutional era, when Qajar autocracy was effectively challenged. Identity was tied to loyalty to Islam and not to the dynasty, except as its members were upholders of the faith. In actuality, a variety of identities and loyalties were the norm, so long as Islam and the monarch were not challenged.

Qajar autocracy was limited by the absence of effective military and bureaucratic institutions; by the absence of centralization, which allowed for private— even competing— military units and authority and which accorded autonomy to regions and groups and their leaders; by fragmentation of society into multitudinous groups divided by geography, language, and religion and by social, cultural, and political affiliations; by the breadth of their realm and the absence of effective communication; and, at times, by an apparent lack of will. Qajar arbitrariness—and power—was generally felt only by those close to the shah or to his governors and their representatives.

Nasir al-Din Shah designated an *ilkhani* [paramount leader] of the Bakhtiyari for the first time in 1867. He was responsible for maintaining order and collecting taxes and conscripts. The *ilkhani* recognized the shah as his suzerain: he remitted taxes, levies, and gifts to the shah and allowed his sons to be kept as hostages at court. He subordinated himself to the shah or his governors. He wore a robe of honor (*khaʿlat*) and the Qajar *kulah* [a conical hat] and received royal deputies and documents with public ceremony and obeisance. The *ilkhanis* and other elite Bakhtiyari expressed Islamic links as well through ties with the *ʿulama*, pilgrimage, and maintenance of shrines. Chosen from the governing elite family, they represented the shah to their tribal people and the tribal people to the shah, and sometimes they had to balance conflicting interests.

The Bakhtiyari confederation was divided into a variety of economic and social units, ultimately headed by the *ilkhani*. It came into being with the creation of the *ilkhani* and its support by the shah. Again, a variety of identities and loyalties were the norm; they ranged from one's family through subgroups ending in *tayafah* (a named subtribe with pastures and migration routes), where critical economic activities were organized. Key unifying Bakhtiyari symbols associated with the *ilkhani* and the confederation included dress—the men's distinctive hat (*khusravi*), cloak (*chuqa*), and full trouser (*shalvar*); myths— some adapted from the dominant Persian culture;[4] and the Luri language (although the Bakhtiyari also included non-Luri speakers).

In addition, there were three distinctive symbols of power relating specifically to the *ilkhani*: the *ilkhani* lineage; the presence of the *ilkhani*, including his tent and camp and later his house or those of the elite families; and especially the *bastagan* system (Garthwaite 1983: 80–81). *Bastagan* (sing. *bastah*) were non-elite Bakhtiyari retainers who performed administrative, political, and military duties for the khans. Although there often were marital links between the khans and *bastagan* families, the essential link was service, not kinship. The *bastagan* as an institution emerged in the late nineteenth and early twentieth centuries, when there were multiple candidates for *ilkhani* and *ilbigi* [deputy].

---

4. Many Bakhtiyari call Firdausi's great Persian epic, *The Shahnamah*, the Bakhtiyari epic and associate its heroes, especially Rustam, with Bakhtiyari qualities and values.

Bakhtiyariness was also associated with the region and its pastoral nomadism as well as with loyalty to the *ilkhani*s and their families and, beyond them, to the shah. There appears to have been little use of the term "Bakhtiyari" as designating nomadic pastoralists before the middle of the eighteenth century. On that basis, identity would seem to have been associated with specific leaders—a critical factor in Bakhtiyari factionalism—presumably in a patron-client relationship.

In the constitutional period of the first decade of the twentieth century and its immediate aftermath, key Bakhtiyari leaders, especially Sardar As'ad II, played important roles in support of the constitution while maintaining a Bakhtiyari identity. Commoner Bakhtiyari support for nationalism and the constitution or for Muhammad ʿAli Shah and his attempted suppression of it (1909) was dependent on the allegiances of the khans with whom they were allied. It was in this period that the Bakhtiyari elite became part of the national elite. Their roles as governors and officials overlapped their traditional roles. The tension between the two roles was like that of the *ilkhani*s, who had to balance the interests of the state with those of the tribal people within the confederation, or their "infinite divisibility."

Sardar As'ad, who articulated Iranian nationalism, was accepted as a nationalist leader by Iranian society. He was also acknowledged by the Bakhtiyari even though he subordinated his Bakhtiyari identity to an Iranian one. Sardar As'ad, like the Bakhtiyari as a whole, accepted a hierarchy of identities and loyalties, depending on circumstances, and did not see them as exclusive or competing.

Tribespeople have long been feared by urban populations in Iran because they were mounted and armed and posed a perceived threat to order, but they have posed no ideological challenge to the religious and political values of the state and society (with the possible exception of early sixteenth-century Safavid pretenders and Nadir Shah in the mid-eighteenth century). The Qajars, with their own tribal background, merely reaffirmed Safavid political values and practice. Beginning with Reza Shah's rise to power in the 1920s, however, the tribes were seen not only as a threat to order but also as a threat to the state and its representation of society and ideology.

Reza Shah's reign marked a new pattern of relationships between tribes and the state in Iran. In an expeditious manner and with physical coercion, he created a polity that accorded with his image of a modern nation-state. He expected that it would preclude tribal organizations and structures and that identities would be subordinated and subsumed under the Pahlavi identity. Nonetheless, tribal structures persisted, although not at the confederation level for the Bakhtiyari, except in the most general sense.

The Pahlavi state became centralized under a bureaucracy and a standing army, and a new active role for the state involved it directly in the economic, political, legal, social, and cultural life of the people. The autonomy of groups and regions was subordinated to the center; their leaders acquiesced or were coopted or executed. Sardar As'ad III, son of the nationalist Bakhtiyari leader, served as Reza Shah's Minister of War. After he had disarmed and suppressed the tribes, he was executed. Centralization of government gave Reza Shah the means to rule as an autocrat. Although he appropriated the traditional symbols of rule, he also utilized Western ones. His ideology of nationalism focused on Iran's pre-Islamic and imperial past and a Western, urban, industrial, and secular future, with Iran restored as a regional power.

Pahlavi Iran did not tolerate competing identities and loyalties; they were to be Irano-Persian-Pahlavi—Dresch's "absolute moral unity." Layers of identity persisted, however, and were tolerated if they were subsumed under the Pahlavi ones, which was the case for the Bakhtiyari. All groups making up Iran generally adapted to the dominant identity.

The leadership of the Bakhtiyari confederation was eliminated by Reza Shah, although a general Bakhtiyari ideology was maintained within its constituent units. Some of the Bakhtiyari elite survived as part of the Pahlavi national elite. They continued their traditional patronage roles for the Bakhtiyari on a diminishing basis. In the World War II era and again in the early 1950s, when autocracy was weakened, there were resurgences of Bakhtiyari tribal identity. The two most important Bakhtiyari rebellions, one during the Azerbaijan crisis following World War II and the other in the summer of 1982, were led by members of the same elite family, and in both instances there was external support for the revolts. In both cases, the Bakhtiyari did not support them. More successful opposition to the state occurred among the Qashqa'i, but it also failed eventually.

The momentum of change intensified under Reza Shah's son, Muhammad Reza Shah, especially during the 1960s and 1970s. Economic resources and the monopoly of power in the shah's hands allowed for implementation of policies such as the "White Revolution"—later stylized as the "Shah and People Revolution." Bakhtiyari identity and pastoral nomadism were weakened through the expropriation of pasture land and education and by the increasing migration of people to urban areas.[5]

The Revolution of 1978–79 and the formation of the Islamic Republic changed the ideology and symbols of the state, but not its form. The Islamic Republic replaced the Pahlavi identity with a religious one, but it too required unchallenged loyalty alongside an Iranian loyalty that once again became dominant in the Iraq-Iran war. Aspects of Westernization, especially of a cultural and legal nature, have been deemphasized in favor of Islam. Until it faced challenges from the Kurds, Turkmen, and Baluch and then the Qashqa'i and Arabs, the Islamic Republic had seemed willing to tolerate groups or regions and even appeared ready to restore some autonomy. As a result of these

5. Ironically, one consequence of postrevolutionary changes has been a resurgence of pastoral nomadism, which has received support from some government offices.

challenges, however, the authority and power of the Islamic Republic were reimposed, and identity has been made even more exclusive, rejecting not only those who are secularized or Westernized but also those the ʿulama regard as nominally Muslim.

Under the Pahlavis, the tribes were regarded as anachronistic and only nominally Iranian. Now, given traditional ʿulama skepticism about the adherence of the various tribes, including the Bakhtiyari, to Shiʿi norms (let alone tribespeople who identify themselves as Sunni),[6] the new Islamic-Iranian identity is also exclusive, although dominant clergy are supportive of the tribal sector of Iranian society. Socialization to Shiʿi norms has been centralized and institutionalized, despite persisting anticlericalism, through religious education and religious requirements for advancement. Even though the confederation no longer exists politically, aspects of it persist in government provincial administration.

Although the Iranian state's representation of tribes has changed dramatically in the twentieth century, Bakhtiyari self-image and representation of themselves continues, with some significant changes. The pastoral tribespeople who have maintained a nomadic life appear to organize their lives around essential economic and social patterns, yet the primary factor seems to be pastoralism and its organization, including concerns about land, attachment to leaders, historical memory, and maintenance of a hierarchical worldview. These socioeconomic relationships have persisted in the "lesser" organizational levels within the confederations (the family, in the case of the Bakhtiyari), despite the elimination of confederation leadership in the twentieth century (Digard 1979, 1983). The memory of the confederation continues as an identifying and unifying factor.

For those Bakhtiyari who have settled in agricultural villages or in towns and cities—the most accurate estimate is that only 250,000 out of the 1 million Bakhtiyari in 1992 still function as pastoral nomads[7]—their Bakhtiyari identity continues, especially membership in a *tayafah*. And their *tayafah* identity, even though it is no longer linked to pastures and migration, continues to be an effective, and perhaps the most important, one for social and economic activites. When Bakhtiyari meet, the first question asked is one's *tayafah*, for it fits the individual into a hierarchical worldview that includes responsibilities and obligations. For those Bakhtiyari of the three large and extended elite families, the first question establishes relationships within them. These elite families, especially the Ilkhani and Hajji Ilkhani, function like a *tayafah* in terms of identity.

For elite and nonelite, nomadic and sedentary Bakhtiyari, education, urban

6. A member of the ʿulama asserted that the Bakhtiyari are not even Muslim (personal communication, May 1967).
7. Sekandar Amanolahi (personal communication, May 1992).

economic opportunities, and urban life in general have brought about significant change.

Increasingly, young Bakhtiyari men are abandoning traditional Bakhtiyari dress for jeans, running shoes, and army fatigues and the *khusravi* for the latest Tehran hairstyles. Bakhtiyari schoolgirls dress like their urban counterparts. Since the Revolution, education is widely available, even for nomads, and holds the promise of jobs, advanced education, and jobs in urban areas. Education is seen by the Bakhtiyari as important for both boys and girls as the way toward a more secure future. Education is also important in combatting the common urban attitude that regards the Bakhtiyari as uncivilized.

As members of the earlier Bakhtiyari elite were socialized to the norms of Iranian-Persian nationalism through Pahlavi-established institutions, the newly emerging Bakhtiyari middle class is being socialized through Islamic Republican institutions, especially schools and the military, to Islamic-Iranian values. And like the earlier Bakhtiyari elite, this new middle class seems little interested in developing a separate Bakhtiyari national identity.

A distinct Bakhtiyari identity persists, however, even for those who are sedentarized and urbanized. It persists at a level acceptable to Pahlavi-Islamic Republic representation—an identity comparable to a regional, cultural one that poses no threat to national identity and loyalty. And for the Bakhtiyari, pastoral nomad or urban, *tayafah* identity and representation continues to serve economic and social functions. After the Iranian Revolution and the establishment of the Islamic Republic, several Bakhtiyari *anjuman* (societies/clubs) emerged in Tehran and Shiraz. Their members were businessmen, engineers, and doctors who do not appear to come from the former elite families. Their activities included publication of a newspaper, *Anshan*,[8] and social and cultural meetings. They have not articulated an explicit political agenda.

Nationalism and the Kurds

Kurdish society is found in more places than Bakhtiyari society, and the Kurds are more heterogeneous. They constitute a far larger population spread over five states, where they have been influenced by nationalist movements in the Ottoman and Russian Empires and in Turkey, Iran, and among the Arabs.

Like the Bakhtiyari, some Kurds are urban, others rural; some are agriculturalists, and others are pastoralists. Some are members of the professional class. Many agriculturalists and pastoralists were—and continue to be—tribally organized, and their elites include landed magnates, religious figures (especially the leaders of Sufi brotherhoods), and pastoral leaders. For tribally organized

---

8. Anshan is the name of an important southern city in ancient Iran. It was located near the southeastern border of the Bakhtiyari and was presumably chosen for that reason.

Kurds, small groups form around essential economic and social relationships (Yalçin-Heckmann 1990). These are comparable to Bakhtiyari units. Although the Kurds were never centralized politically, confederations as large as those of the Bakhtiyari existed.

Nationalist leadership and support for Kurdish nationalism derive from twentieth-century political, economic, and social changes. Urbanization and the emergence of new elites have been especially important. For these elites, Kurdish identity is largely cultural and political. It is often a response to the nation-state's policies, including policies of suppression. Among agricultural villagers and pastoral nomads, tribal identities and organization continue to serve socioeconomic functions, and this sometimes conflicts with Kurdish nationalism.

Ruth Mandel argues that Alevi (a Shiʿi religious sect centered in Turkey) identity is constantly negotiated (Mandel 1990: 153–71). Taken further, one could argue that the majority of the Kurdish population, rural or recently urbanized, continues to imagine a variety of identities, depending on circumstances (Yalçin-Heckmann 1990: 303–304). Their primary identity, however, remains oriented around family, economic activities, and religion. Nationalist identity is contextual, which may account for the Kurds' failure to achieve nationalist goals of autonomy or a nation-state.

The urbanization or rural-urban migration of the past two decades, better characterized as the "ruralization" of cities (Hourani 1985, 1990), has probably resulted in an intensification of traditional identities, including religious ones. Some Kurds support nationalists, but on a traditionalist rather than a nationalist basis. Others have rejected traditional leaders who appeal to nationalist terms if they are seen as a threat to the traditional order. This may have been the case for Shaykh Saʿid in the early 1920s.

Kurds in small communities and rural areas continue to identify with traditional leaders, especially Sufi shaykhs or regional magnates. Shaykh ʿUbayd Allah, Shaykh Saʿid, and Simku Aqa were probably not nationalist leaders as much as they were members of traditional elites who sought personal aggrandizement by using a mix of traditional and nationalist rhetoric. The suppression of such leaders' attempts to unify the Kurds, even on a traditional basis, resulted in powerful ethnic and national symbols. Shaykh Saʿid became such a symbol.

Despite his status and commanding leadership, Shaykh Saʿid failed for a variety of reasons. Kurds in what was to become the Republic of Turkey may have seen nationalism as a threat to their socioeconomic well-being, as well as to their traditional worldview. Shaykh Saʿid's rebellion grew out of Kurdish nationalist movements that possibly date to 1921 (Olson: 41–42).[9] Just as

---

9. Prior to the abolition of the caliphate in 1924, the traditional order was defended by Mustafa Kemal, later styled Atatürk (Father-Turk), the great Turkish nationalist, Westernizer, and secularizer. As founder of the Republic, he was opposed by Kurds in general.

nationalism posed a challenge to the established order in the West, so it did in the Middle East. Earlier in the twentieth century and only in specific circumstances, however, have Kurdish tribal peoples—in their "infinite divisibility"—supported nationalist leaders, which helps explain the frustration of Kurdish nationalist aims. The experience of Kurdish leaders contrasts with that of Atatürk, who succeeded as a Turkish nationalist leader. Atatürk's success was the result of postwar conditions in the 1920s, the loss of non-Turkish areas of the empire (except for Kurdistan in Eastern Anatolia), the incompetence and acquiescence of the Ottomans to the dismemberment and occupation of Anatolia, and his own ability.

Urban backgrounds and education in Ottoman schools characterized the first Kurdish nationalist leaders, some of whom espoused Turkish nationalism. For example, Ziya Gokalp (Olson 1989: 16), who articulated Turkish nationalism before World War I, was a Kurd. Some middle-class Kurds have also accepted a Turkish identity within the Republic; others have retained cultural Kurdish affinities while rejecting political nationalism. Regional, social, cultural, and political divisions among Kurds—including their manipulation by Middle Eastern and Western states—have also frustrated Kurdish nationalist leaders.

Kurdish nationalism could have been seen by tribal people as a threat, especially during the establishment of the Turkish Republic in the 1920s, which brought the government army down upon Kurdish opposition. Or such events may have appeared to be another form of exploitation and the leaders political opportunists. Rural life has always been precarious in the Middle East. Economic and political organization requires an adaptability to changing conditions and resists centralization and domination, which inhibit response to changes.

Nationalism and its potential for change can also represent domination. Just as some of the old symbols are rejected by the emerging middle class, which provides leadership for nationalist movements, so too are new nationalist symbols and power sometimes seen as inappropriate by tribal people, especially pastoral nomads. They are perceived as domination by another name. To become a nationalist may be seen as abandoning the social mainstream of tribal society and thus as threatening to the individual as well as to the group.

The Turkish Republic's repression of the Kurds may have been more extreme than that of the Pahlavis in Iran, and it continues today. "Kurdish" political organization has not been tolerated. Such repression gives nationalist notions negative legitimacy. The impact of Iraq's state terrorism against the Kurds in 1991–92 remains to be seen. With lives and property at stake in the aftermath of the recent Gulf War, some Kurds in Iraq and Turkey have accepted nationalist leaders; others have opted for traditional or government leaders. Some have remained in their communities; others have fled. Nationalism, raditionalism, religious fundamentalism, and "apoliticalism" all represent alternate, even overlapping, responses to repression.

Contemporary Nationalism: Kurds and Bakhtiyari

How can we account for the presence of a nationalism among Kurds and its absence among the Bakhtiyari? Tribal people still conceive of themselves as members of a particular family, extended family, camp, subtribe, and tribe. To be a member of a tribe—or, more accurately, of a family (*tayafeh*, in the case of the Bakhtiyari)—meant access to pastures, water, and migration routes, and affiliation with regional and national leaders. Membership in a *tayafeh* provides a structure for social and economic interaction and relationships in an alien urban world. A specific territory and leaders add another dimension to identity—that is, memory or history—which provides a framework for the whole range of social, cultural, and political activities. The context, whether past or present, determines the nature and level of identity.

Historically, political negotiations were necessary for making decisions about herding, camping, or migrating, about insuring access to land for pastoralism, agriculture, water, and marketing, and about affiliating with other groups or leaders, whether tribal or government. Tribal groups, including confederations, were polymorphic in nature. They formed and, in some cases, disappeared. Tribal leaders, through the exercise of tribal power and organization, formed states. Many different confederacies, states, and empires have emerged: the Aqqoyunlu dynasty and empire in Anatolia and Iran, the Ottoman empire, and the Qajar dynasty in Iran. In Afghanistan and Central Asia, weak states emerged, and tribes retained great autonomy and power well into the twentieth century (Canfield 1991).

Change can be seen especially within the Kurdish population, where nationalists have provided leadership. These nationalists represent the values and backgrounds of a new middle class, especially the new professional middle class, which has adopted Western-style education and values. Some of these nationalists seek leadership opportunities. Kurdish tribal and religious leaders have also advocated nationalism as a way to reinforce their traditional roles and to broaden their base of support. Non-Kurds, including Western government officials, social scientists, and journalists,[10] have also advocated Kurdish political entity.

At the level of basic socioeconomic organization, especially the family, there may be little difference between the Bakhtiyari and the Kurds of Iran. One significant difference, however, is the role of shaykhs of various Sufi groups among the Kurds. Another would be the greater politicization of the Kurds following the White Revolution and the discriminatory state policies—such as uneven development—that resulted in the highest rate of demonstration in Iran

---

10. See, for example, *The Cambridge Encyclopedia of the Middle East and North Africa* (1988: 460–73), which has a category called "Peoples without a Country." It includes Armenians, Kurds, and Palestinians.

in 1977 and November 1978 (Parsa 1991). Also critical in Iranian Kurdistan was the organization of the Kurdish Democratic Party, with its Turkish and Iraqi influences, and the key role played in it by shopkeepers and other urban residents.

The new middle class, which would provide both the leaders and the core for Kurdish nationalist movements, can also be found among the Bakhtiyari,[11] although Bakhtiyari nationalism has yet to emerge. Bakhtiyari traditionalists, like their Kurdish counterparts, might regard a Bakhtiyari nationalist movement as irrelevant, if not threatening, to the social and economic order. Another critical factor is the history of the Bakhtiyari confederation and society. The confederation's elite—and closely associated with them, the *bastagan*, who represent the *ilkhani*'s and khans' nonelite network—have subordinated their Bakhtiyari identity to Iranian nationalism. The socialization of other Bakhtiyari to Iranian norms through Pahlavi and Islamic Republican institutions and their subordination of Bakhtiyari identity and representation to Iranian ones is similar. In mid-1992, it may be that Iranian Kurds are following the same pattern.

Conclusion

One last point returns us to the problem of perception, both in the West and in the Middle East, and the persistent misunderstanding of the nature of tribal society and its role in the contemporary Middle East. Tribal structures are adaptable, and the basic socioeconomic structures continue—are even adapted to urban settings—in spite of the extraordinary changes that have occurred. When "tribes" figure in contemporary history, as they have dramatically in the last decade in Afghanistan or in Turkey with the Kurds, they do so in terms of the state's or others' representation of society. In both the Afghan and Turkish context, "tribes" does not prefigure a resurgence of tribal power but a way of organizing society for a specific military or political purpose.

Tribal structures have proved adaptable, and they have persisted, although not on the scale of the past. The Islamic Revolution of 1978–79 in Iran masked Reza Shah's more profound change in the nation-state's representation, a representation that does not allow for competing identities and loyalties, including tribal ones. Beginning with Reza Shah, new internal frontiers of official identity were inculcated through state-controlled education and media.

Nationalist, modern, and Western "frontiers" under the Pahlavis and Islamic "frontiers" under the Islamic Republic set acceptable limits for the identities and allegiances of the population within Iranian boundaries. The Bakhtiyari

---

11. The Treaty of Sèvres (1920) brought a Kurdish state into being for a brief period after World War I, but the Treaty of Lausanne (1923) recognized Turkish sovereignty.

have accepted those boundaries. The *"ought"* (Reynolds 1985: 399–400) or the "moral unity" (Dresch 1990: 281) in this case has been enforced by the nation-state. The Iranian case is not unique: the same phenomenon has occurred in Turkey, Iraq, and Soviet Central Asia. The Kurds present a more complex case. Clearly, in both Iraq and Turkey, many Kurds regard themselves as a nation that should find expression as a nation-state; this is less clear for the Kurds in Iran. And in twentieth-century Kurdish history, the outcome of a Kurdish state continues to be uncertain and dependent not just on a Kurdish notion of "ought," but on the role of Middle Eastern states as well as others.

References

Anderson, Benedict (1983). *Imagined Communities: Reflections on the Origin and Spread of Nationalism.* London and New York: Verso.
Bates, Daniel G. (1984). "Kurds." In *Muslim Peoples: A World Ethnographic Survey,* I, ed. Richard V. Weekes, pp. 421–27. Westport, Conn.: Greenwood Press.
Beck, Lois (1984). "Qashqa'i." In *Muslim Peoples: A World Ethnographic Survey,* II, ed. Richard V. Weekes, pp. 631–37. Westport, Conn.: Greenwood Press.
——— (1990). "Tribe and the State in Nineteenth- and Twentieth-Century Iran." In *Tribes and State Formation in the Middle East,* ed. Philip S. Khoury and Joseph Kostiner, pp. 185–225. Berkeley: University of California Press.
Canfield, Robert, ed. (1991). *Turko-Persia in Historical Perspective.* Cambridge: Cambridge University Press.
Caton, Steven C. (1990). "Anthropological Theories of Tribe and State Formation in the Middle East: Ideology and the Semiotics of Power." In *Tribes and State Formation in the Middle East,* ed. Philip S. Khoury and Joseph Kostiner, pp. 74–108. Berkeley: University of California Press.
Crossley, Pamela Kyle (1990). "Thinking About Ethnicity in Early Modern China." *Late Imperial China* 11, no. 1 (June): 1–35.
Digard, Jean-Pierre (1979). "De la necéssité et des inconvénients, pour un Baxtyâri, d'être Baxtyâri: Communauté, territoire et inegalité chez des pasteurs nomade d'Iran." In *Pastoral Production and Society.* Paris and Cambridge: Cambridge University Press.
——— (1983). "On the Bakhtiari: Comments on 'Tribes, Confederation and the State.'" In *The Conflict of Tribe and State in Iran and Afghanistan,* ed. Richard L. Tapper, pp. 331–36. London: Croom Helm.
Dresch, Paul (1990). "Imams and Tribes: The Writing and Acting of History in Upper Yemen." In *Tribes and State Formation in the Middle East,* ed. Philip S. Khoury and Joseph Kostiner, pp. 226–51. Berkeley: University of California Press.
Eickelman, Dale F. (1989). *The Middle East: An Anthropological Approach,* 2nd ed. Englewood Cliffs, N.J.: Prentice Hall.
Garthwaite, Gene R. (1983). *Khans and Shahs: A Documentary Analysis of the Bakhtiyari in Iran.* Cambridge: Cambridge University Press.
——— (1984). "Bakhtiari." In *Muslim Peoples: A World Ethnographic Survey,* I, ed. Richard V. Weekes, pp. 81–84. Westport, Conn.: Greenwood Press.
Glass, Charles (1990). *Tribes with Flags: A Dangerous Passage through the Chaos of the Middle East.* New York: Atlantic Monthly Press.
Hourani, Albert (1985). "Political Society in Lebanon: A Historical Introduction."

Inaugural Lecture of the Emile Bustani Middle East Seminar, October 3 (Cambridge: Massachusetts Institute of Technology, Center for International Studies).
——— (1990). *Times Literary Supplement*, March 2–8, pp. 219–20.
Irons, William (1974). "Nomadism as Political Adaptation: The Case of the Yomut Turkmen." *American Ethnologist* I: 635–58.
Khazanov, A. M. (1984). *Nomads and the Outside World*. Cambridge: Cambridge University Press.
Khoury, Philip S., and Joseph Kostiner, eds. (1990). *Tribes and State Formation in the Middle East*. Berkeley: University of California Press.
Mandel, Ruth (1990). "Shifting Centres and Emergent Identities: Turkey and Germany in the Lives of Turkish Gastarbeiter." In *Muslim Travellers: Pilgrimage, Migration, and the Religious Imagination*, ed. Dale F. Eickelman and James Piscatori, pp. 153–71. Berkeley: University of California Press.
Mostyn, Trevor, ed. (1988). *The Cambridge Encyclopedia of the Middle East and North Africa*. Cambridge: Cambridge University Press.
Olson, Robert (1989). *The Emergence of Kurdish Nationalism and the Sheikh Said Rebellion, 1880–1925*. Austin: University of Texas Press.
Parsa, Misagh (1991). Personal communication, Hanover, New Hampshire (December).
Reynolds, Susan (1985). "What do We Mean by 'Anglo-Saxon' and 'Anglo-Saxons'?" *Journal of British Studies* 24 (October): 399–400.
Spooner, Brian (1983). "Who Are the Baluch? A Preliminary Investigation into the Dynamics of an Ethnic Identity from Qajar Iran." In *Qajar Iran: Political, Social and Cultural Change 1800–1925*, ed. Edmund Bosworth and Carole Hillenbrand, pp. 93–110. Edinburgh: Edinburgh University Press.
Tapper, Richard L., ed. (1983). *The Conflict of Tribe and State in Iran and Afghanistan*. London: Croom Helm.
——— (1988). "Ethnicity, Order and Meaning in the Anthropology of Iran and Afghanistan." In *Le Fait Ethnique en Iran et en Afghanistan*, ed. Jean-Pierre Digard, pp. 21–31. Paris: Editions du CNRS.
——— (1990). "Anthropologists, Historians, and Tribespeople on Tribe and State Formation in the Middle East." In *Tribes and State Formation in the Middle East*, ed. Philip S. Khoury and Joseph Kostiner, pp. 48–73. Berkeley: University of California Press.
van Bruinessen, Maarten M. (1978). *Agha, Shaikh, and State: On the Social and Political Organization of Kurdistan*. Utrecht: privately published.
——— (1992). *Agha, Shaikh, and State: The Social and Political Structures of Kurdistan*. London: Zed Books.
Yalçin-Heckmann, Lâle (1990). "Kurdish Tribal Organisation and Local Political Processes." In *Turkish State, Turkish Society*, ed. Andrew Finkel and Nükhet Sirman, pp. 289–312. London: Routledge.

Part IV
Pakistan

IX

ISLAM AND THE STATE
IN PAKISTAN

Vyacheslav Ya. Belokrenitsky

As is the case with countries like Turkey, Egypt, and Iran, Pakistani history is marked by the competitive and antagonistic political and ideological currents which are rooted in the concepts of Islam and Muslim solidarity. These currents can be divided into two broad categories: secular/modernist, and traditionalist/fundamentalist. The secular/modernist current, represented in Pakistan by figures like Muhammad Iqbal (c. 1876–1938) and Muhammad 'Ali Jinnah (1876–1948), predominated from the early 1930s to the 1970s. After the humiliating defeat of Pakistan's armed forces in East Bengal in 1971 and the creation of Bangladesh, the search for a national identity began anew and brought about the growing influence of a traditionalist/fundamentalist sentiment. This period of reappraisal in Pakistan coincided with the tide of Islamic activism in Arab countries and in Iran, another stronghold of Islam. Islamic revivalism continues today, and the Pakistani experience is a significant part of it.

Pakistan differs remarkably from the rest of the Indian subcontinent in climate, environment, economy, and culture. It straddles the two broadly defined cultural areas of South Asia and the Middle East. Indeed, Pakistan may, to some extent, be regarded as constituting part of Southwest or Central Asia rather than South Asia. From the point of view of ethnic composition, only eastern Punjabis and *muhajirs* (post-1947 migrants who came primarily from India and their descendants) can be considered South Asians. The Pakhtun and Baluch are of Iranian origin, while western Punjabis and Sindis claim their origins in both South Asian and the Middle East.

For the past nine hundred years, the Indus Valley and the central and western parts of the Punjab have constituted a frontier zone between the Indian and Turko-Persian peoples. The area has been associated at different times with states and empires to its east and west, although for much of its history, it formed part of northern and central India, which was ethnically and culturally Turko-Persian (Canfield 1991).

Although the number of Muslims is almost equal in Pakistan, Bangladesh, and India, they comprise only about 20 percent of the population of the region. This means that the place of Islam and the relationship between religion and politics differs considerably in the respective countries (see, for example, Wright 1984). In India, Muslims are a minority population, whereas in Pakistan and Bangladesh, they constitute the overwhelming majority.

The situation in Bangladesh is significantly different from that of Pakistan. Bangladesh is more or less ethnically and linguistically homogeneous. Minorities live almost exclusively in the Chittagong Hill Tracts. This homogeneity makes it unnecessary for religion to play an integrative role, although externally—vis-à-vis another part of the Bengali language region (West Bengal and India)—Islam fulfills a nation-building function.

While no single pattern exists for relations between religion and politics in South Asia, I would suggest that Pakistan has much more in common in this respect with the countries to its west and northwest—for example, Iran and Afghanistan—than with India and Sri Lanka.

In the first part of this chapter I discuss three themes. The first is the encounter between Muslim India and the British, the gradual Muslim revival, and the different trends in its framework and their connection with the movement that led to the formation of Pakistan. The second outlines the recent history of Pakistan, which I divide into two periods: from the 1940s to the 1960s, when the state was basically a secular one; and from the 1970s to the 1990s, when the state became increasingly Islamic. The third issue is the controversy between Islamic Pakistani nationalism and ethnic nationalisms. In conclusion, I discuss how Islamization is related to an international ideological context.

Muslim Awakening and the State

Pakistan emerged as an independent state through a combination of factors and trends that marked the final days of colonial India, but the roots of the politicization of Indian Muslims can be traced to the first decades of the rule of the East India Company over the territories of Mughal India and the first encounter between indigenous—chiefly Islamic—administrative and legal systems and European institutions. Changes in the prevailing local order had become profound in the 1820s and 1830s, initially in Bengal, then in the main British center in India. During this period the traditional legal system, based on principles of Islamic codes of personal, civil, and criminal law and those of the Hanafi school (*madhhab*) (which were collected at the order of the last great Mughul, Aurangzeb, in the voluminous *Fatawa-i Alamgiri*), were replaced by a mixture of elements derived from *shari'a* and British juridical norms. English judges administered justice with the help of Islamic legal scholars called *mawlawi*s (Collins 1988a: 680).

The defeat of the anti-British forces in the mutiny of 1857–59 and the establishment of direct British rule over the whole of Mughal India speeded up the demise of the old legal system. With the adoption of the Penal Code of 1860 and the Code of Criminal Procedure the following year, the role of the Muslim judges was drastically reduced. In 1864, the Institute of *mawlawis* was abolished, and English judges began to interpret Islamic public law (Collins 1988b: 541–43).

It should be stressed that the sociopolitical regime established by the British stimulated the growth of Muslim communalism, despite the fact that the British probably aimed at keeping it to a minimum. In some views of an Islamic state (see examples in Masud [1990]), Muslims as a community submit to state authority, whether that authority be *khalifa* or sultan, provided that the rulers adhere to the provisions of the *sharica*. This was generally the case in Mughal India, although its rulers were compelled to introduce certain concessions to Islamic norms to meet the demands of a non-Muslim majority (Gilmartin 1988: 13).

The decline of the Mughal Empire and its final abolition forced Muslim theologians (the *culama*) to confront the necessity of finding a place in the new sociopolitical order, where they were deprived of close links to state power. They realized that they must appeal directly to the Muslim masses to enliven and renew the spiritual life of the community. As a result of this appeal, there was an Islamic resurgence in India, which was based on the writings of Shah Wali Allah. In 1867, this resurgence resulted in the organization of Dar ul-'Ulum in Deoband (Metcalf 1982; Alavi 1986: 28–32).

Parallel with the process of Islamic revival and the strengthening of different fundamentalist and traditionalist organizations was the development of Islamic modernism and intellectual trends close to what one might call secular, lay ideology. These trends were popular among the traditional Muslim salaried class who had lost their positions of prominence in the early days of the British Raj. In an effort to regain their former professional and social status, they were compelled to set aside their prejudices about European education and overcome the fear that their children would cease to be Muslims if they attended Christian schools (Chhabra 1962: 76).

Modernist ideas were first reflected in the social activities and literary work of Sir Sayyid Ahmad Khan (1817–98), one of the founders of Aligarh Muslim University, the center of Indian Islamic modernism. The number of Indians receiving a European education increased considerably in the 1870s and 1880s, and after World War I the process accelerated dramatically. The process of strengthening Muslim political identity was also helped by the British policy of taking account of and nourishing the complex structure of Indian society.

The gap between Muslims and non-Muslims in education, social status, and material well-being was most evident in Bengal and northern India. In the northwestern region of the subcontinent, the situation was very different. There Muslims constituted the majority, in both urban and rural areas, and the Muslim elite was much more safely ensconced in the traditional society. Furthermore, the British faced a significantly altered Mughal system of law and order in the northwest. In the Punjab they replaced a hybrid Sikh administration. Sind gained its independence from the Mughal Empire in 1711, almost a hundred and fifty years before it was annexed by the British in 1843.

Throughout the second half of the nineteenth century, the colonial administration attempted to remain impartial toward Muslims and non-Muslims. This was reflected in the attitude of both central and provincial governments. In certain quarters of the British bureaucracy, however, there was pressure to abandon this policy, and in 1900–1901, two significant administrative actions underlined the importance of the Muslim factor. First, a new province called the Northwest Frontier, populated primarily by Muslims, was carved out of the Punjab. Second, the Land Alienation Act was passed. It discriminated against non-Muslims in the Punjab (primarily Hindu money-lenders and traders) (Government of India 1914). The Muslim position was further strengthened by other decisions of the Anglo-Indian administration. Chief among them were the division of Bengal in 1906, which created a Muslim majority in East Bengal, and the separation of Sind from Bombay in 1935, which increased the number of predominantly Muslim provinces.

In the first half of the twentieth century, secular and modernist trends in the Muslim awakening proved stronger than traditionalist and fundamentalist trends. The main objective behind the former was a political one: achieving autonomy and/or sovereignty for Indian Muslims. The real driving force of this movement emanated from the Muslim elite's fear of losing status, power, and wealth in the event of British withdrawal and subsequent Hindu rule. The feeling grew stronger in 1937–39, years when the Indian National Congress held power in several states.

A second current of traditionalist and fundamentalist feeling espoused the spread of Islamic values in India, the revival of traditions of Muslim rule over the country, and the building of a traditional Islamic state based on the principles of shari*a.

Only during the election campaign of 1946 did groups of the *ulama in the Punjab, who were close to traditionalist organizations and represented "popular" Islam, decide to support the Muslim League and its call for a separate Muslim state. Although this support was of considerable importance, Pakistan came into being chiefly due to the secular-modernist political movement (see, for example, Hardy 1972; Sayeed 1978; Dani 1981).

From Muslim State to Islamic State

The first phase of Pakistani history (1947–71) was characterized by the predominance of secular trends. The country was not a theocracy or theodemocracy but a nation-state run by civil and military bureaucracies and politicians drawn from landowning aristocrats and the families of industrial tycoons.

Many leading figures of the second current in Muslim politico-ideological life, the *ʿulama*, had changed their minds after Pakistan became a reality. The most important factor in effecting this change was the decision of Mawlana Mawdudi to settle in Pakistan, where his idea of establishing the true Islamic order could be implemented.

The efforts of religious figures to change the character of the state initially met with considerable opposition, and the religiopolitical organization Jamaʿat-i Islami suffered a defeat in the beginning of the 1950s. Compelled to act as an ordinary party in the parliamentary type of political system, Mawdudi's organization was unsuccessful in mobilizing mass support, as was clearly demonstrated by the results of the 1970 general elections.

The issue of the state secularizing is very controversial in the Islamic world (Abbott 1966; Ahmad 1988; Ahmad 1988: 229–46; Rosenthal 1965). On the one hand, since there is no church or clerical hierarchy in Islam, it seems impossible to separate church from state. On the other, since Islam penetrates into every corner of individual and social life, it determines and regulates both spiritual and sociopolitical spheres. Thus it is difficult to see how the state in the world of Islam can have secular features.

In its first phase, Pakistan was not in any way an Islamic state, but it could not be considered a secular one either. In the Objectives Resolution adopted by the Constituency Assembly in 1949, Islamic principles were very directly stated. They were repeated in the preamble to the constitution of 1956, which proclaimed Pakistan an Islamic republic. Ideological battles over the second constitution (approved in 1962) ended in favor of conservative Islamists (fundamentalists and traditionalists), and their influence increased in the second half of the 1960s.

The second phase of modern Pakistani history began in 1971, the year of a new split in the subcontinent, with the formation of Bangladesh. The year was marked by growing Islamization of economic, political, and social life. In the early 1970s, Islamic phraseology was used more successfully by the forces representing the secular/modernist current. Islam as a raison d'être of Pakistan was included as a cornerstone of Islamic socialism, a slogan later raised by the Pakistan People's Party (PPP) and its leader, Zulfiqar Ali Bhutto. In the late 1960s, when the PPP was founded, socialism seemed to play a leading part in its ideology.

Soon after the party came to power, socialism and Islam changed places. Islamic concepts were extensively used in the text of the 1973 constitution. Concern about the growing role of Islamic elements in Pakistani politics was amply demonstrated by the Bhutto government's decision in 1974 to declare members of the Ahmadiyya sect non-Muslims. Pakistan's foreign policy became oriented, to a large extent, toward the Islamic world, with oil-rich Muslim countries beginning to act as aid donors. Socialistic modernist Islamization came to an end in 1977, and with the military's assumption of power, the second ideological current became for the first time a leading one.

It should be emphasized that in the composition of this politico-ideological current, certain changes occurred in the mid-1970s, at the time the Pakistan National Alliance was formed to counter the PPP. The current was joined by some sections of secular-modernist origin, politically represented by offshoots of Qa'id-i Aᶜzam's Muslim League.

General Muhammad Zia ul-Haq, as Chief Martial Law Administrator and President, promulgated a number of Islamic laws and regulations. Besides playing a legitimizing role for the army, generals violated the constitution with their coup d'état, Islamization proved a rallying factor for centripetal forces in the country and an important instrument of foreign policy.

Islamization, as carried out by the military government, affected credit and capital and fiscal, legal, and social arrangements. In an attempt to eliminate usury, modern banking practices were substituted, with procedures for sharing profits and losses. The state took care of collecting Islamic taxes, *zakat* [alms] and ᶜ*ushr* [tithe]. *Zakat* committees were established to insure that the sums collected reached the deserving ("Islamization of the Economy" 1985: 1–18). Islamic penal laws (*hudud*) were introduced, and special Shariᶜa benches were created in the High and Supreme Courts. The observation of Islamic social requirements pertaining primarily to the role of women were demanded by the state authorities. Pakistan under Zia ul-Haq turned out to be one of the few countries approaching the status of an Islamic state. In some aspects, Pakistan was ahead of clergy-ruled Iran and following in step with Saudi Arabia and the Arab Emirates (Esposito 1987).

The death of Zia ul-Haq brought a change in Pakistan's political life. In the general elections of 1988, the PPP won the majority of seats in the parliament, and its leader, Benazir Bhutto, formed the government. The return to power of modernist/secularists was too short-lived to change the trend of the politico-ideological process, however. Furthermore, the position of the government was weak. It faced strong opposition in the National and Provincial Assemblies and was flanked by both the president and the generals. The process of Islamization was not reversed during Bhutto's period in power. Indeed, additional steps toward Islamization were taken, partly to embarrass the government. In May 1990, the senate (the upper chamber of the parliament) passed the Shariᶜat Bill. It went further in changing basic provisions of the constitutional set-up than Zia-ul Haq's Shariᶜa Ordinance of June 1988. The bill, which calls for insuring the enforcement of *shariᶜa*, contains the provision that "*shariᶜa* shall be the supreme law of Pakistan . . . and shall have effect, notwithstanding anything contained in any other law, custom, or usage" (*Viewpoint*, May 24, 1990: 13). After the Bhutto government was dismissed, the president promulgated the Qisas and Diya Ordinances with the aim of further Islamicizing the Pakistani penal code.

The victory of the Islami Jamhuri Ittihad [Islamic Democratic Alliance] in the 1990 elections raised the question of how far Islamization would go. After the elections, the ruling alliance included parties representing almost all ideological and religiopolitical shades and currents, from fundamentalists through traditionalists, although some of them stood apart from modernists of a non-socialistic brand. It is now a matter of no surprise to see the political heirs of the Qa'id-i A'zam and Maulana Maududi in one boat, and this boat seems to drift with the winds of time from the bank of secularization to that of Islamization.

Moreover, it seems that there is a real barrier between Islamicization's not adversely affecting economic progress and measures which can impede it. It seems that the policy of economic liberalization, which was followed by several consecutive Pakistani governments, may continue and prove successful, regardless of further steps toward Islamizing Pakistani society and the economy, but any overreaching drift from the principles of modern economic and social life might have a retrogressive effect and stand in the way of further progress.

Islamic versus Ethnic Nationalism

The term "Islamic nationalism" is, to a certain extent, a contradiction in terms. Islam is simultaneously national and trans-national. Princely and empire-type state formations were of course well known to Islamic civilization. Modern "nation-state" concepts were only introduced during the colonial epoch in the interaction of European and Muslim societies. Pakistani nationalism is one of those modern ideologies which aims at establishing and preserving the sovereignty of one nation, whether derived from the notion of ethnicity or nationality or from more than one ethnic entity. It relies upon the "two-nations" theory advocated by Jinnah. The idea that the Muslims of India constituted one nation (Muslim nationhood), as Islam determined a specific social order, was put forward but never elaborated, perhaps because of the difficulties of going too deeply into the subject (Ahmad 1988: 230; Naim 1979).

Ethnic nationalism or subnationalism is also quite a new ideological concept. Each of the four major ethnic nationalisms of Pakistan has its peculiar features. The most developed and politically active Sindi nationalism relies upon the long historical tradition of pre-Muslim India or Harappan civilization, with the archaeological site of Mohenjo-Daro serving as its main symbol. Before 1947, the national culture of the Sindis was developed, to a considerable extent, by the activities of Sindi Hindus. The literary Sindi language came of age only in the 1920s, and its present-day written form developed largely after the creation of Pakistan, when Sindi Hindus emigrated to India (Ageev 1986: 250–63).

Baluchi nationalism is still younger and now of lesser significance in comparison with Sindi but potentially of an explosive character, with its traditions of waging prolonged and vehement struggle against Pakistan's central authorities and the army.

The national culture of Afghans or Pushtuns is a complex phenomenon, with some remarkable differences between large tribal and territorial units. In Pakistan alone, there are three parts in predominantly Pushtun territory: North-Western Frontier Province, Federal Administrative Tribal Area, and North-Western districts of Baluchistan Province. Inspired by virtually the same historical and literary sources, Pushtun nationalism is divided. Probably its time has not yet come.

The case of Punjabi nationalism is a very special one. Punjabis constitute approximately 60 percent of the country's population. Despite this majority, their mother tongue, Punjabi, is neglected, and Urdu, a Persianized variant of Hindustani and the acknowledged medium of Muslims of northern India and the Deccan, continues to serve as a standard language of education in high schools; in colleges and universities, it shares this position with English. Haphazard efforts to develop literary Punjabi have recently become more consistent, but there is not ample ground for a takeoff of Punjabi nationalism.

Major ethnonationalistic trends are weakened by the growing strength of second-order nationalisms or subnationalisms (relying upon self-identities of smaller ethnic groups traditionally incorporated into larger ones) such as Brahui (Brohi) in the Baluchi area and Hindko in the Pushtun. The most important of them is the Siraiki subnationalism in the western and southern Punjab.

One common feature of ethnic nationalisms is their secular character. Islamic elements are certainly present in the national cultures, but Islam does not constitute a rallying point in ideologies of this type.

National movements in Pakistan made their appearance soon after the creation of the state, and from the very beginning, there have been two major currents among intellectuals and politicians: socialistic, and liberal/democratic. Socialist and pro-Communist thinking was quite influential at the time of the Second World War and immediately thereafter. This can be explained by the military successes of Stalin's Soviet Union and the uncertain nature of the postwar sociopolitical evolution in the world.

Characteristic of the influence socialistic forces had in the 1940s is the fact that the author of the Muslim League Programme of 1944 was Daniel Latifi, a leftist who was close to some Communist Party members. It is also not coincidence that Jinnah, an adherent of liberalism and private economy, used the term "socialism"—or rather, "Islamic socialism"—in his speeches in 1947 and 1948. This preoccupation with ideas of social reformation resulted in an ethnic/national character of opposition to the ruling circles of the newborn country and the latter's efforts to impose one language (Urdu), one ideology (Pakistani), and one social model (Western).

From the late 1970s, the crisis of socialistic thinking among ideologues of ethnic nationalisms became progressively more manifest, and the strength of leftist parties and organizations in all the provinces of Pakistan dwindled. Correspondingly, one can observe the growing strength of the other current: liberal/democratic—politically represented by ethnically oriented, nonideological parties and movements such as Muhajir Qawmi Mahaz, Jiye Sind, and others. The change of paradigm from socialistic to liberal was well pronounced in Sind, where the popularity of leftist and Communist intellectuals like Rasul Bakhsh Palejo and Jam Saqi abated and was succeeded by that of figures such as Muhammad Ibrahim Joyo.

It is interesting to note that Islam, as the basis of statehood, is totally rejected by Joyo. Accepting the stand taken by Jinnah, he vigorously refuted the policy of Islamists: "Even though the Qa'id-i A^czam [Jinnah] never used the phrase 'Islamic state,' self-righteous, half-baked Muslim priests, full of self-conceited rhetoric as their chief weapon, . . . pushed forward, claiming superiority of their truth in Islam, to contend for their sole right to build and run Pakistan as an authentic Islamic state" (Joyo 1990: 3). Elsewhere he emphasized that "Islam as a primarily metaphysical system, like all other metaphysical systems, had no potential left to integrate whole societies, not to say varied societies" (Joyo 1987: vii), meaning that there is no Pakistani society as such, only Sindi, Punjabi, Pushtun, and other societies.

Conclusion

The ideological situation in the world differs significantly from that of the decades immediately following the Second World War. The late 1940s and 1950s, with the Cold War between East and West, saw ideological rivalry spilling into the newly independent countries. The futility of ideological struggle between capitalism and socialism or Communism, proclaimed by certain Western intellectual circles in the 1950s, seemed to be unconvincing to most of the intelligentsia until the late 1980s. Now the rivalry of ideologies based on secular principles seems to have come to an end, although this is not accepted unanimously. In any case, the international ideological climate has recently suffered a drastic change, and the intensity of conflicting secular ideas has diminished. It remains to be seen whether the ideological vacuum will be filled by a new kind of opposition or whether a qualitatively different situation in the field of international relations will emerge.

Beginning in the early 1970s, the Islamic factor has come to play an important role in interstate and intrastate relationships, in national and international politics. An Islamic "boom" affects internal affairs in many Muslim countries and in communities of Muslims in non-Muslim countries. Pakistan, naturally, is no exception and not only reflects the Islamic resurgence but contributes significantly to this process.

Muslim sentiments in Pakistan will almost certainly continue to play an important role in ideological and political life and in the lives of individuals (as indicated by Kurin) and of institutions (as illustrated by Novossyolov). This is to be expected from a country with almost complete religious homogeneity. What is not certain is which trend or current of Islamic forces will have the upper hand. With leftist Islamic socialist trends profoundly shaken and reduced to a microscopic dimension, the main controversy would probably involve the centrist-modernist and fundamentalist groups, but the possibility is there for these controversies to remain subdued if challenged by centrifugal forces united around slogans of ethnic nationalism and separatism.

Much depends on future economic considerations, which would be considerably influenced by external factors. The success of the present economic liberalization policy and steady economic improvement will provide a chance for strengthening modernist elements among Islamic—or, putting it in Urdu, *Islam Pasand* [Islam loving]—forces. Should a slackening of the pace of national economic growth occur, economic troubles and social tensions would help fundamentalist and traditionalist groups to gain and hold on to people's imaginations and to channel popular sentiment to the attainment of goals that can be characterized as retrograde, although they may contain elements of cultural value. In the international field, it might lead to actions inspired by Islamic, Muslim solidarity. At the same time, developments like these will help to breathe life into political movements of an ethnonationalistic character and once again put Pakistan under pressure from within.

References

Abbott, F. (1966). "Pakistan and the Secular State." In *South Asian Politics and Religion*, ed. Donald E. Smith, pp. 352–70. Princeton: Princeton University Press.

Ageev, Valery F. (1986). *Noveishaia istoriia Sinda* [Modern History of Sind], special supplement on Sindi literature. Moscow: Nauka Publishing House (Urdu edition: Karachi: Pakistan Publishers, 1990).

Ahmad, Iqbal (1985). *The Concept of an Islamic State*. Stockholm.

Ahmad, Mumtaz (1988). "Pakistan." In *The Politics of Islamic Revivalism*, ed. Shireen T. Hunter, pp. 229–46. Bloomington: Indiana University Press.

Alavi, Hamza (1986). "Ethnicity: Muslim Society and the Pakistan Ideology." In *Islamic Reassertion in Pakistan: The Application of Islamic Laws in a Modern State*, ed. Anita M. Weiss, pp. 21–48. Syracuse: Syracuse University Press.

Canfield, Robert L., ed. (1991). *Turko-Persia in Historical Perspective*. Cambridge: Cambridge University Press.

Chhabra, C. S. (1962). *Social and Economic History of the Punjab (1845–1901)*. Jullender: Punjab Book Press.

Collins, Daniel P. (1988a). "Islamicization of Pakistan's Law," *The Oxford History of India*, 4th ed. Delhi: Oxford University Press.

——— (1988b). "Islamization of Pakistani Law: A Historical Perspective," *Stanford Journal of International Law*, 24, no. 2 (Spring): 511–84.

Dani, Ahmad Hasan, ed. (1981). *Founding Fathers of Pakistan*. Islamabad: Qaid-i Azam University.

Esposito, John L. (1987). *Islam and Politics*, 2nd ed. Syracuse: Syracuse University Press.

Gilmartin, David (1988). *Empire and Islam: Punjab and the Making of Pakistan*. Berkeley: University of California Press.

Government of India. (1914). *Punjab Land Administration Acts and Rules Having the Force of Law Thereunder*, vol. I: *Acts*. Lahore: Civil and Military Gazette Press.

Hardy, Peter (1972). *The Muslims of British India*. London: Cambridge University Press.

"Islamization of the Economy" (1985). In *Pakistan Economic Survey, 1984–1985*. Islamabad: Government of Pakistan.

Joyo, Muhammad Ibrahim. (1990). Paper presented at Goethe-Institut seminar, Karachi, March 3.

—— (1987). "Introduction." In *Sorrows of Sind*, ed. G. M. Mehkri, pp. 1–16. Hyderabad, Sind: Sindi Adabi Board.

Masud, Muhammad Khalid (1990). "The Obligation to Migrate: The Doctrine of *hijra* in Islamic Law." In *Muslim Travellers: Pilgrimage, Migration, and the Religious Imagination*, ed. Dale F. Eickelman and James Piscatori, pp. 29–49. London: Routledge; Berkeley and Los Angeles: University of California Press.

Metcalf, Barbara Daly (1982). *Islamic Revival in British India: Deoband, 1860–1900*. Princeton: Princeton University Press.

Naim, C. M., ed. (1979). *Iqbal, Jinnah and Pakistan: The Vision and the Reality*. Syracuse: Syracuse University Press.

Rosenthal, E. I. J. (1965). *Islam and the Modern National State*. Cambridge: Cambridge University Press.

Sayeed, Khalid B. (1978). *Pakistan: The Formative Phase, 1857–1948*. Karachi: Pakistan Publishing House.

Viewpoint (1990). May 24, p. 13. Lahore.

Wright, Thomas F., Jr. (1984). *Methodology of Research on Indian Muslims*. Lahore: University of the Punjab, Centre for South Asian Study.

X

THE ISLAMIZATION OF WELFARE IN PAKISTAN

Dimitri B. Novossyolov

The Islamization of Pakistan's social life was the product of a political decision taken by the country's military, with General Muhammad Zia ul-Haq, Pakistan's president from 1978 to 1988, at its head. For some scholars, Zia's apparently genuine piety, which no doubt contributed to his decision to Islamize, has deflected attention from state-sponsored "Islamization" as a means to secure legitimacy for military rule. Only later did his regime try to broaden the social bases of its support.

In the preceding chapter, Vyacheslav Belokrenitsky provided an overview of the Islamic and Muslim currents which have shaped politics and the state in Pakistan. In this chapter, I argue that the state's takeover of Islamic taxes—*zakat* and *ʿushur*—which had previously been voluntary, profoundly altered the nature of these religious obligations. The complex networks of local committees to collect and distribute these taxes created a broad base of local representation at a time when democratic institutions were absent in Pakistan. Local and regional committees acted as mobilizing centers for the government, something alien to the basic concept of Islamic welfare.

Like other elements of the state apparatus, these committees were widely perceived as corrupt and inefficient, although politically active elements of the population appreciated the uses to which they could be put. The analysis of how Islamic welfare legislation was implemented in Pakistan suggests the limits of state-sponsored Islamization when such measures fail to receive widespread popular support. It also suggests how state sponsorship profoundly modifies the meaning and practice of religious obligations.

Islamization in Pakistan, in contrast to many other countries, was clearly a movement from the top down. Inclusion of some elements of Islamic law (*shariʿa*) into the criminal code could not decisively put such aims into effect. For this reason, Zia ul-Haq's socioeconomic program concentrated additionally on dealing with usury by creating an interest-free banking system. Far more significant, however, was the introduction, in 1980, of a kind of Islamic social-security system based on compulsory payment by Muslims of a "clearing" tax (alms to the deserving, or *mustahaqin*) in the form of *zakat*.

Zakat—and *ushr*, its agricultural equivalent—is one of the five pillars of Islam on which the entire edifice rests.[1] Unlike *salat* [obligatory prayer], *sawm* [fasting], *hajj* [pilgrimage to Mecca], or *jihad* [holy war], *zakat* implies a Muslim's duties relative not only to god (*huquq-i elahi*) but also to a fellow being (*huquq-i ebad*). Theoretically it means social justice through the redistribution of material resources to those in need. In fact, a network has been established in Pakistan to collect and distribute the revenues, which amount to billions of rupees. This system has had unprecedented consequences for Pakistani society.

Although the Islamic welfare system has proven quite viable for more than ten years in Pakistan, some "experts," mostly those of Pakistan's neo-Marxists,[2] deny that the authoritarian regime has actually achieved any social transformation—a projection of their political antipathy onto the institutions that time has actually shown to be successful. On the one hand, this criticism unavoidably leads to an oversimplification of the current system and a vulgar class analysis. Hassan Gardezi maintains that "a few changes were also introduced in order to extend Shari῾a into the areas of taxation and finance, such as compulsory payment of *zakat*, . . . but these have no more than cosmetic value" (Gardezi 1990: 24; see also Haque 1983). A similar view is shared by Ziaul Haque, a Pakistani expert who described the Islamization of the 1980s: "Under this process, rituals were practically used . . . and interpreted . . . as a social and economic system, whereas in practice, these rituals were used to promote the interests of the rich elites, the capitalists, feudals" (Haque 1990: 24).

By focusing attention on the self-evident necessity of changing the sociopolitical structures that "perpetuate the exploitation," these researchers abandon in advance the idea of the major role these new institutions (*zakat* and *ushr*, among others) could play in society (Khan 1986). Such an approach fails to consider that, whatever the initial motivation of the regime leaders, the newly introduced institutions are in harmony with the historic roots and religious traditions of Pakistani society, and they tend to become a major factor of social development which provides, thanks to its intrinsic dynamics, a marked countereffect on the entire network of social links existing in the country.

On the other hand, a thorough examination of the *zakat* and *ushr* system

---

1. Technically, only *zakat* is considered a Qur'anic "pillar." In legislative practice in Pakistan, however, *ushr* is treated in the same manner as *zakat*.

2. By Neo-Marxist, I mean those left-oriented intellectuals who adopt Marxist class-analysis for their social studies of the Third World. They tend to be critical both of "state socialism" in eastern Europe and of "late capitalism" in the West, believing that the latter brings about neocolonial exploitation of the developing world and leads to the emergence of an "egoistic comprador bourgeoisie."

did not prevent a certain idealization of its role by some U.S. researchers. Ann E. Mayer, for example, argues that "in terms of case and efficiency of administration, the current Pakistani *zakat* system seems to perform extremely well" (Mayer 1986: 71). Grace Clark also speaks in glowing terms of *zakat* collection, which, she feels, "has demonstrated that the government can collect a tax impartially and efficiently, without corruption" (Clark 1986: 3).

This chapter attempts to further some aspects of the research undertaken by Mayer and Clark between 1982 and 1984. Unfortunately, I was unable to carry out field research comparable to theirs in Pakistan during my stay there in 1986–87 because of limitations imposed by both Soviet and Pakistani authorities. Thus the data for this chapter were collected through interviews with Pakistani nationals residing in Karachi, mostly white-collar workers at the Pakistan Steel Mill Corporation. In general, those interviewed were rather critical about the effectiveness and practical outcome of the *zakat* collection and distribution system. Most emphasized the difference between paying money to a state treasury and voluntary donations, which are viewed by well-to-do families as a moral obligation.

A second important source of data were Pakistani periodicals, primarily English-language newspapers (*Dawn* [Karachi], *Nation* [Lahore]), the Urdu-language *Nawa-e Waqt* (Lahore), weekly magazines (*Viewpoint* [Lahore], the *Pakistan and Gulf Economist* [Karachi]), and monthlies (*Herald* [Karachi] and *Newsline* [Karachi]). Despite varied orientations (*Dawn* is moderately liberal and business-minded; *Muslim* is moderately nationalist; *Nawa-e waqt* is conservative and close to "Islamic" parties), none of these periodicals doubted the necessity of preserving *zakat* in Pakistan. They explain the system's inadequacies by the low moral qualities of the people involved. Yet all the publications are clearly reticent on the issue. The impression is that the few materials covering corruption cases in the *zakat* system reveal only the tip of the iceberg. Critical and analytic discussions are rare.

Pakistan's *Zakat* System Structure and Principles

Examination of the salient features of the Zakat and ʿUshr Ordinance 1980, shows that the ordinance has its own key and contains elements having no precedents in the practices of other Muslim countries. These are the newly introduced and well-developed tax collection and distribution system, which utilizes the existing administrative machinery, and techniques designed to assure the smooth collection of revenue. The Qur'an prescribes compulsory payment of *zakat* by a true Muslim from visible (*zahir*) rather than hidden (*batin*) wealth; in contrast, the Zakat and ʿUshr Ordinance virtually declares a state monopoly on the right to gather and distribute the money collected through taxation of exposed wealth. Furthermore, Qur'anic prescriptions concerning exposed wealth are interpreted quite freely. The idea was to adjust relevant seventh-century dicta to the realities of modern forms of financial savings and thereby secure the maximum influx of financial resources.

Admitting that a large portion of movable and immovable property (for example, dwelling structures, shops, machine tools, transport facilities, and furniture) is exempt from *zakat* taxation (although the wealth tax is still deducted), *zakat* is compulsorily deducted with respect to eleven different bank assets, including savings bank accounts, deposit receipt accounts, and shares of companies and statutory corporations. Also subject to *zakat* taxation are other forms of property such as gold, silver, livestock, and property involved in commerce. Agricultural produce is subject to ʿushr (Zhmoida 1988: 76). In reality, tangible effect is achieved by compulsory withdrawal of money from bank accounts, effected every year on the first day of Ramadan. The withdrawn sum is 2.5 percent of the annual savings. All accounts are subject to taxation if the total volume of deposited wealth exceeds the established equivalent of Nisab (at least 87.47 grams of gold or 612.36 grams of silver [Zakat and ʿUshr Ordinance 1980]). As of April 1989, this was equivalent to 3,400 rupees, or $135 to $140 at current rates (*Morning News*, April 8, 1989).[3]

Zakat collection and disbursement is characterized by a centralized and multistep structure which corresponds generally to the country's territorial divisions and by the structure's entanglement with the state's machinery. Also characteristic are the principles of assignment, election, and voluntary application when setting up relevant committees.

"To provide policy guidelines for the assessment, collection, and disbursement of *zakat* and ʿushr and exercise general superintendence and control over the conduct of affairs of the *zakat* fund" (*Dawn*, February 2, 1979), a Central Zakat Council (CZC) was set up. Committee members are nominated by the president, and its chair is a judge of a High Court or the Supreme Court. It is composed of secretaries in the Ministries of Finance and Religious Affairs, three ʿulama, and some other officials (Zakat and ʿUshr Ordinance 1980). The CZC is quite active: between 1980 and 1990, it held forty-five meetings authorizing the release of 22 installments from the Central Zakat Fund to the provinces (*Dawn*, August 24, 1989). The four provincial councils (nominated by the governors) have a similar structure composed of top bureaucrats and ʿulama, who supervise the routine activities of the Provincial Chief Administrator, Zakat. The councils are responsible for allocating funds to the districts, either as a flat rate per community or proportional to population.

The work of identifying those in need and the corresponding disbursement rests with lower-level bodies: district-level bodies or *tahsil zakat* committees (subdistrict administrative units). In addition, there are local *zakat* committees (LZC) established in wards in urban areas and at the village level in rural areas. Administrative control over committee composition and the election of com-

---

3. As of June 1989, 2,015 rupees were equivalent to $95.

mittee chairs remains intact at all levels, differing only in form and extent: the lower the level, the weaker the control. A district committee, for example, necessarily includes (since 1983) a local deputy commissioner as its vice chair, whereas a *tahsil*-level agency includes an assistant commissioner. All members of district *zakat* bodies, including the chairs, are subject to appointment by a higher-level provincial council; in contrast, *tahsil zakat* committee members are all delegated from the LZC of a particular area. LZC members are elected by vote at a general meeting of the area's residents (Zakat and ʿUshr Ordinance 1980). All told, there were 36,642 local *zakat* bodies in the country as of July 1988 (*Pakistan and Gulf Economist*, July 2–8, 1988: 27).[4]

The central *zakat* structure is under the direct control of bureaucrats from the Ministry of Finance. In general, a centralized and somewhat hierarchical system of *zakat* and ʿushr recovery enables an efficient control by the authorities, who can use the system for other purposes—including political ones.

Zakat Disbursement

The resources of the *zakat* fund are delivered (based on population) through provincial funds, although the basic concept of *zakat* is assistance based on need. Between 1980 and 1989, the provinces disbursed 8,006.86 million rupees (approximately $500 million).[5] The fund also retains a considerable sum to support various welfare and relief programs. In the 1987–88 fiscal year, this sum was 600 million rupees out of a total of 2.1 billion rupees (Akhtar 1989: 427; *Pakistan State Bank Annual Report, 1987–1988*). This means that *zakat* collection is a vital source of additional financial assistance for the administration, which handles it as it does budgeted funds—deciding on its own how and where to use them.

In a similar manner, the provinces pass on about half to the LZCs; the remainder is supposed to be spent primarily on stipends for students (about half of the retained funds) and for those studying at *dini madrasa*s (mosque religious schools) (about 20 percent of the retained funds) (*Dawn Economic Review*, November 4–10, 1989). However, as will be seen, this routine is frequently not observed.

There are numerous problems facing local *zakat* bodies. According to the

---

4. The distribution of *zakat* committees by province is: Punjab, 23,125; Sind, 6,851; North West Frontier Province, 3,932; Baluchistan, 2,616; Islamabad Capital Territory, 118.

5. The formula for apportionment of central funds to the provinces is: Punjab, 59 percent; Sind, 20 percent, NWFP 14 percent; Baluchistan, 6 percent; Islamabad Territory, 1 percent (*Dawn Economic Review*, November 4–10, 1989). The funds allocated were: Punjab, 4,690.5 million rupees; Sind, 1,590 million rupees; North West Frontier Province, 1,113 million rupees; Baluchistan, 477 million rupees; Islamabad Territory, 78.8 million rupees; allocations to different institutions, 57.78 million rupees (*Pakistan and Gulf Economist* 8, 54, December 23–29, 1989, p. 19).

ordinance, priority recipients (covered by the Qur'anic category of *tamlik*) include the poor and destitute, handicapped persons, orphans, widows, and hospitals for the poor, as well as training schools designed to impart skills to the needy (Zakat and ʿUshr Ordinance 1980). In addition, LZC regulations emphasize the rehabilitation of *mustahaqin*, which must receive no less than 45 percent of the total funds spent (*Dawn Economic Review*, November 4–10, 1989).

In fact, the basic form of support is a subsistence allowance disbursed once every six months. Despite inflation, the amounts disbursed over the past six or seven years showed virtually no increase: they ranged from 50 to 100 rupees a month per individual ($2.30 to $4.80) and 100 to 150 rupees a month for the head of a deserving family ($4.80 to $7.10), plus 50 rupees for each dependent ($1.50) (*Nawa-e Waqt*, July 17, 1989). An average of 7.7 percent of the country's households were entitled to rehabilitation allowances; of these, according to statistics, only 68 percent had an increase in their incomes from *zakat* grants (*Dawn Economic Review*, November 4–10, 1989; Akhtar 1989: 425–27).

Still, the *zakat* system can be seen as relatively efficient. According to the Federal Bureau of Statistics' *Survey of Social and Economic Impact of Zakat* (December 1988), 68 percent of the LZC chairs characterized *zakat* as helpful in alleviating recipients' problems, and 6 percent felt that recipients' problems had been permanently resolved. At the same time, 72 percent saw a need for improvement in the existing system. They called for larger *zakat* funds and the creation of more industrial establishments (*Survey of Social and Economic Impact of Zakat* 1988).[6]

A major obstacle to the efficient functioning of the *zakat* system is conceptual limitations. The *tamlik* principle stipulates that only individuals may be recipients. Even when money is donated to an institution, it may be done only in the form of stipends, grants, or allowances to students. Pakistan's central authorities tend to bypass the religious taboo, however. *Tamlik* does not mention construction of houses, for example, but Pakistan launched an ambitious program in 1989–90 to provide for the construction of 75,000 dwelling units for the needy at a cost of about 25,000 rupees apiece ($1,200) (*Dawn*

---

6. Some other data of interest were: (a) 79 percent of the households utilized *zakat* grants for household expenses, and the remaining 21 percent spent the sums for such purposes as the treatment of patients, marriage, education, payment of debts, etc.; (b) about 21.4 percent of the households that received cash for rehabilitation used the money to start a business, 9 percent purchased animals, another 9 percent spent it for repairs and construction of houses, and the balance was used for payment of school and college fees, purchase of books and school supplies, tools and instruments to start work, etc.; (c) to explain their failure to increase their incomes, 49 percent reported that their business did not flourish, 3 percent felt that the amounts given were too small, 10 percent attributed it to bad health, and 10 percent had used the sum for household expenses; (d) of the recipient households, 3.5 percent earned 300 rupees or less, 29 percent had a monthly income between 300 and 500 rupees, and 3 percent reported an income above 500 rupees.

Economic and Business Review, November 11–17, 1989). The program was exploited for propaganda purposes and claimed by the Pakistan People's Party administration as a major achievement in combatting poverty.

Corruption and Misuse of Funds: Problems in the *Zakat* and *'Ushr* System

Zia ul-Haq has been quoted as saying that utilization of *zakat* funds "would be free from the corrupting influence of public administration" (Ahmad 1990). Unfortunately, his words remain wishful thinking. A system so closely intertwined with the state's apparatus apparently cannot avoid adopting its vices, and rhetoric about "the religious duty of a Muslim" or the "sacrosanct nature" of the tax cannot guarantee against misuse of *zakat* funds. Corruption is made easier by the redistributive nature of the program and its multilevel administration, where funds have to pass through four levels of bureaucracy.

At the local level, *zakat* committees are dominated, as a rule, by the most influential and well-to-do community members—primarily landowners in the countryside—who have close links to the local bureaucracy and who act, especially in villages, as community spokespersons when dealing with local or higher-level officials. As a result, some of the money received by LZCs settles in the pockets of those committee members and civil officers who are involved in the disbursement process. In some urban localities, a *zakat* applicant must secure, in succession, a written consent from the *pesh imam* [mullah] of his mosque, the signatures of four community members, a signature from a municipal committee's councilor, and finally, a consent from the police. The list of persons involved in some way in *zakat* funding is large indeed, especially in towns. There a needy person is less likely to be in close contact with his community and thus less likely to claim *zakat* funds, even if he or she is eligible to do so.

The accumulation of money available to many LZCs—and to persons having access to the funds—is further aided by the more-or-less uniform allocation of money to each local committee in the provinces (according to available data, such allocations in Sind Province amount to 16,000 rupees [$760] for each of the committees) (*Dawn Economic and Business Review*, November 4–10, 1989). As a result, some LZCs are unable to use the accumulated funds while others could use more than they receive. It is manifest that such "leveled disbursement" is far from perfect, but it survives because it is viewed favorably by many people of influence.

Corruption is facilitated, of course, when half the LZC members are illiterate. The situation is worse in the countryside, where a quarter of the committees contain no literate members at all (Clark 1986). Most of the committees have a mullah as chair; however, the mullah (especially in villages) is frequently dependent himself upon local bosses, who may have allotted a plot of land for the mosque or who have provided financial support for its activities. Thus he is unable to make decisions himself. Assigning a secretary to each LZC to look after the administrative side of *zakat* disbursement also failed to help solve the problem of mismanagement and embezzlement. Inquiry into the functioning of LZCs in Peshawar District as early as 1989 showed that most of the secretaries had not even passed middle school, and many were aged and/or illiterate. As a result of the inquiry, fifty-one secretaries were dismissed for malpractice in Peshawar District alone (*Dawn Economic and Business Review*, April 22–28, 1989).

When misuse of funds occurs, accountability is impeded by the loose hold authorities have on LZC members, who are nominated by their community and enjoy influence there. (For example, in February 1986, K. K. Bhatia, Director of the Sindh Anti-Corruption Committee, pressed charges of misappropriation of funds against seventy-six *zakat* and *'ushr* committees; virtually none was found guilty, and none was dismissed from his/her post [*Dawn*, February 24, 1986].) According to one estimate, there were as many as 2,000 cases of embezzlement of *zakat* funds in 1989 ("Handling Zakat with Care" 1990). It is not unusual to find cases of *zakat* committee chairs relieved of their duties even at the district level (see, for example, *Nation*, December 12, 1990).

The corruption is of a "vertical" nature: each layer of the bureaucracy involved in redistribution of *zakat* money receives a share of the funds misappropriated at the local level. Thus it is not surprising that the authorities concerned do not insist on an audit of LZC funds. Local committees prepare fictitious lists of persons in need, which are not made public, and the amounts disbursed are lower than those recorded in the books of LZCs. *Mustahaqin* signatures on financial documents are often secured dishonestly.

Malpractice at the province level is frequent as well. Major projects involving central and provincial *zakat* funds (for example, construction of buildings, training and rehabilitation centers, etc.) often go to favored companies through collusion with corrupt functionaries. There are also allegations that many centers have existed only on paper for a lengthy period of time.

Large-scale corruption is also condoned by various groups and associations which hope to drag the *zakat* apparatus into a political struggle. Both the ruling authorities and the opposition use *zakat* as a rhetorical weapon to make particular points.

Ideological Framework

As has been noted, Zia ul-Haq and his administration, in an attempt to ground the legitimacy of their government in a Muslim state, declared the establishment of a just "Islamic economic order" the main purpose of their activities. This order, they asserted, was to be an alternative to capitalism and socialism (Haq 1983). According to Zia, this order was to be based on the principle of *ihsan*, by which he meant providing equal opportunities in life to all, and *ʿadl*, which meant an equal opportunity to all to earn wealth and justice in the distribution of wealth. *Zakat* was incorporated as a key element of the *ʿadl* concept, although it was usually viewed by Pakistani Islamic ideologies as an independent and permanent means of dealing with the problems of poverty. Fazle Haq, one of Zia's closest associates, saw effective enforcement of the *zakat* system as a necessary condition of the "truthfulness" of an Islamic state.

The meanings of Zia's pronouncements were generally reduced to the statement that a person's persistent observance of religious duties would result in the disappearance of "worldly problems." By introducing compulsory *zakat*, the state and its pious leaders undertook, as it were, to put into effect these duties of every Muslim. Zia took advantage of the mass media (which was under his control) in an attempt to persuade the well-to-do stratum of society to assist the "Leader of the Nation" in accomplishing his "divine mission" of ridding the country of poverty through *zakat* collection and distribution.

The opposition, in its confrontation with the military, was criticizing, not "Islamic" steps as such, but the conjunctive motifs behind them and the attempt to perpetuate authoritarian rule by using the screen of "Islamization." This explains the opposition's severe criticism of the *zakat* system, which it saw as inadequate, and its charges that the system was riddled with corruption.

The Political Role of the *Zakat* and *ʿUshr* System

By establishing a *zakat* system largely dependent on bureaucracy, the authoritarian regime sought, among other things, to secure itself against contingencies at all levels of state administration. In the absence of democratic institutions, this system allows for fairly broad representation, the inclusion of the locally powerful and the powerless poor. Of course, one should not overestimate the role of the *zakat* system as the basis of the ruling regime. Neither should one view LZCs as cells for a progovernmental political party. Yet, for the lower strata of towns and villages, the LZCs have become a source of financial support, sanctified by religion. Thus, under certain conditions, the LZCs could function as mobilizing centers.

This was manifestly proven in December 1984, prior to a referendum on Islamization and Zia ul-Haq's retention of his post. Some of the *zakat* committees took part in the propaganda campaign, seeking to persuade the lower class that General Zia alone could guarantee *zakat* disbursements on a regular basis. The role of the *zakat* committees was also prominent when Prime Minister Mohammad Khan Junejo reconstituted the Muslim League in late 1985 and early 1986. The league actively styled itself as a bastion against "anti-Islamic forces," but in fact it owed much to *zakat* committees, which contributed appreciably to the party's reestablishment. After an eight-year absence from the political scene, the league lacked the necessary career functionaries for its mass meetings in Karachi and Multan. The *zakat* committees of Punjab and Sind, together with the provincial bureaucracy, performed many of these functions.

Upon resumption of an open political struggle in 1986, the politicizing of the *zakat* system accelerated. From 1986 to 1988, the opposition in provincial assemblies elected on a nonparty basis repeatedly accused the government of maladministration of *zakat* funds, which imparted a political character to a social problem. This politicizing of the *zakat* system proceeded rapidly after August 1986 when the ban on participation by local councilors was lifted, allowing them to take part in party activities. The close ties between *zakat* committees and the councilors made this a natural step.

The increasingly political confrontations were felt at the local level, where the Pakistan People's Party (PPP) attempted to strengthen its antigovernment campaign. To check this, the Muslim League cited Section 21 (1) of the Zakat and ʿUshr Ordinance, which prohibits party activism by leaders of *zakat* committees. The critical phases of the interparty struggle saw dismissals of committee chairs on a mass scale, especially during the 1988 and 1990 election campaigns. The opposing sides apparently used *zakat* funds to enlist supporters and to bribe voters. It became common to see misappropriation of funds through the use of bogus names and institutions. After the general elections of 1988, Ehsan ul-Haq Piracha, Minister of State for Finance and a PPP member, ordered an investigation into the alleged misappropriation of 410 million rupees ($22 million) by Nawaz Sharif, head of the Muslim League, from the provincial *zakat* funds of Punjab (*Muslim*, December 11, 1988). Unfortunately, there are no concrete data concerning the investigation's results.

Six months later, upon assuming power in Azad Jammu and Kashmir (AJK) in June 1990, PPP leaders took the unprecedented step of dissolving all the district, *tahsil*, and local *zakat* councils in the state. The move was a response to Sardar Sikanhar Hayat's misuse of resources. As former AJK premier, Hayat had, on the eve of the state elections, allocated "in a haphazard manner" half a million rupees to a progovernmental Urdu daily paper, *Azadi*, which was published in Muzaffarabad. Some Pakistani press editions reported that workers and supporters of the ruling All-Jammu and Kashmir Muslim Conference in AJK and the Islami Jamhuri Ittihad [Islamic Democratic Alliance] (IJI), the main opposition to Benazir Bhutto, were "rewarded generously" from the *zakat* fund as well. Some activists received as much as 100 thousand rupees ($4,800) (*Dawn*, July 2, 1990; August 15, 1990).

In October 1990, following the so-called constitutional coup of August 6, Bhutto's party was returned to power. Charges by the anti-PPP caretaker cabinet served as a pretext for dismissing *zakat* committee chairs in the districts of Larkana and Dadu, Bhutto and PPP strongholds. The dismissals were ordered by the Sind Minister for Zakat, but they were formally initiated by the deputy commissioners who led the district bureaucracy (*Sind Express*, October 5, 1990).

In 1989–90, when a direct confrontation between the PPP-led central government and the IJI-led Punjab provincial cabinet became fact, the struggle for control over the distribution of central and provincial *zakat* funds became part of the general political struggle. Under prevailing conditions, Islamic "sacrosanct" funds were being brazenly—and increasingly—used as an additional means of mass mobilization, and the PPP attempted to deprive the provincial cabinets of access to the resources in question. The ultimate aim was to "federalize" the system by virtually eliminating the provincial level of *zakat* distribution and bringing the lower structural elements out from under provincial jurisdiction. If implemented, this plan would have enabled the Bhutto administration to appoint district *zakat* committees and their chairs, thereby maintaining almost complete control over the system. In case of a budget deficit, the PPP could secure more support and, more important, a way to finance popular social programs.

The peculiarity of the situation was that, without a two-thirds majority in the National Assembly, the administration could introduce but not pass amendments to the Zakat and 'Ushr Ordinance. Thus, to create a favorable sociopolitical climate, the PPP preferred (according to official propaganda) to "expose the vulnerability to corruption of the *zakat* distribution system envisaged and implemented by the Zia regime . . . to secure the support and the loyalty of some influential circles" (*Dawn Economic and Business Review*, April 22–28, 1989). The Zia government was subject to particularly sharp criticism because of the misappropriation of funds for the 1988 election campaign by the Punjab cabinet and reports of gross abuses of resources in the wake of floods that struck the province that year.

In the spring of 1989 there were several populist-type "appeals" in the press addressed to the Bhutto administration. They called for "streamlining" the system and removing the "defects" which had resulted in colossal economic damage to the poor. As if in reply, the government instituted, in May 1989, two-member scrutiny committees in every district to probe into the reported irregularities (*Dawn*, May 12, 1989). Each committee included a district auditor and a government official, an obvious violation of the 1980 Zakat Ordinance, as the opposition quickly pointed out.

It was an open secret that the PPP's aim was to crush the system of *zakat* committees in Punjab, which remained appointed rather than elected, contrary to the same law, for more than seven years (in other words, since their establishment by Zia). It is not surprising that the old committees had supported the Muslim League since 1986. The committees were also the base of influence for Nawaz Sharif, the league's provincial leader and Bhutto's main rival. Fully aware of this fact, the Prime Minister planned to effect the reelection of local *zakat* committees after personally appointing all the district chairs to guarantee the loyalty of the system. In short, the *zakat* administration was taken over by the federal government.

To make this innovation legal, a special provision was included in the Finance

Bill passed with the federal budget in June 1989. *Zakat* and *ushr* were made part of the bill, despite the opposition's vehement protests (*Muslim*, June 25, 1989). By this change in the regulations, officials of the Provincial Zakat Council, being provincial government officials, were not directly responsible to the Central Zakat Council in Islamabad. Without formally introducing the change into the Zakat and 'Ushr Ordinance, the Bhutto administration nominated the Federal Zakat Committee, which was answerable to Parliament, where the PPP held the majority. The political nature of such an action is clear.

To mitigate somewhat the effect of the government's action, by which the provincial cabinet was denied the use of *zakat* institutions to consolidate his position, Nawaz Sharif announced in May 1989 the establishment of the Bayt ul-Mal (Islamic charity fund), with an initial capital of 100 million rupees. The Bayt ul-Mal, which became operative in January 1990, is not financed from government resources but from voluntary *zakat* and *sadaqa* [alms] (*Nation*, May 27, 1989). Bayt ul-Mal, however, seems not to be especially efficient, and its activities are unavoidably propagandistic.

The dismissal of Bhutto in August 1990 prevented further changes in the *zakat* system, either functional or organizational. The PPP used the general elections of October 1990 to continue its expansion of *zakat* applications through a comprehensive interpretation of *tamlik*. In its election manifesto it suggested using the funds for new programs and to assist social groups not previously seen as deserving *Mustahaqin* (principally, for unemployment benefits) ("Pakistan Democratic Alliance Manifesto" 1990). Today, the IJI, which emerged the winner of the elections and is enjoying a solid majority both at the center and in the provinces, evidently has other priorities, and additional reforms, along with the struggle surrounding *zakat* funds, are a matter for the future.

Some other attempts to utilize *zakat* resources for partisan purposes rest with the fundamentalist Jamaʿat-i Islami [Party of Islam] (JI). Making good use of the congenial atmosphere of the Zia years, the JI intensified its work among students of *dini madrasa*s [religious schools]. They have traditionally had much political influence, and the JI views *madrasa*s as an important channel for promoting its interests. In North West Frontier Province, for example, where the JI's position is relatively strong, every district has a religious school, with 500 to 600 students in attendance at each. Many students go on to become *imam*s in mosques (*Herald*, October 1987: 66). By the late 1980s, large numbers of JI supporters were recruited from *dini madrasa*s. The party is therefore active in lobbying for allocation of sometimes disproportionately large *zakat* sums for students of these institutions. In addition to the *zakat* that *madrasa*s receive directly from provincial funds, religious schools in North West Frontier Province receive funds from the local committees, an obvious misappropriation of funds. JI activists also try to participate personally in the disbursement of *zakat* money.

Attempts have also been made to utilize *ushr* collection structures for political purposes. *'Ushr* has replaced the Land Revenue and is supposed to be charged at 5 percent of agricultural production exceeding 948 kg of wheat (or its equivalent, in the case of other crops) (Zakat and 'Ushr Ordinance 1990). Under the existing system, the assessment is made by the district *zakat* and *'ushr* committee, following a protracted, inaccurate, and somewhat artificial procedure involving various irrigation, agricultural, and revenue agencies and local deputy commissioners, among others. This convoluted process, combined with numerous exemptions, enables most landlords to escape payment. Furthermore, all *'ushr* funds are to be spent where they are collected, which places them at the disposal of local *zakat* and *'ushr* committees.

As noted above, LZCs are under the control of local "strong men," and this impinges on the system's efficiency. According to Firuz Qayser, former advisor to the Prime Minister, who prepared a special report, the yield from *'ushr* collection could be enhanced 500-fold if the system were properly implemented (*Muslim*, June 23, 1989). Unlike *zakat*, *'ushr* collections seem negligible. When the tax was first introduced in 1982–83, the country-wide collection amounted to some 304 million rupees ($14.4 million). The yield dropped to 128.9 million rupees in 1986–87 ($6.13 million) (Akhtar 1989: 427–29). According to Qayser, it was "minimal" in 1989.

Despite certain innovations, the *'ushr* assessment and collection system relies heavily on the outmoded and corrupt land-revenue system. Under such a system, key positions are held by *lambardars* (local tax collectors who often inherit their positions). They keep land-tenure records and collect the so-called *patwari* taxes from the rural population, reserving a fixed portion for themselves. The introduction of a local system was intended to abolish this century-old institution, but the old system has been purposely retained. *Lambardars* have played an important role in local politics for decades (in the colonial period, they helped the British suppress rural insurgencies).

Just prior to the election of October 1990, the Muslim League-led Punjab caretaker government convened a 50,000-member *lambardar* congress. The party's support for this institution was reiterated, and a series of concessions for *lambardars* was announced. The most important was a grant of 12.5 acres of land for each and the inclusion of *lambardars* on *'ushr* committees, plus a 5 percent allowance for *'ushr* collection. This can only be viewed as a form of political bribery, and the impact of such measures on the efficiency of *'ushr* recovery (poor as it was even before that) could only be negative.

According to some estimates, each *lambardar* is in a position to influence from 250 to 1,000 voters (*Newsline*, October 1990: 58). There is reason to believe that *lambardar* support was one of the decisive factors that assured a landslide victory for the Islamic Junhuri Ittihad in the province.

The practice of using *zakat* funds for varied purposes has thus become rather popular, but the evidence that has surfaced merely hints at the extent of the problem. The corruption of the *zakat* system deserves further research.

Conclusion

Ten years of experience with the *zakat* system's functioning demonstrates convincingly that the institution has gained firm ground in Pakistani society. However, the efforts to create agencies designed to encourage the proper moral climate in society through maintenance of its "Islamic" spirt have actually failed (hence the withdrawal from the political scene of Information Minister Raja Zafar ul-Haq, Zia's protegé and a prominent adherent of Islamization and the so-called *Islah-e Muashra* [spiritual reform]).

During his time in power, Zia attempted, although in vain, to establish a corps of *Nazmin-i Salat*—persons (165,000 in Punjab Province alone) supposed to be attached to each mosque to persuade people in the congregation to say their daily prayers and report every fortnight to the government on the state of morale in their jurisdiction (*Viewpoint*, June 28, 1990; see also Barna 1986). In May 1989, Nawaz Sharif, in his capacity as Chief Minister, spoke openly in favor of including members of the district and *tahsil* administration into *salat* committees, which would be given the power to issue character certificates and have charge of certain financial funds. These were in fact attempts to establish parallel administrative and ideological structures (similar to *zakat* committees) to bring life to routine political issues. However, so far no such plans have come to fruition.

Zia ul-Haq's efforts to introduce parallel "Islamic" legal procedures by the so-called *qadi* courts have also failed because the change directly affects lawyers and would result in confusion in the administration of justice.

The *zakat* system remains one of the few products of the Islamization policy in the Pakistani social sphere. Maintaining the system serves the interests of both recipients of financial aid and the officials responsible for its disbursement (in conditions of a corruption-laden society, the latter are unwilling to disregard the system's "advantages"). The *zakat* structure's serving as a pillar for those in power has always been present. Political parties will undoubtedly continue to fight for influence in the rather popular *zakat* committees.

Still, Islamization-initiated institutions that are of a purely ideological and, consequently, artificial nature or those that infringe on the rights of influential groups of society have no chance of long-term existence in Pakistan. We may note in this connection that secular traditions inherent in both state power and legal procedure remain deeply rooted. We can expect antagonism between temporal and religious traditions to be a major part of the social struggle in years to come.

References

Ahmad, Mushtaq (1990). "Law and Morality in Taxation." *Dawn*, June 4.

Akhtar, Rafique (1989). *Pakistan Year Book, 1989–1990.* Karachi and Lahore: East and West Publishing House.
Barna, Minhaj (1986). "The Issue of Islamisation." *Muslim,* April 18.
Clark, Grace (1986). "Pakistan's *Zakat* and *ʿUshra* as a Welfare System." In *Islamic Reassertion in Pakistan: The Application of Islamic Laws in a Modern State,* ed. Anita M. Weiss. Syracuse: Syracuse University Press.
Federal Bureau of Statistics (1988). *Survey of Social and Economic Impact of Zakat* (December).
Gardezi, Hassan N. (1990). "Religion, Ethnicity, and State Power in Pakistan." *Viewpoint,* June 21, 15, 45.
"Handling Zakat with Care." (1990). *Dawn,* September 26.
Haq, Zia ul- (1983). Presidential Address. *Pakistan Times,* March 20.
Haque, Ziaul (1990). "Islamisation in Pakistan (1977–1988)." *Viewpoint* 16, 7, September 27.
——— (1983). "Pakistan and Islamic Ideology." (1983). In *Pakistan, The Roots of Dictatorship: Economy of a Praetorian State,* ed. Hassan Gardezi and Jamil Rashid, pp. 367–83. London: Zed Press.
Khan, Omar Asghar (1986). "Shariat and Islamisation: Economic Aspects." *Muslim,* July 27.
Mayer, Ann Elizabeth (1986). "Islamisation and Taxation in Pakistan." In *Islamic Reassertion in Pakistan: The Application of Islamic Laws in a Modern State,* ed. Anita M. Weiss. Syracuse: Syracuse University Press.
"Pakistan Democratic Alliance Manifesto" (1990). *Dawn,* October 16.
Pakistan State Bank Annual Report, 1987–1988.
Zakat and ʿUshr Ordinance (1980). Islamabad: Pakistan Publications.
Zhmoida, Irina Viktorovna (1988). *Pakistan: Vnutrennie i vneshnie faktory ekonomicheskogo razvitiia* [Pakistan: Internal and External Factors of Economic Development]. Moscow: Nauka Publishers.

Periodicals Cited:
   Dawn. Karachi.
   Dawn Economic and Business Review. Karachi.
   Dawn Economic Review. Karachi.
   Herald. Karachi.
   Morning News. Hyderabad.
   Muslim. Islamabad.
   Nation. Lahore.
   Nawa-e-Waqt. Lahore.
   Newsline. Karachi.
   Pakistan and Gulf Economist. Karachi.
   Sind Express. Hyderabad.
   Viewpoint. Lahore.

XI

ISLAMIZATION IN PAKISTAN
THE SAYYID AND THE DANCER

Richard Kurin

In the preceding chapters, Belokrenitsky and Novossyolov have painted with broad strokes the implications of Pakistan's recent Islamization movement. The former sees this movement as part of an on-going dialectical history of sometimes competing, sometimes merging social ideological forces—the traditionalist and fundamentalist, on the one hand, and the secular and modernist, on the other. The latter examines the appropriation and exploitation of an Islamic religious precept—alms-giving (zakat)—through its institutionalization by the state. This chapter brings these larger tensions between religion and politics, state power and morality, tradition and modernity down to the level of individuals.

In this chapter, I examine how two Pakistanis have construed their Muslim identities in the context of the Islamization movement in Pakistan. Although these people are chosen somewhat arbitrarily, their roles, circumstances, ambivalences, and actions reveal how government policies and large-scale social movements are articulated at the level of personal experience, ideas, motivations, emotions, and interactions. In doing so, the chapter rounds out the discussion of Islamization in Pakistan. It also reveals a strain in American social scientific work—a concern with social actors—often absent in Soviet scholarly traditions, although certainly not in Russian literature.

Islam and "Being Muslim"

"Islam" generally refers to a code of conduct; "Muslim" refers to people. A state may be Islamic, in that its institutions are informed by and realize concepts, values, and relationships enshrined in a recognized corpus of "Islamic" thought and expression: the Qur'an, Islamic law (shari'a and fiqh), the sayings of the Prophet (hadith), and, in some cases, forms of community consensus. Yet ideas of an Islamic state are always subject to historical and contextual articulations of what such a state might be. Selections are always made from a wide reservoir of Islamic ideas. And even when particular ideas are dominant, others may be present as alternatives or remain latently embedded in the social order.

A state may be Muslim to the extent that its population is composed of people identified as Muslim. A nation with a vast majority of Muslims can be an Islamic state (for example, Saudi Arabia and Iran), but it need not be if characterized by other principles and codes (for example, Turkey and Indonesia). Muslim minorities often exist within non-Islamic states (for example, the United States and the former Soviet Union), but they may have sometimes controlled the state and defined it as Islamic (for example, the Indian Sultanate).

While Islam consists of a code of conduct, worldview, legal system, values, and normative practices, Muslims are people who articulate parts of that ideational repertoire in their daily lives through verbal, mental, emotive, and physical actions. It is difficult to identify any society in which Islam offers the only available set of symbols, meanings, and codes. Indeed, much of Islamic culture draws upon Judeo-Christian, local, regional, and occupational traditions. Contemporary Islam coexists with various "cultures": colonialism, socialism, "Third Worldism," the new technoglobalism, and various regional, local, tribal, and familial cultures.

Few Muslims are cognizant only of Islamic symbols and ideas, and even the most conservative Muslim clerics dip into other cultural streams to make their arguments and state their positions (Fischer 1980: 73–76, 147–70; Maududi 1972: 85–123). The juxtapositions of cultural forms are sometimes dramatic—for example, the philosophy of *hudud* punishments (executions and amputations) and the conceptual underpinnings of shopping malls in Saudi Arabia. Cultural syntheses such as Islamic socialism and Indonesian Islam may attempt to reconcile ideas and traditions relevant to a society, while dual legal systems may, in contrast, deter conflict by separating competing ideas and traditions.

Islam exists in multicultural contexts, and so do Muslims. One may be a Muslim and also partake of many other identities, since identity is never singular and monolithic. There are many ways to be Muslim—Sunni, Shiʿa, Ahmadiya, Ismaili, and others—although the question of who is Muslim has been vigorously debated. Differences between Barelis, Deobandis, Wahhabis, and others and affiliations and loyalties to Sufi masters (*pirs*) point to diversity within a larger Muslim community. People who are Muslims are also politicians and soldiers, intellectuals and poets, farmers and sailors, parents and children, Pathans and Arabs, Kuwaitis and Iraqis. In certain situations, throughout a day or over a lifetime, the codes for various roles and identities may be switched, and one or more identities may be foregrounded. Sometimes various identities are articulated and conjoined; at other times they are compartmentalized. Sometimes identities are juxtaposed in creative or dysfunctional ways or encapsulated within others.

One of the main tensions in the Muslim world revolves around the relationship between Islam as code and Muslims as people. Pakistanis, among others, have asked, "Should the nation-state be an Islamic one or a state for Muslims?" The issue is not unique to Muslims. Jews, for example, are ambivalent about Israel. It is a state for people who are Jewish and also a state in which Jewish ideas, values, and traditions inform its institutions and practices—often with considerable ambiguity. American Christian fundamentalists raise strong feelings, even as they realize that the United States will never formally become a Christian state. In India, a growing Hindu political movement threatens that country's secular democracy by advocating a state run on Hindu ideas and principles, although India includes large Muslim, Christian, and Sikh minorities. And germinating in Central Asia are the seeds of yet another conflict: the tension between nationalism and religion as organizing principles of new, post-Soviet states.

Adherents of theocratic states might argue that the dichotomy between religion and politics is a false one. A state for Hindus must be a Hindu state and likewise for Jews, Muslims, and Christians. Here the argument has been that the ideas, norms, and traditions that make people feel Muslim, for example, will die out if not supported or promulgated in the social institutions of the state. Secular democratic, socialist, and Communist states promote ideas and values that conflict with particular religious cultures and reduce people to being Muslim, Jewish, or Christian in name only.

Islamization in Contemporary Pakistan

Pakistan's history reflects the tension between an Islamic state and a state for Muslims. It grew out of an anticolonial movement and owes its rise to a Muslim nationalism that developed alongside and within the Indian freedom movement. Pakistan was seen by its advocates, independence leaders, and settlers as a place for Muslims (Alavi 1986). It was a place (*istan*) where Muslims could control wealth, land, and institutions and be free from restraints imposed by others (Naim 1979; Sayeed 1967; Gilmartin 1988). Some saw Pakistan as a place where the destiny of the Muslim community could be realized: purity, faith, unity, and discipline—the higher spiritual aspirations associated with the values of a religious community (Kurin 1981; Naim 1979; Weiss 1986). The relationship between Pakistani statehood and religion has long been a subject of debate among politicians, secularists, Muslim modernists, religious scholars (*ulama*), and Pakistanis in general.

Pakistan has always been a nation with a vast Muslim majority. In the 1951 census for both East and West Pakistan, Muslims constituted about 88 percent of the population; roughly 10 percent (largely in Bengal) were Hindu; Christians and Buddhists accounted for the remainder. Since the separation of an independent Bangladesh, the population of contemporary Pakistan has been 97 percent Muslim. Pakistan has also adopted many symbols that could be considered Islamic. Its first constitution (1956) contained a provision (Article 198) "that no law shall be enacted which is repugnant to the injunctions of Islam." The 1962 constitution made Pakistan an "Islamic Republic" and proclaimed the sovereignty of Almighty Allah. The 1973 constitution made Islam the state religion by trying to "help Muslims live in accordance with the fundamental principles of Islam" and made Qur'anic instruction "compulsory for all Muslims" (Article 31), declaring that "all the existing laws are to be brought into conformity with the injunctions of Islam" (Article 227).

The use of prayer in official circumstances, the shrouding of national addresses in the language of Islam, and official visits to pilgrimage centers reflect the attempt to define the state in Islamic terms. Successive governments have also had to decide which expressions of Islam were to be foregrounded, appropriated, or ignored. Constitutional and legal reforms have often dealt with the ʿulama and the legalistic, rationalistic, and normative formulations of Islam and the degree to which they should drive the practice of the state. Some governments have encouraged the institutionalization of Islamic laws and precepts more than others—witness, for example, the decades-long debate over the extent to which Pakistan's family laws should encode Islamic law.

Governments have also had to deal with the influence of Sufi leaders (pirs), their followers—who number in the millions—and the numerous sufi shrines, which serve as focal points of religious activity. Senior government officials have sought to control contributions at such shrines, to affect the succession of spiritual leaders, to politically mine their networks of followers, and to be seen as respecting sufi saints by attending, for example, their annual death anniversaries (ʿurs). And governments have not been beyond exploiting Muslim identity—defining groups as Muslim or non-Muslim—as a means of coping with political crises.

The debate over the extent to which Pakistan should be an Islamic state reached a pinnacle with the overthrow of Zulfiqar Ali Bhutto and the Islamization program of Mohammed Zia ul-Haq. The Pakistan National Alliance (PNA), a coalition of diverse political parties opposed to Bhutto, used the idea of instituting a nizam-i mustapha or nizam-i Islam—an Islamic order—in its campaign to mobilize popular support in the 1977 national elections.

Zia, who ousted Bhutto in a July 1977 coup and became Chief Martial Law Administrator and then President in 1978, instituted a specific strategy to make Pakistan an Islamic state. Islamization included the establishment of shariʿa courts to set aside laws repugnant to Islam, the establishment of hudud punishments (Weiss 1986), economic reforms that placed banking, alms-giving (zakat), and taxation (ʿushr) in a state-managed Islamic context (Burki 1986; Clark 1986; Mayer 1986), and the promulgation of Islamic education. In 1984, Zia's government defined the Ahmadiya movement as non-Muslim and held a national referendum to gauge public support for his Islamization policy.

While against Zia and military rule, opposition groups throughout the 1980s were reluctant to openly attack Islamization as wrongful policy. This reluctance has continued since Zia's death (1988), Benazir Bhutto's subsequent assumption of power, and her fall. Muslims in Pakistan have not been passive recipients of attempts by state authority to define and institute an Islamic order. Whether supporting, opposing, or ignoring these policies, individual Muslims play an active role in interpreting Islamization, finding its relevance to their lives, and changing their ideas and behaviors over time.

The Sayyid and the Dancer

It has long been a tradition in American social science to understand historical events, cultural processes, and social relationships through the examination of individual lives. Cultural anthropologists from Franz Boas on have used insights gained from their key informants to describe and analyze local culture. Sociologists such as Talcott Parsons and Edward Shils (1951) recognized the theoretical importance of the individual as a social actor within a larger analytical framework.

Analysis of social action at the level of the individual requires an understanding of how cultural values and social relationships are manifested in motivations and meaningful behavior. Scholars such as Oscar Lewis (1963; see also Lewis et al. 1977) have used oral biography and personal narrative to bring to life for nonspecialists such abstract notions as poverty and revolution. Although usually presented in less dramatic ways, American ethnographers tend to generate extensive life histories and "everyday accounts" as a tool for description and analysis, an opportunity often denied to Soviet researchers.

Scholarly examination of ideas of the person (for example, Dumont 1970; Geertz 1973 [orig. 1966]) neither excludes treatment of other units of society nor does it see biography as the cause or explanation of complex social and cultural history. Rather, social scientists have examined personal lives in order to understand the impacts and articulations of larger social processes on those who participate in them. In so doing, scholars have found a richness of meaning often overlooked in discussions of grand categories or descriptions of institutions.

How do individuals in Pakistan understand Islamization? How has it affected their lives? Individual biographies can help us understand what it is to be a Muslim and how Islamization affects notions of self, other, and society. In this chapter, I examine the biographies of Sayyid Ahmed Shah, who lives in a small Punjabi village, and Jabina Abbas, a woman dancer from Karachi. Their experiences offer insights into how government policy affects individuals.

I have known Sayyid Ahmed Shah since 1977 and Jabina since 1976. I lived with them and their families for over a year and have revisited them several times over the last fifteen years. Our friendships began at the time of Zulfiqar Ali Bhutto's demise and the initiation of the Islamization movement. I was able to learn a great deal about the impact of these events upon these individuals; subsequent visits and numerous contacts have allowed me to follow the course of their lives.

Sayyid Ahmed Shah

Ahmed Shah is a *sayyid*, a purported descendent of the Prophet Muhammad. His family has long been resident in the rural Punjab and traces its roots to those *sayyid* families credited with the conversion of Punjabi peasants to Islam in the fourteenth and fifteenth centuries. His family holds a large amount of cultivable land and earns its livelihood from its produce.

Sayyid Shah lives in Chakpur, a village of some 2,000 inhabitants, located ten miles from his parental home. He farms about five acres. The land is owned by the village and let to him under a traditional barter agreement (*seipi*) in return for his services as a traditional physician (*hakim*). He diagnoses illness and prescribes dietary, herbal, and medicinal cures.

He also delivers sermons (*taqrir*) over the mosque loudspeaker and gives advice on religious and spiritual matters. He is a follower (*murid*) of the Sufi Barkat Ali, an influential Punjabi *pir* who made service to the rural poor an important part of one's spiritual duty. For Barkat Ali, this included growing crops, educating and caring for children, and provision of healthcare needs. Sayyid Shah has strongly internalized and endorsed this notion of community service as part of his spiritual development.

Ahmed Shah's faith in Allah is strong, yet it has its tensions. He and other villagers annually commemorate the death of Ahmed Shah's son, who died at the age of six. After his marriage, Ahmed Shah had five daughters, whom he loved. However, he longed for a son and offered many *dua* (discretionary prayers), wondering why Allah would not fulfill the dream of such a devoted and true Muslim. Finally Allah endowed his wife with the spirit, and a boy was born. Some years later, the boy contracted typhoid and died. Ahmed Shah was grief-stricken. He could not understand why Allah would grant his prayers and then take his son away. Ahmed Shah had two graves dug side by side, each topped with a fine, whitewashed grave marker: one is for his son, the second for the Qur'an. The annual commemoration of the death marks both the separation of the boy's soul from his father and its union with Allah. Sayyid Shah feels this profoundly: he is happy, pained, awed, and shaken.

Jabina Abbas

Jabina Abbas is a middle-aged mother and housewife living in a middle-class Karachi neighborhood. She was trained as a classical dancer by her father, a musician and teacher in his own right. Jabina's mother is a converted Hindu. Jabina's father and her mother's brother were fellow students with her husband, apprenticed to a music teacher (*ustad*) in prepartition India.

She was born in Junagadh, a princely state on India's Gujarati coast, about

200 miles from present-day Pakistani territory. Junagadh's Muslim ruler wanted to accede to Pakistan at independence but was opposed by the Indian government, which wanted a plebiscite instead. Indian troops forced the prince out; Junagadh became part of India; and Jabina's family, like many other Muslims, left for Karachi.

Jabina grew up in a musical household; she, her younger brothers, and her father practiced constantly. Music became their livelihood. After Jabina's father died, the family, led by Jabina, became very successful. They gave concerts, and she danced at government and corporate functions. For a time, they had a training school for other musicians. The family, which was quite accomplished, participated in many international tours. Jabina's performances won awards from the Zulfiqar Ali Bhutto government and enough cash for the purchase of land and a house for her extended family.

Though proud of her success, she faced difficulties. As the oldest child and as someone with experience in affairs outside the home, she supplanted her mother as head of the household. Her younger brothers deferred to her. Her sense of responsibility and the feeling that she had to look after her family forced her to put off planning for a marriage until she was well beyond the age when most Karachi women do so.

Jabina's brothers were supportive of her career but hoped, with their mother, that Jabina would marry and have her own life. Their wives looked forward to the day when Jabina would leave, thus allowing them to manage their husbands' household. The brothers' support of Jabina's career was tempered by ambivalence, since her presence signalled that their income was inadequate to support the household. They also had to listen to neighbors, who resented Jabina's career and success, suggesting that her dancing was improper for a virtuous woman and in conflict with the tenets of Islam.

A Culture of the Person and Society

Both Jabina and Sayyid Ahmed, along with many others in Pakistan, share a general concept of the "person." This concept, while generally associated by Pakistanis with Islamic discourse, is implicitly derived from, historically tied to, and culturally resonant with aspects of Jewish theology, pre-Socratic metaphysics, Greco-Roman-Arabic medical theory, pan-Mediterranean and southwest Asian folk knowledge, Kantian anthropology, and ideological systems diffused to Latin America and Southeast Asia (Kurin 1981, 1984, 1988).

Ahmed Shah and Jabina, like most Pakistanis, think of a person (*shakhs*) as having a spirit (*ruh*), intellect (*ʿaql*), life energy (*nafs*), and body (*jism*). The body is material in nature. *Nafs* is a force issuing directly from the body and is associated with innate heat, blood, carnality, desire, and sexuality. *Ruh*, associated with light (*nur*) and spirituous or nonelemental forms of matter, is given by Allah and enters the fetus in about the fifth month of pregnancy.

Unlike *nafs* or body, it continues after death. Life in this world is made possible by the union of the spirit and body. The meeting point is the heart, and the union of the two allows for the development of a distinctly human intellectual/moral faculty, *ʿaql*. Intellect enables people to think, to use language, to have a conscience, to exert control over their nature.

ʿAql combines and mediates otherwise mutually exclusive orders of existence, making humans distinctive beings distinguished from angels and animals. Angels, composed of spirit, do not have physical bodies; they have intuition and the ability to speak, but not sensation, and are thus removed from the needs and demands of the physical world.

Animals, on the other hand, while possessed of *nafs* and *jism*, have a deficiency in terms of spirit. They possess some mental faculties indicative of *ʿaql* (for example, sensation); but they lack others (for example, intuition, imagination) which make moral choice possible. Animals cannot order their lives or control their destiny. They are by nature amoral. Animals are generally accorded hot dispositions because they are composed of bodily matter and *nafs* and act in non-intellective ways, blindly fulfilling bodily wants and desires.

Given this general view, a human being can be seen as both angel and animal, as well as a combination of the two. To the extent that a person engages in spiritual pursuits, he or she is angelic; to the extent that a person engages in physical pursuits, he or she is animalistic. In humans, both animal and angel qualities coexist in a uniquely balanced state. As Sayyid Shah says, "What separates man from animals is that man has a path, a road, a canon by which he can make decisions and be conscious of what he does. This faculty, *ʿaql*, means that we can have some control over what we do and that we do not blindly follow instincts."

This attempt to exert control, to moderate man's dual nature, is dynamic and involves the ever-constant struggle between the raw energy of life (*nafs*)—the terrible, powerful, active, hot aspects of one's nature—and the spirit (*ruh*)—the sedate, beautiful, passive, cool nature. The battleground is the heart, the seat of *ʿaql*, thought, and emotions. It is this shifting balance between the necessity of order and the intractability of physical existence that defines the stage for human action in this world.

Given this general idea, it is possible to speak of the person and his or her constituents in a variety of ways. As Jabina learned, "The *ruh* has two parts, one pure (*pak*) and the other impure, and the *nafs* also has two parts, one pure and the other impure. *ʿAql* is that which joins the two." The spirit is corrupted by the body, but the body is controlled and thus ennobled by the spirit. *ʿAql* may be seen as either an element of *ruh* or *nafs* or in opposition to either of them. For example, spiritual knowledge may be opposed to intellectual knowledge, or knowledge, as discipline and control, may be opposed to body-rooted physical elements and emotions.

The person, in this construct, is said to have an inner nature associated with the spirit and an outer one associated with the body and its energy. The inner aspect of the person implies the internalization of the spirit of Allah, the ultimate reality from without brought into the self to give it order. The outer aspect of the person, the extension of the corporeal body and its energy, is something within projected into the temporal and transient material world.

Different kinds of persons effect different kinds of balances or states with regard to this struggle. Pakistanis readily elaborate on how gender differences, age differences, and ethnic differences relate to the particular struggles and relative primacy of spiritual and physical forces.

Public Articulations, Private Understandings

Sayyid Ahmed Shah

Prior to the formal "Islamization" program initiated by Zia, Sayyid Shah saw his role in life as making people better Muslims. The local population consists largely of small peasant farmers, agricultural laborers, village crafts- men, and service providers who support agricultural production. Ahmed Shah is the only *sayyid* in the village. The largest segment of the population (about 80 percent) are the Nunari, who, according to the oral historical accounts of their *mirasis* [genealogists], were converted to Islam by Makhdum Jahaniyan in the fourteenth century and by Jilani *pirs* in the fifteenth century. The next largest group, the Bhattis, were supposedly Rajputs, also converted to Islam by various *pirs*.

When I first met Sayyid Shah, he saw other villagers in a negative way. "People in this village lack *ʿaql*," he said. "They are very much like animals. They don't know the difference between what is clean and what is dirty, between what is right and what is wrong. They don't know how to eat properly or how to wash themselves. They only think of their own advantage and filling their own carts [with crops]. They wouldn't help anyone unless they saw some advantage in it."

Sayyid Shah saw his role as resonant with those of Rumi, other *sufis*, and theologians such as Maulana Maududi. Hindus and peoples converted to Islam were associated with the *nafs*, hot, carnal, sensual, animalistic lifeways. For Sayyid Shah, "the only difference between man and animals is the *qanun* [the law]. This is the way so that we know how to eat, wear clothes, recognize our parents. The people in Chakpur do not act in an Islamic way. They know very little about it and do not follow. They will receive punishment on judgment day. This is because they are like animals, exerting no control over their actions."

Sayyid Shah saw his role as providing an example, leading the way for others through the exercise of *ʿaql*. His strategy was to be personally virtuous, serving humanity through his ministration of *desi tibb*, giving sermons over the village loudspeaker, and pointing out ways of proper behavior in conversations and meetings with other villagers. He was generally regarded as virtuous and had their respect. He regulated his diet in a manner that encouraged his "cool" nature. Sayyid Shah told me: "Sayyids and all people should eat a cold breakfast, not tea or egg, but *lassi*, *dahi*, fruit, and *chapati*. This keeps the mind from drying up and keeps us active and aware so we can pray and do *zikr* in the best manner." He regarded his Punjabi neighbors as having hot dispositions, making them prone to eating hot foods, engaging in lustful sex, and being too aggressive.

Sayyid Shah's promulgation of Islamic teachings was sometimes less appreciated than his work as a physician. He gave daily sermons over the mosque loudspeaker. During Ramadan, for example, he talked about the significance of fasting. At other times he talked about the Prophet Muhammad or why it was important to read the Qur'an. His *zikr* was in Arabic and his sermons and commentaries usually in Urdu, which made them difficult for all but a few villagers to understand. Occasionally he spoke in Punjabi.

In his speeches he typically included a section on how bad, sinful, criminal, and terrible "we" are, asking Allah's forgiveness, compassion, and blessing. Some villagers regarded Sayyid Shah's sermons as a nuisance. Indeed, Sayyid Shah was happy to have an anthropologist living in the village because I was interested in his sermons. After I had lived in Chakpur for some weeks, Sayyid Shah began to come to my hut late at night and often kept me up for hours rehearsing what he would say the next morning. I finally showed him how to use my tape recorder, and he recorded his sermons for me.

Sayyid Shah did not acknowledge any close friendships. If he approached men playing cards under a tree, they stopped playing out of respect. If someone was playing music on the radio when he came near, they turned down the volume. Only occasionally did people ask his advice or opinion about a topic having to do with Islamic practice. People seemed to trust his opinion more than they did that of the village *maulvi*, who was regarded as less knowledgeable and lax in his duties. This did not keep Sayyid Shah from telling people they were not behaving properly, however. Indeed, proper behavior, with or without Qur'anic reference, was regarded by Sayyid Shah as "being Islamic." Exhibiting compassion, acting righteously, being kind were all "Islamic" acts, as they invoked cooler, more spiritual actions.

Zia's Islamization program did not change Sayyid Shah's life or outlook. Information about Zia's policies and actions came to Sayyid Shah through the radio, newspapers purchased in town, and general discussions with relatives and followers of his *pir*. He generally agreed with Zia's attempt to make Pakistan an Islamic society. For Sayyid Shah, village society specifically and Pakistani society generally lacked the order to be gained from following Allah's *qanun*. As Sayyid Shah put it: "Man is a prisoner on this earth. The *qanun* is the constraint which binds him to follow the rules. If he didn't, he'd be an animal."

Sayyid Shah felt that people have a choice between doing right or wrong.

"Desire and greed make Muslims go astray." Unfortunately, without Islamization, Pakistani society encouraged desire and greed. *Shaitan* [Satan] had an easy time of tempting people: "People must conquer Satanic things to follow the right path." Still, while Islamic institutions—courts, schools, teachers, rulers—could encourage following of the *qanun*, Sayyid Shah believed it was up to each person to obey Allah and "follow the teaching of the Prophet Muhammad."

One of the major consequences of the government's Islamization policy in Chakpur was a limitation on the distribution of opium and other drugs. Several village addicts suffered visibly from the closing of the nearby opium store. The government provided a medicinal substitute at a hospital ten miles away, but this did not appease the handful of Chakpuris dependent on the drug. Sayyid Shah felt sorry for them. He noted that "Man must love and fear God. On one hand, Allah is merciful and forgiving. On the other hand, He is a stern judge." Sayyid Shah personally believed that Allah did not make it easy for humans but that they had responsibility for following God's law and "passing the test."

Sayyid Shah agreed with Zia that *hudud* punishments would control the population: "A leader has to be merciful and just. Fear and justice will prevent people from doing bad things. When they do bad, punishments should be strictly enforced." Many Chakpuris challenged this stance, even in discussions with Sayyid Shah (Kurin 1985). They argued that Nunari men and women were hot people with strong sexual urges and desires. For them, the ordinances concerning adultery and fornication seemed overly harsh, considering the state of human nature and their own temperaments. Given the "uncontrollable" nature of such urges and desires, it was difficult for many to understand the severity of the punishment. Besides, many in Chakpur were engaged in sexual affairs.

While Sayyid Shah emphasized the force of external agency to achieve proper conduct, he was not without his own sense of internal struggle—born, perhaps, of his own misfortunes. While he might dismiss his Nunari covillagers as *jangli*—wild, uneducated, and youth-like—he nonetheless understood their very human problems. In talking about his family and his role as husband and father, he said: "A person who does not feel pleasure—a person who pits his piety against his desires and wins, killing his desires—is a person who will not be able to love."

Jabina Abbas

From 1976 to 1978, Jabina did not generally cast her relationships in a language that was explicitly Islamic, though it resonated with associated ideas. She was deciding whether to continue her career and grappling with the difficulties faced by women in Pakistani society. She was also wrestling with a conflict between her own desires and her responsibilities toward her family. This was reflected in her discussions about marriage, which often included stories of failed marriages and illustrated how the insensitivity of husbands led to the degradation of wives intent on upholding their honor.

Jabina hoped to have a marriage characterized by mutual understanding, kindness, respect, and obedience. "Each should respect, obey, and understand the other. It isn't just the wife's job to do this," she said. She wanted to decide on her own husband. Commonly called a "love marriage" in urban Pakistan, this is "making a marriage of one's own accord" (*apni marzi se shadi karna*), as opposed to relying on one's parents' decision. The rationale for parents' making a marriage for their children is that young people do not have sufficient *ʿaql* to make a sound decision. They are likely to be swayed by emotions and physical desires. But older, more experienced men and women, Jabina felt, possess sufficient *ʿaql* to weigh marriage considerations rationally.

Jabina was aware of the Islamization program through speeches and rallies held in Karachi and coverage of debates about its consequences in the newspapers, on television, and in family discussions. A new mosque being constructed down the block from Jabina's residence provoked discussion about the spate of mosque-building in Pakistan. Jabina found it ironic that so many mosques were being built and so much money being spent when hospitals, clinics, schools, and orphanages were needed. "Is this Islam for show? Is this the real Islam?" she asked.

She was distressed that neighbors used the language of "Nizam-i Islam" to deride her career and accomplishments. Music and dance, she and her brothers were told, were "against Islam." She was aware that some neighbors, relatives, and family friends spoke negatively of her involvement in music and dance, and this upset her: "I am not a stone. I have my feelings. I have done good things and behaved properly. These people talk as though I were a prostitute." Jabina saw no reason to be ashamed of her career. Opportunities for domestic and local performances dried up during the initial Islamization period, though there was still a demand for her participation in international cultural exchange programs. She found it ironic that she and her brothers could represent Pakistan abroad but not at home.

Jabina's notion of Islam was very broad and somewhat relativistic. She had no doubt about her own identity as a Muslim: she kept the Ramadan fast, said *namaz* on Fridays, and believed in obeying Allah's word. "Of course we should obey the word of God. Any fault in this world is not God's, but man's." She felt that some people, such as *pirs*, were especially blessed, but she did not follow a *pir*. Many Islamic teachings are also common to other religions, she asserted. "There are things we should do no matter what our religion. These are honorable things to do. It's a matter of being human. They are right whatever our religion."

Jabina's battle during the initiation of Islamization was with a society which she felt had too base a view of itself. She saw herself as a kind, respectful person who had human feelings and desires. She operated rightfully, rationally, and with the best of intentions. Even in her dancing she emphasized the importance of mental discipline and bodily control, and she never considered her dancing to have an erotic or sexual aspect. She felt unjustly accused because other people had "dirty minds," because other people were so dominated by their *nafs*. She did not want to fight against others and felt that the most important struggle (*jihad*) was fought within oneself. She was confident that she had lived a life in which her spiritual nature—her beliefs, actions, and ennobling emotions—had precedence. She had, as she said many times, "a clean heart" or "clear conscience" (*saf dil*).

Jabina's brothers gave up their musical careers between 1978 and 1980 and secured mid-level sales and clerical jobs for private firms. Her youngest brother, then in college, pursued a degree in pharmacy. Jabina's resident sisters-in-law began to instruct their children in daily readings of the Qur'an. The frequency of saying *namaz* in the household increased substantially, as did her brothers' attendance at *jama* [Friday] prayers in the neighborhood mosque. By 1980, Jabina had ended her performance career and given up a lifelong dream of starting her own dance school. In 1982, she married and moved into a modest home about half a mile from her mother's house. Her husband was a mid-level white-collar worker whom she had known for some time.

Conclusion: The Impact of Islamization

By 1986–87, villagers in Chakpur had completed the construction of a new facade and addition to the village mosque. More newborn children were given traditional names drawn from the Qur'an and Muslim history than traditional Punjabi names. About a dozen boys studied the Qur'an with the village *maulvi*, as they had in the decade before. The incidence of pilgrimage to Mecca, daily recitation of *namaz*, and other Islamic duties seemed about the same, although perhaps a few more people held to the Ramadan fast than in the previous decade. Most people in Chakpur were skeptical about the government's Islamization program. They did not see a more just or moral society nor one that made it easier for them to operate as good Muslims, as good human beings. Indeed, they felt that the government's Islamization program impinged on them through the agricultural taxation policy and threats to change land-inheritance patterns.

Sayyid Shah continued in his previous role: villagers were still relatively hot and uncivilized, and his role was to cool them down and civilize them through adherence to the teaching of Islam. If anything, the Islamization program gave him greater coercive power to do so. He could point to the state and to the broader society as agreeing with him, and thus he painted his neighbors as more marginal. Rather than being an isolated voice, as he was prior to Islamization, Sayyid Shah was able to speak with a louder, stronger, and more compelling voice.

Interestingly, Sayyid Shah no longer spoke alone. A well-respected older woman in the village, who headed her family and held sizable acreage, had, during the Islamization period, begun to teach Islamic practices and history to a handful of village girls. She was also appointed to the area's *zakat* committee. Being a Nunari and a woman, she was well positioned to exert moral suasion vis-à-vis other village women and thus offered an alternative voice to that of Sayyid Shah. Her message and style was more familial, less ominous and stern than the Sayyid's. Still, each acknowledged the good work of the other.

By the same time, Jabina had given birth to a child, a daughter. Her career as a dancer and her family's musical history had receded. She saw herself as a good wife in an honorable and successful marriage. Her external practice of Islam did not change, and she still held to the primacy of conscience rather than external force or subscription to a particular code as determining whether one was a good Muslim. She remained skeptical of the Islamization program and, when I visited in 1988, was distressed at the breakdown of civil order in Karachi. Islamization had not made her neighborhood or the city a better place to live. For all the speeches, social changes, and hopes, Karachi was less civil, less honorable, and less a place of mutual understanding. For her, the Islamization of Pakistani society had failed.

Interestingly, its effects were still being felt in her family's household. Her youngest brother had married a stewardess. While Jabina's sister-in-law brought needed income into the family, there was considerable pressure for her to give up her career. Stewardesses are often derided for having to deal with unrelated males and are imputed to be less than honorable. By 1990, Jabina's sister-in-law had made enough money to help purchase a new home for her and her husband, and she gave up her career. By the year's end, Jabina's two other brothers found working and living in Karachi difficult. They travelled to New York to work in a clothing store and began to play music again, part-time, in a restaurant, with the intention of bringing over their families to settle.

Islamization in Pakistan did not come suddenly into the lives of Sayyid Shah and Jabina Abbas but was part of an ongoing process of self-awareness and decision-making with regard to their definition of themselves and their society. It had the effect of heightening some thoughts, emotions, and actions and bringing them into relief in relation to others. Neither Jabina or Sayyid Shah were passive receptacles of government policies but actors who negotiated and articulated the meanings of those policies and orientations in their own lives. Islamization empowered certain institutions, roles, and rhetoric and disempowered others. Whether as explicit government policy or as the daily attempt of Muslims to use Islamic ideas and values to conjure meaning, it will continue to do so.

References

Alavi, Hamza (1986). "Ethnicity, Muslim Society, and the Pakistan Ideology." In *Islamic Reassertion in Pakistan*, ed. Anita Weiss, pp. 21–48. Syracuse: Syracuse University Press.

Burki, Shahid Javed Burki (1986). "Economic Management within an Islamic Context." In *Islamic Reassertion in Pakistan*, ed. Anita Weiss, pp. 49–58. Syracuse: Syracuse University Press.

Clark, Grace (1986). "Pakistan's *Zakat* and *'Ushr* as a Welfare System." In *Islamic Reassertion in Pakistan*, ed. Anita Weiss, pp. 79–96. Syracuse: Syracuse University Press.

Dumont, Louis (1970). *Homo Hierarchicus: An Essay on the Caste System*. Chicago: University of Chicago Press.

Fischer, Michael (1980). *Iran: From Religious Dispute to Revolution*. Cambridge: Harvard University Press.

Geertz, Clifford (1973 [orig. 1966]). "Person, Time, and Conduct in Bali." In *The Interpretation of Cultures*, ed. Clifford Geertz, pp. 360–411. New York: The Free Press.

Gilmartin, David (1988). *Empire and Islam: Punjab and the Making of Pakistan*. Berkeley: University of California Press.

Kurin, Richard (1981). "Person, Family and Kin in Two Pakistani Communities." Ph.D. Dissertation, Department of Anthropology, University of Chicago.

——— (1984). "Morality, Personhood and the Exemplary Life: Popular Conceptions of Muslims in Paradise." In *Moral Conduct and Authority: The Place of Adab in South Asian Islam*, ed. Barbara Metcalf, pp. 196–220. Berkeley: University of California Press.

——— (1985). "Islamization: A View from the Countryside." *Asian Survey* 25, no. 8: 852–62.

——— (1988). "The Culture of Ethnicity in Two Pakistani Commmunities." In *South Asian Islam: Moral Principles in Tension*, ed. Katherine Ewing, pp. 220–247. Berkeley: University of California Press.

Lapidus, Ira (1984). "Knowledge, Virtue and Action: The Classical Muslim Conception of Adab and the Nature of Religious Fulfillment in Islam." In *Moral Conduct and Authority: The Place of Adab in South Asian Islam*, ed. Barbara Metcalf, pp. 38–61. Berkeley: University of California Press.

Lewis, Oscar (1963). *The Children of Sanchez*. New York: Random House.

Lewis, Oscar, Ruth Lewis, and Susan Rigdon (1977). *Four Women: Living the Revolution, An Oral History of Contemporary Cuba*. Urbana: University of Illinois Press.

Maududi, Maulana S. A. (1972). *Purdah and the Status of Women in Society*, trans. al-Asha'ari. Lahore: Islamic Publications.

Mayer, Ann (1986). "Islamization and Taxation in Pakistan." In *Islamic Reassertion in Pakistan*, ed. Anita Weiss, pp. 59–78. Syracuse: Syracuse University Press.

Naim, C. M., ed. (1979). *Iqbal, Jinnah and Pakistan: The Vision and the Reality*. Foreign and Comparative Studies/South Asia, no. 5. Syracuse: Maxwell School, Syracuse University.

Parsons, Talcott, and Edward Shils, eds. (1951). *Toward a General Theory of Action*. Cambridge: Harvard University Press.

Rahman, Fazlur (1982). *Islam and Modernity: Transformation of an Intellectual Tradition*. Chicago: University of Chicago Press.

Sayeed, Khalid bin (1967). *The Political System of Pakistan*. Boston: Houghton Mifflin.

Weiss, Anita (1986). "The Historical Debate on Islam and the State in South Asia." In *Islamic Reassertion in Pakistan*, ed. Anita Weiss, pp. 1–20. Syracuse: Syracuse University Press.

Conclusion

THE LIMITS OF "EXPERT" KNOWLEDGE

Muhammad Khalid Masud

Recent political changes in the Middle East, Eastern Europe, and the former Soviet Union have made us realize how limited our "expert knowledge" actually is. This is particularly true in the case of Muslim politics. Some attempts have been made to analyze these limitations—indeed, this chapter grows out of my own participation in one such endeavor.[1]

Two well-known scholars of comparative politics, Gabriel A. Almond and G. Bingham Powell (1966: 2–12), have severely criticized the approaches of American political scientists studying non-American political systems. First, they said, these studies are Eurocentric and belong to the area study tradition. Second, the studies are configurative and offer little or no systems analysis. And finally, they are formal studies only of institutions, rules, regulations, and ideologies; they do not examine how these systems perform politically. Almond and Powell urged that studies in comparative politics be based on comprehensive scope, precision, and realism. They should also include a study of the intellectual order of individual societies.

This advice applies to the study of Muslim politics as well. Nearly ten years ago, James A. Piscatori, a political scientist, pointed out that "to date there have been only a few empirical studies that try to go beyond the impressionistic and general and take the measure of Islam's current political activity. . . . Islamic politics is an elusive and contentious subject to study" (Piscatori 1983: 1–2).

The frustration that Piscatori voiced speaks eloquently of the limitations of expert knowledge about Muslim politics. In this chapter, I attempt to pinpoint those limitations and offer some comments.

---

1. "Other Orients: Soviet and American Perspectives on Muslim and Middle Eastern Societies and Politics," conference held in Hanover, N.H., and Washington, D.C., April 4–11, 1991.

Methodology

Perhaps the foremost limitation arises from the methodology employed in most studies of Muslim politics. The categories, classifications, and paradigms used for analysis and prediction are inadequate.[2] The category of nation-state, for example, assigns fundamental significance to territory,[3] yet territory is an unstable variable in modern Muslim states. Events in India, Pakistan, Bangladesh, Palestine, Central Asia, and Eastern Europe illustrate the point quite graphically. Language, ethnicity, and culture are also difficult to define territorially, and recent political developments in the Middle East, Asia, and Europe suggest that it is not a nation that defines a state, but a state that defines a nation.

Historically, nation-states have been seen by political historians as resulting from the breakup of empires (Sonn 1990: 2–30). Empires of course required a legitimacy that transcended ethnic, racial, and linguistic loyalties, and this was often provided by religion. Such legitimacy is not required for nation-states, however. Since there has not yet been a proper historical analysis of the nation-state and its continuity in Muslim political thought, let me note only that most Muslim nation-states are not the product of the breakup of great Muslim empires.

The most notable exception, of course, is the Ottoman Empire, which produced both kingdoms and Arab nationalism. Arab nationalism, however, was as extraterritorial as religion. The modern Muslim states of Asia and Africa arose from the demise of European colonial empires, which did not base their legitimacy on religion. It is thus obvious that the empire/nation-state/secularism paradigm is irrelevant to Muslim nation-states.

An exaggerated focus on territory has thus prevented any real understanding of the Muslim conception of national and political identity. This focus probably grows out of a view of international relations in which loyalty to religion necessarily means territorial expansion. In Tomara Sonn's words, "When the religion on which the legitimacy is based claims universal applicability, it is by nature expansive, rejecting the inviolability of geographical borders on which national stability is based" (Sonn 1990: xi). Piscatori has discussed Bernard Lewis's and Adda Bozeman's views about Islam, which are very similar (Piscatori 1986: 42).

In analyzing Western writers' views on Islam and international relations,

---

2. Albert O. Hirschman (1979) cautions that the search for paradigms may prove a hindrance to understanding social phenomena. Referring to two studies of politics in Latin America, he shows how one provides an understanding without a paradigm, while the other is frustrated because a single paradigm spawns thirty-four hypotheses.

3. A recent study defines nation-state as "a combination of . . . two concepts: it is a nation or group of people with a common identity who accept territorial limitations, or it is a geographically limited territory whose inhabitants have developed some sense of common identity" (Sonn 1990: 20).

Piscatori notes that "it is almost inevitable that, insofar as Islam is a factor in international relations, it will work to the disadvantage of the West" (Piscatori 1986: 43). Quoting Lewis ("foreign policy is a European concept . . . alien and new in the world of Islam"), Bozeman ("Islam is inimical to the core idea of the state"), and J. B. Kelly ("the animosity borne by the Muslim Arab world for the Christian West is of such intensity that it was bound sooner or later to cause the Arab maxim of the 'the enemy of my enemy is my friend and malevolent foe'"), Piscatori finds Western writers looking at the role of Islam in Muslim states from the perspective of Cold War ideology (Piscatori 1986: 43). On the other hand, as long as there is a consensus among modern Muslim intellectuals on the acceptance of "nation-state" as a fact of life, Islam plays a significant and integrative role for the definition of national and political identity among Muslims.

Empirical evidence "point[s] to a single conclusion: Islam is one of the more powerful sources of social and political identities for Arabs" (Carrol 1986: 189).[4] Terrance G. Carrol ascribes this to the fact that Islam is a political religion, and that Islam, more than any other religion, calls upon its followers to display their commitment publicly (Carrol 1986: 189). Vyacheslev Ya. Belokrenitsky makes a similar observation in the case of South Asian states. He notes in his chapter that the ethnic and linguistic homogeneity among Muslims in Bangladesh makes it unnecessary for religion to play an integrative role, but in other areas Islam fulfills a nation-building function.

Aside from the complexity of "nation-state" as a category, most approaches and frameworks for studying Muslim politics have been ideologically oriented. They usually employ deterministic frameworks for their analysis, and modern scholars have seen a diminishing role for religion since secularism meant democracy, freedom, progress, and development. Unfortunately, such frameworks have not been employed as temporary tools, as was initially intended. Worse still, the frameworks were often developed for other disciplines or areas, and this has presented serious problems for their application to Muslim politics: either the time span between the framework's development and its application was so long that some of its postulates were outdated, or it was not seen as a framework that had to be amended over time. Dale F. Eickelman (1985) observed, for example, that Weber's typological characterization of domination was an improvement over that of Marx and Engels, yet in his study of the transition from theocracy to monarchy, Eickelman found it nearly impossible to conceive of practical situations in which the two forms of domination were pure and clear.

Another example of the limitations of borrowed or outdated frameworks is

---

4. Based on studies in Lebanon in 1957–58 and 1971, in Kuwait and the Gulf states in 1976–77, among Arab students in Boston in 1979–80 and Arab university students in the United States, and on surveys conducted by a number of researchers at various universities in the United States between 1966 and 1970 (cited in Carrol 1986: 189).

J. Koren and Y. D. Nevo (1991). In this study the authors used source criticism to study the history of the Islamic state. Ignaz Goldziher applied source criticism—which was originally developed for the analysis of language and literature—to a study of Islamic history in Jerusalem. A number of these findings have since been refuted by other scholars. Despite this, Koren and Nevo also used source criticism, which led them to suggest that the Islamic state originated in Syria, not in the Hijaz.[5]

Perhaps the second most difficult category to define is "Islam," where the problem is with the referent by which it is defined. The diversity of these referents and the efforts to find a "realist" definition—a search for "essential" characteristics—has been emphasized by most scholars. Kevin Reinhart (1990), who has analyzed use of the term Islam in recent studies, observes that Duncan Black MacDonald described Islam in essentialist terms and thus for him Islam produced a characteristic form of government. Reuben Levy, H. A. R. Gibb, and others have followed this essentialist line. Marshall Hodgson criticized this approach as imprecise and spoke about "Islams" to emphasize the diversity in Muslim societies. Anthropologists and sociologists have subsequently revised this and have written about unity in this diversity. Now scholars are proposing a translocal phenomenon—Cosmopolitan Islam (Reinhart 1990).

While efforts have been made to find a realist definition, conceptual or nominalist definitions of Islam have not received an equal emphasis.[6] A definition for Islam has been complicated by the choice of referents. A realist definition, for example, uses Muslims, and sometimes *ulama*, as the referent. Michael Curtis's (1981) chapters on religion and politics in Egypt, Saudi Arabia, and Turkey are examples of such a definition. He refers to *ulama* in order to analyze Islam in politics in these countries. Some studies refer to Islam as a name or a technical term and define it lexically and technically. Very few have treated Islam as a concept. William Roff (1987: 1) has recently suggested yet another definition—"being Muslim."

The *ulama* rose as an organized group or as political parties only in the twentieth century. They have their own training institutions, printing presses, periodicals, and publication programs. They also have national networks linked to international organizations. Some studies have been made of the *ulama*, and scholars have urged that further research be done (Esposito 1990: 8). However, while the modernity of this phenomenon should be stressed, more precision is required to distinguish among the various religious groups—*sufi* groups (like

---

5. Earlier, Moshe Sharon (1988: 228) had claimed the birth of Islam in Jerusalem under the Umayyads.

6. I rely on G. W. Paton (1964: 62–68) for this classification. He argues that the accepted method of definition is to discover the genus to which a thing belongs and the particular characteristics that distinguish it from other characteristics or mere incidents. But the need for clarity demands that we be explicit about what we are referring to—a word, a thing, or a concept. Thus, a definition may be nominalist, realist, or conceptual, depending on its respective referents.

Naqshbandia), juridical groups (like the Hanafis and Malikis), sects (like the Shiʿa, Deobandi, and Barelawi), Daʿwa groups (like Tablighi Jamaʿat), and neo-ʿulama (scholars graduating from modern institutions).[7] Such a distinction is necessary because not all these groups stress participation in politics.

We should also study their popular appeal. Occasional electoral victories (as in Algeria) do not explain their lack of electoral success on other occasions. We need to look too at some popular postulates and paradigms about the ʿulama. The paradigms of conflict, for example, where the role of religious groups is often described as oppositional, are incorrect, since there are always some religious groups that support governments.[8] In some political systems, they are part of the ruling elite.[9]

"Tribe" is another complex category. As Gene R. Garthwaite's chapter points out, notions of tribe have not yet been scientifically analyzed. While Soviet scholars have dealt with "tribe" within a Marxist-Leninist framework of economic evolution, others saw "tribe" as linked to the notion of nation. Both have some common elements—language and culture, for example—but often "tribe" is perceived as a primordial social organization, lower than state in terms of political evolution.

In referring to various tribes in Iran, Garthwaite observes that the Bakhtiyari tribes were organized as confederations. Thus they had political representation in a state structure. Some tribes, as Garthwaite points out, developed strong nationalistic sentiments while others did not. Such observations are very valuable in correcting the general notion of a tribe as a nonpolitical group.

It is clear that we must pay serious attention to terms and concepts in our discourse on Muslim politics. Some terms used by scholars for modern political concepts and institutions have historical semantic contexts that may carry some of the same ideas and meanings. *Khilafa* and *imama*, for example, are sometimes used as Islamic names for state and government. They are not neutral terms, however. We must not overlook the fact that they also have theological and polemical connotations, since they originated in political contexts as discussed in theological texts. Although the terms are often used interchangeably, the debates in early Islam and again during the Abbasid period on whether the ruler should be called Khalifat Allah [deputy of God] or Khalifat Rasul

---

7. For a study of ʿulama in Islam and its various manifestations, see Algar (1987). For the very significant and more politicized role of the neo-ʿulama—as opposed to the traditional ʿulama—see Van Dijk (1981) and Masud (1990).

8. Both al-Azhar ʿulama in Egypt and Ansar in the Sudan supported their governments (Curtis 1981: 77–88, 307–19).

9. In medieval Muslim politics, we often find the ʿulama as a part of the ruling elite. The Maliki ʿulama in Spain were partners in the Umayyad and the Almoravid political systems (Masud 1977: 49–65; Masud 1991). In India the ʿulama were always part of the ruling elite, whereas most sufis were generally opposed to participation in politics (Hardy 1958: 465; Nizami 1978). Sajida Sultana Alvi (1989: 107) has observed, however, that "the extent of the ʿulama's influence fluctuated with the personality of the ruler."

Allah [successor to the Prophet] reflect the theological context in which the religious legitimacy was being discussed. Similarly, the term *imam* also refers to the leader of ritual prayers.

Debates on the definition and application of these terms began very early in Islamic history. Early rulers were called Khalifa or Amir al-Muminin, and the political developments of the civil wars between the Khawarij and the Shiʿat ʿAli and between the Umayyads and the Abbasids were framed in theological terms. Modern scholars therefore find it very difficult to separate the political from the theological and juridical doctrines (Lambton 1978: 948). Abuʾl Aʿla Mawdudi prefers the term *khalifa* to *hakim*, as the latter is an attribute of God alone (Mawdudi 1960: 235).

One significant aspect of the theological context is that for the Shiʿa, *imama* is a matter of fundamental principles (*usul*); for the Sunnis, it is a matter of detail (*furuʿ*). Yet, because of its polemical context, both Sunnis and Shiʿa treat the subject in books on *kalam* [theology] rather than in books on law. We do not find separate chapters dealing with political theory or constitutional law in *fiqh* [law texts], although problems of detail regarding public and constitutional laws are scattered throughout *fiqh* books (Mawdudi 1960: 221). No doubt there are books exclusively on the rules of government—Abuʾl-Hasan al-Mawardi's (d. 1058) *al-Ahkam al-Sultaniyya*, for example—but they were never incorporated in the juridical texts.

Even though the Sunnis consider *imama* a juridical subject and not one of the fundamentals to be discussed in books of theology, invariably a full chapter is devoted to a discussion of *imama* at the end of theological texts. Hasan Hanafi (1988: 166ff.) disagrees with these approaches and deals with the question as a fundamental principle of Islam.

The rules, regulations and models of state and government have changed over the years, which has prompted the addition of new terms for political authorities: sultan, padishah, amir, and nawab, for example. We need a precise analysis of these terms and their historical contexts.

Sources

Studies of Muslim politics have usually been studies of scholars by scholars for scholars, which misses the essential ingredient of the political process: the masses. Scholars write about Islamic politics and Islamic political theories using texts written by the scholars of the classical, medieval, and modern periods (for example, Rosenthal 1958; Lambton 1985; Lewis 1988). These are literary sources, and they suffer from that inherent limitation. Furthermore, they are historical interpretations of literary texts written retrospectively. Texts on Muslim political theory to which most scholars refer may be divided into four genres, or traditions: mirror, philosophical-ethical, juridical, and theological.

The mirror genre is an *adab* (literary) tradition. It includes books written by government functionaries and consists of manuals of governance like Abu'l-Fadl ʿAllami's (d. 1602) Aʾin-i Akbari. This tradition has produced primarily advice literature, what is known as mirror books, such as Abu Hamid al-Ghazali's (d. 1111) Nasihat al-Muluk. The mirror genre approaches politics humanistically; and it refers either to pre-Islamic precedents, as in Shihar al-Din al-Qalqashandi's (d. 1418) Subh al-Aʿsha, or to non-Islamic models, as in Nizam al-Mulk al-Tusi's (d. 1092) Siyasat Name. From the medieval period onward, this tradition refers to the Sassanid statecraft model of the West and South Asia, in which the ruler has absolute power. The religious elite or ʿulama are given a distinct role because religion and government are considered twins.

The philosophical-ethical genre of literature approaches political theory in Aristotelian fashion. Aiming to achieve happiness, it looks for ideal types. Examples of this tradition are Abu Nasr al-Farabi's (d. 950) al-Madinat al-Fadila and Muhammad al-Dawani's (d. 1502 or 1503) Akhlaq-i Jalali.

The juridical genre treats constitutional and administrative law as separate from the legal compendia, although employing the principles of jurisprudence. It does not refer to pre-Islamic or non-Islamic precedents, but it attempts to consolidate and systematize Muslim political practice. The best-known example of this tradition is Mawardi's al-Ahkam al-Sultaniyya. Similar treatises also serve as an implicit criticism of contemporary political systems. Sometimes the criticism is quite obvious, as in Ibn Taymiyya's (d. 1328) al-Siyasat al-Sharʿiyya.

The theological genre treats the imamate as a matter of creed, and it considers obedience to the imam as a religious obligation. Contributors to this tradition discuss issues such as whether rebellion against the imam is ever justified or even whether the rule of the first four caliphs was really valid.

These genres differ both in their emphasis and in their approach to political questions. The terms and categories such traditions develop, therefore, should be used with great caution, for they often carry medieval nuances.

As noted above, the study of modern Muslim politics tends to focus on literary, official, and elite sources. Even the study of popular movements often concentrates on the literature they issue and the official statements they publish (Esposito 1990: 5). The press in fact has become a primary source in the study of Muslim politics, and this is unfortunate; for in Muslim countries it is often controlled directly or indirectly by government, and it tends to support the official viewpoint. That the radical press is equally unreliable in providing an accurate picture of the political process can be seen from the two studies in this book that discuss Islamization in Pakistan: the insights that Richard Kurin offers are not available in official or literary sources; and Dimitri B. Novossyolov shows that while Islamization appears viable and successful from official sources, observations at the personal level reveal very real problems.

Some recent studies have used other literary sources—novels, drama, poetry—and they have provided more insights about the political processes than official or political texts. An example of such a study is David B. Edwards's chapter, which illustrates the power of metaphor in political poetry. It also gives evidence that the poetics of politics is not entirely Islamic. This is a significant comment on the popular view of politics, for the popular image of the political leader—in contradistinction to literary and classical Islamic political theory—is of a powerful, vengeful king. There is emphasis on social hierarchy, genealogy, and honor.

Folk literature in general has a pessimistic view of politics. Kings and rulers are usually repressive; benevolent kings are rare. The role of religion is suprarational and magical (indeed, saints are venerated more than jurists). In short, the worldview in folk literature sees political power as absolute and personal. We need more in-depth studies of such literature, which is often oral, to relate to the political attitudes of the masses.

Language

A significant limitation is imposed by various semiotic aspects of language. By this I mean lack of attention to language as a means of communication in the political process. One aspect is word choice: selecting words that will gain sympathy and support and avoiding words or meanings that may arouse hostility. Afghans, for instance, called themselves Mujahidin because that is a prestigious and acceptable term among Muslims. The American press and scholars called them "freedom fighters" or "the resistance movement" to avoid association of the terms *mujahidin* and *jihad* [holy war].

The semantic of political slogans is another area that needs further study. Identifying how and when slogans become popular, lose their popularity, and change meaning would provide insight into the semantics of political contexts.

A third area of concern is the complicated process of translating political terms from one language to another, and the translator attempts to transfer the political concept of one community into that of another. The translator's choice of words reflects his or her decision to convey some senses and avoid others. The translation of nationalism as *qawmiyya* or *wataniyya*, for example, reflects very different emphases (Piscatori 1986: 107–109), as does the translation of sovereignty as *hukm*, *hakimiyya*, or *siyada*.[10] "State" implies very different conceptions when translated, respectively, as *riyasa*, *dawla*, *saltana*, or *mamlika*.

Acceptability

Another significant limitation comes from the writer's conception of his audience. When an analysis is written for state policymakers, the choice of

---

10. ʿAbd al-Hamid Mutawalli (1978: 165) refers to Mawdudi's translation of *hakimiyya* as sovereignty, while Mutawalli prefers to translate it as *siyada*. Muhammad Amara (1987: 185–222) is also critical of Mawdudi's translation. In analyzing Mawdudi's use of *hakimiyya*, Amara finds it synonymous with *uluhiyya* [divinity]. With such a connotation, the concept of sovereignty leads necessarily to a theocratic view of state.

words, paradigms, and framework differs dramatically from an analysis written for the press or for a Muslim audience. The main reason for the difference is the criterion of acceptability and the author's conception of the reader's expectations.

A recent development has been the growing number of Muslim communities in Western countries. They are well organized and articulate and insist on representing a Muslim point of view. Pressure is building to determine the criteria of acceptability, and this has an influence on the framework that a study will assume.

Personality

Finally, I should speak about personal limitations. Muslim criticism maintains that a non-Muslim cannot understand Islam and the Muslim view of politics. Studies by non-Muslim scholars or by Muslim scholars trained in Western universities are termed "Orientalist" (Masud 1991: 14). Although this criticism is exaggerated, the personality of the scholar studying Muslim politics is important for understanding the problems, framing the questions, and exploring the data. The scholar's training, cultural literacy, nationality, position, religious background, worldview, and attitudes toward the contemporary world order all play a vital role.

The chapters in this volume point, explicitly and implicitly, to some of the limitations of expert knowledge. There is a need for a constant revision of paradigms, a critical view of sources, and a comprehensive approach to the study of Muslim politics and societies. I hope that this book will generate deliberations along these lines.

References

Algar, Hamid (1987). "ʿUlama." In *Encyclopedia of Religion*, vol. 15, ed. Mircea Eliade, pp. 115–17. New York: Macmillan.

Almond, Gabriel A., and G. Bingham Powell (1966). *Comparative Politics: A Developmental Approach*. Boston: Little, Brown.

Alvi, Sajida Sultana (1989). *Advice on the Art of Governance: Mau'izah-i-Jahangiri of Muhammad Baqir Nam-i-sani, An Indo-Islamic Mirror of Princes*. New York: State University of New York Press.

Amara, Muhammad (1987). *Abuʾl Aʿla al-Mawdudi waʾl Sahwat al-Islamiyya* [Abuʾl Aʿla al-Mawdudi and the Islamic Awakening]. Cairo: Dar al-Shuruq.

Carrol, Terrance G. (1986). "Islam and Political Community in the Arab World." *International Journal of Middle East Studies* 18: 185–204.

Curtis, Michael, ed. (1981). *Religion and Politics in the Middle East*. Boulder: Westview Press.

Eickelman, Dale F. (1985). "From Theocracy to Monarchy, Authority and Legitimacy in Inner Oman, 1935–1957." *International Journal of Middle East Studies* 17: 3–24.

Esposito, John L. (1990). "The Study of Islam: Challenge and Prospects." *Middle East Studies Association Bulletin* 24, no. 1: 1–11.

Hanafi, Hasan (1988). *Min al-ʿAqida ila al-Thawra* [From Faith to Revolution], vol. 5. Cairo: Madbuli.

Hardy, Peter (1958). "The Muslim Ruler in India." In *Sources of Indian Tradition*, vol. I, ed. William Theodore De Bary, pp. 455–500. New York: Columbia University Press.

Hirschman, Alberto O. (1979). "The Search for Paradigms as a Hindrance to Understanding." In *Interpretive Social Science: A Reader*, ed. Paul Rabinow and William M. Sullivan, pp. 163–79. Berkeley: University of California.

Koren, J., and Y. D. Nevo (1991). "Methodological Approaches to Islamic Studies." *Der Islam* 68, no. 1: 87–107.

Lambton, Ann K. S. (1978). "Khalifa in Political Theory." In *The Encyclopedia of Islam,* 2nd ed., vol. 3, pp. 947–50. Leiden: Brill.

——— (1985). *State and Government in Medieval Islam*. Oxford: Oxford University Press.

Lewis, Bernard (1988). *The Political Language of Islam*. Chicago: University of Chicago Press.

Madelung, William (1971). "Imama." In *The Encyclopedia of Islam*, 2nd ed., vol. 3, pp. 1163–69. Leiden: Brill.

Masud, M. K. (1977). *Islamic Legal Philosophy*. Islamabad: Islamic Research Institute.

——— (1990). "The Obligation to Migrate: The Doctrine of Hijra in Islamic Law." In *Muslim Travellers: Pilgrimage, Migration and the Religious Imagination*, ed. Dale F. Eickelman and James Piscatori, pp. 29–49. London: Routledge.

——— (1991). "Orientalism." In Ministry of Education, *Highlighting the History of the Islamic World in School Curricula*, pp. 12–31. Islamabad: Government of Pakistan.

Mawdudi, Abu'l Aʿla (1960). *Islamic Law and Constitution*. Trans. Kurshid Ahmad. Lahore: Islamic Publications.

Mutawalli, ʿAbd al-Hamid (1978). *Mabadi Nizam al-Hukm fi'l Islam* [Principles of the System of Governance in Islam]. Alexandria: Ma'arif.

Nafisi, ʿAbdullah al- (1989). *al-Harakat al-Islamiyya: Ru'ya Mutaqbaliyya, Awraq fi'l Naqd al-Dhati*. Cairo: Madbuli.

Nizami, Khaliq Ahmad (1978). "Aspects of Muslim Political Thought in India during the Fourteenth Century." *Islamic Culture* 52: 213–40.

Paton, G. W. (1964). *A Textbook of Jurisprudence*. Oxford: Oxford University Press.

Piscatori, James A. (1983). *Islam in the Political Process*. Cambridge: Cambridge University Press.

Reinhart, Kevin (1991). "The Limits of Expertise." Paper presented at conference on "Other Orients: Soviet and American Perspectives in Muslim and Middle Eastern Societies," Hanover, N.H., and Washington, D.C., April 4–11.

Roff, William, ed. (1987). *Islam and Political Economy of Meaning: Comparative Studies of Muslim Discourse*, "Introduction," pp. 1–10. London: Croom, Helm.

Rosenthal, E. I. J. (1958). *Political Thought in Medieval Islam*. Cambridge: Cambridge University Press.

Sharon, Moshe (1988). "The Birth of Islam in the Holy Land." In *The Holy Land in History and Thought*, ed. Sharon, pp. 225–35. Leiden: Brill.

Sonn, Tomara (1990). *Between Quran and Crown: The Challenge of Political Legitimacy in the Arab World*. Boulder: Westview Press.

Van Dijk, C. (1981). *Rebellion under the Banner of Islam: The Darul Islam in Indonesia*. The Hague: Martinus Nijhoff.

NOTES ON CONTRIBUTORS

Abdujabar Abduvakhitov is Scientific Secretary of the Institute of Oriental Studies in the Uzbekistan Academy of Science, Tashkent. He received a Ph.D. from the State University of Tashkent in 1990 and earlier studied Arabic at al-Azhar University in Cairo. In addition to his dissertation, "The Ideology and Practice of the Muslim Brotherhood in Egypt and Syria," he has published articles in Russian and Uzbek on contemporary Islamist movements in Central Asia and the Middle East. Since 1990, he has also been a coeditor of *Maverannahr*, an Uzbek political and scholarly journal.

Vyacheslav Ya. Belokrenitsky is the chair of the Near and Middle East Department, Institute of Oriental Studies, Russian Academy of Sciences in Moscow. His writings include *Small-Scale Industries in Pakistan Economy* (Moscow: Nauka Press, 1972), *Pakistan: Specific Features and Problems of Urbanization* (Moscow: Nauka Press, 1982), and *Capitalism in Pakistan: History of Socio-Economic Development* (New Delhi: Patriot Publishers, 1990).

Richard W. Cottam is University Professor of Political Science (Emeritus) at the University of Pittsburgh. His books include *Nationalism in Iran* (1964, revised 1978), *The Rehabilitation of Power in International Relations* (with Gerard Gallucci, 1978), and *Iran and the United States: A Cold War Case Study* (1988), as well as numerous contributions to edited books and scholarly journals. His research interests include Middle Eastern politics, American policy toward the Middle East, and international relations theory.

David B. Edwards is Assistant Professor of Anthropology at Williams College. A graduate of the University of Michigan, he has held a Mellon Post-Doctoral Fellowship at Washington University in St. Louis and has conducted extensive field research in Pakistan and Afghanistan. His publications include "Mad Mullahs and Englishmen: Discourse in the Colonial Encounter," *Comparative Studies in Society and History* (1989), and "Origins of the Anti-Soviet Jihad" in *Afghan Resistance: The Politics of Survival*, ed. Grant M. Farr and John G. Merriam (1987). He is currently completing a book entitled *Pretexts of Rebellion: The Cultural Origins of Pakhtun Resistance to the Afghan State*.

Dale F. Eickelman is Ralph and Richard Lazarus Professor of Anthropology and Human Relations at Dartmouth College. He has spent more than seven years in the Middle East since the late 1960s, including extensive field research in Morocco and the Sultanate of Oman. His publications include *Muslim Travellers: Pilgrimage, Migration and the Religious Imagination* (coedited with

James Piscatori, 1990), *The Middle East: An Anthropological Approach* (1981; 2nd ed., 1989), *Knowledge and Power in Morocco* (1985), *Moroccan Islam* (1976), and numerous scholarly articles and contributions to edited books. He is a former president of the Middle East Studies Association (1991) and was a 1992 Guggenheim Fellow.

Gene R. Garthwaite is Professor of History and the chair of the Asian Studies Program at Dartmouth College. His research centers on Iranian social history. His *Khans and Shahs: The Bakhtiyari of Iran* was published in 1983. He is currently working on a general history of Qajar Iran (1796–1925), the Bakhtiyari oral tradition, incorporating the Lorimer Collection of Bakhtiyari prose and poetry as an historical source, and also on "A Study of State-Tribe Relationships in Iran: The Impact of Reza Shah's Reign on Luristan-Bakhtiyari-Fars." He is a former member of the Board of Directors of the Middle East Studies Association.

Victor G. Korgun is a senior researcher in the Near and Middle East Department of the Institute of Oriental Studies, Russian Academy of Sciences, Moscow. He is the author of *Afghanistan: the 1820s and 1830s* (1979), and *Afghan Intelligentsia in Political Life* (1983), the coauthor of *The History of Afghanistan* (1982), and the author of articles on sociopolitical problems in modern Afghanistan. He has made numerous trips to Afghanistan since 1966 as an interpreter, advisor to the Afghan Youth Organisation, participant in international seminars, and lecturer for the Soviet diplomatic mission and military units. Since 1980, he has been the secretary responsible for scholarly problems of the joint Soviet-Afghan Commission on the Social Sciences. His current scholarly interests include social structures of modern Afghan society. In 1990, he was a visiting scholar at the University of Nebraska in Omaha.

Georgy M. Korniyenko was in the Soviet diplomatic service from 1949 to 1986. As minister-counselor of the USSR Embassy in Washington, he was involved in the 1962 Cuban missile crisis. From 1977 to 1986, he was First Deputy Foreign Minister of the USSR. From 1986 to 1988, he was First Deputy Chief of the International Department of the Central Committee of the Communist Party. Since then he has been Senior Research Scholar at the Institute of Oriental Studies, Moscow. His major publications are *Truth and Lies Concerning SS-20 Missiles* (1989), *The Origins of the Cold War* (1990), and *Something New about the Caribbean Crisis* (1991). His current research interest is the settlement of the Afghanistan conflict.

Richard Kurin is Director of the Smithsonian Institution Center for Folklife Programs and Cultural Studies and Professorial Lecturer in Social Change and Development at The Johns Hopkins University School of Advanced International Studies. He received his Ph.D. in anthropology from the University of Chicago and has published broadly on South Asian kinship, religion, and ethnicity, and on issues of development and cultural policy.

Alexei V. Malashenko is Head of the Religious Studies Section in the Institute of Oriental Studies, Russian Academy of Sciences, Moscow. He received his Ph.D. in 1978 from Moscow State University, where his thesis topic was Islam in Algeria. In 1972, and again from 1974–1976, he served as Arabic translator in Algeria and Egypt. He was formerly an advisor to the Soviet scientific mission in Libya (1979–80) and from 1983 to 1986 was an editorial advisor to the *World Marxist Review*, Prague.

Muhammad Khalid Masud has taught Islamic law at Ahmadu Bello University in Zaria, Nigeria; at Qaid-i Azam University in Islamabad, Pakistan; and at the International Islamic University in Islamabad. He is the author of *Islamic Legal Philosophy* (Islamic Research Institute: Islamabad, 1977), of *Iqbal and the Concept of Ijtihad* (in Urdu), and of numerous articles on law and social change in Islam.

Dimitri B. Novossyolov received his Ph.D. from the Institute of Oriental Studies, Moscow, in 1989. His thesis examined the "Socio-Political Crises of 1968–1969 and 1977 in Pakistan: A Comparative Analysis." He is currently Junior Research Fellow in the Pakistan Section of the Institute. His publications include "The Place of the State in Pakistan" (Moscow, 1985), "Islamization of the Political System in Pakistan, 1977–1985" (Moscow, 1985), and "The Role of the Army in the Socio-political Crises of 1968–1969 and 1985" (1988). His research interests include the integration of traditional institutions into modern political processes in Pakistan, the evolution of the *biradari* and clan systems and their political influence, and the Islamic factor in Pakistan's political process.

Martha Brill Olcott is Professor of Political Science at Colgate University. She is the author of *The Kazakhs* (1987) and the editor of *The Soviet Multinational State*. Olcott has also written nearly two dozen articles and chapters in scholarly books. She has travelled throughout the Commonwealth of Independent States and visits the region regularly.

INDEX

Abduvakhitov, Abdujabar, 6, 7, 8–9, 12, 69, 79–97
Abu-Lughod, Lila, 117
Afghanistan: Amin, Hafizullah, 104, 110–11, 116, 119, 127; Daud, Muhammad, 101–104, 127; ethnic identities, 12; Islamic resistance, 109–29; Marxism in, 40–41, 105–107, 116, 127–28; 1978 revolution, 104; People's Democratic Party of Afghanistan (PDPA), 103–104, 107, 111, 115, 116–17, 119, 123–27; poetry, political, 11, 114–29; reforms, pre-1978, 101–103; Soviet invasion, 3, 9–11, 25–26, 111–13, 114; in Soviet policy, 5, 9–11, 40–41; Taraki, Nur Muhammad, 11, 40, 104, 105, 110–11, 114, 115, 122–23, 127
Atatürk, Mustafa Kemal (1881–1938), 1, 21
Azerbaijan, 5, 6, 35, 38, 39, 65, 69, 73, 74, 137

Bakhtin, Mikhail, vii
Bakhtiyari, 11, 131, 134–39
Belokrenitsky, Vyacheslav Ya., 12–13, 149–59, 160, 175

Caton, Steven C., 117
Central Asia: compared to Baltic states, 53; demography, 49, 54–55; economic conditions, 54–55; Islamic movements, 6, 7, 53, 59, 60, 81; languages, 52, 59; liberalization, 52–53, 67; mafia in, 6, 56, 91; and Middle East, 4, 5; political elite, 6, 8, 49, 51, 52, 53, 54; Russian control over, 52, 90–91; Russian settlers, 8, 9, 49–50, 55, 59, 94
Cold War: great power rivalry, 4, 19–37; in Middle East, 29–31, 38–39
Comaroff, John, 4
Communism: and Islam, 6, 63–78, 157. See also Communist party
Communist party: in Pakistan, 157; in Central Asia, 49, 52, 55, 56, 90–92
Commonwealth of Independent States, 3, 49
Cottam, Richard W., 2, 4–5, 19–37, 45

Dresch, Paul, 130–31, 144

Edwards, David B., 9–11, 12, 14, 114–29, 196–97
Eickelman, Dale F., 192
Esposito, John, 12
ethnic identity: in Central Asia, 4, 14, 92–94,

132–33; in Pakistan, 155–57. See also Bakhtiyari; Kurds; Stalin, Joseph, ethnic policies

Ferghana Valley (Uzbekistan), 9, 55, 84, 86, 88, 92–94
"fundamentalism," Islamic: 2, 5, 7, 69–77, 103. See also Islam; Islamic movements
Fussell, Paul, 117

Garthwaite, Gene R., 11–12, 130–45, 194
Gorbachev, Mikhail, 3, 51, 52
Gulf Crisis (1990–1991), 2, 27–29, 31–32, 44–46
Gul Shaʿir (Afghan poet), 123–26

Hussein, Saddam, 24, 27, 31, 32, 33, 42, 44–45

Iran: and Central Asia, 5; nationalism, 21–22; under Qajar rule, 11, 134, 136; revolution, 1, 2, 134, 137–38; Muhammad Reza Shah Pahlevi (1919–1980), 1, 137; Reza Shah Pahlevi (1878–1944), l, 134, 136, 137, 143; Russian/Soviet policy toward, vii, 40; U.S. policy toward, vii, 5, 21–23, 25, 28. See also Musaddiq, Muhammad
Iraq, 4, 24, 27. See also Hussein, Saddam
Islam: as code of conduct, 175–76; and Communism, 63–77; Jadidi (reform), 50, 79–80; "fundamentalism," Islamic, 2, 5, 7, 69–77, 103; in modernization theories, 1, 2, 10, 20–21, 191; "Soviet," 7, 66–69, 81–82; studies of, 2–3, 14; Sufi orders, 66, 80, 134, 178, 193. See also Central Asia, Islamic movements; Islamic movements; jihad; mujahid; Muslim; Pakistan; Islamization; shariʿa (Islamic law); Spiritual Directorate of the Muslims of Central Asia and Kazakhstan (SADUM); ʿulama; ʿushr (tithe); zakat (alms tax)
Islamic movements: educational goals, 7, 68, 79–84, 88, 94; Islamic Renaissance Party, 57, 71–72, 76, 85, 86, 87, 95, 96–97; pan-Islam, 6, 95; reformist, 50; Tajikistan, 56, 72, 76; Tatar role in, 67–68, 73; Uzbekistan, 8, 71, 72, 76, 78–97. See also Islam; Uzbekistan; "Wahhabis"
Israel, 20, 21, 23, 24, 25, 29, 34–35, 40, 43, 44

Jadidi (reform) Islam, 50, 79–80